PSYCHOANALYSIS AND THE PARANORMAL

PSYCHOANALYSIS AND THE PARANORMAL

LANDS OF DARKNESS

edited by

Nick Totton

LONDON NEW YORK

First published in 2003 by
H. Karnac (Books) Ltd.
6 Pembroke Buildings, London NW10 6RE

British Library Cataloguing in Publication Data

A C.I.P. for this book is available from the British Library

ISBN 1 85575 985 3

10 9 8 7 6 5 4 3 2 1

Edited, designed, and produced by The Studio Publishing Services Ltd, Exeter EX4 8JN

Printed in Great Britain

www.karnacbooks.com

Occultism is another field we shall have to conquer. . . . There are strange and wondrous things in these lands of darkness. Please don't worry about my wanderings in these infinitudes. I shall return laden with rich beauty for our knowledge of the human psyche.

Jung to Freud, 1911: McGuire, 1991, p. 223

If I had my life to live over again I should devote myself to psychical research rather than to psychoanalysis.

Freud, quoted in Jones, 1957, p. 392

CONTENTS

ACKNOWLEDGEMENTS

The chapter by J. Marvin Spiegelman has appeared in *Quadrant: Journal of the C. G. Jung Foundation for Analytical Psychology, Volume* XXX (1), Winter 2002, pp. 57–73. The chapter by Edward Emery has appeared in *Psychoanalytic Quarterly*, Volume 89, April 2002. I am grateful to the editors of both journals for permission to publish here.

M. Lietaert Peerbolte's chapter is a shortened and revised version of Chapter 1, Book II, from *Psychic Energy in Prenatal Dynamics; Parapsychology; Peak Experiences: A Paraphysical Approach to Psychoanalysis and Transpersonal Psycho-dynamics* (Wassenaar: Servire, 1975). The publishers are no longer in business, and it has not proved possible to trace Peerbolte's heirs; an appropriate fee will be payable in the event that those heirs approach Karnac Ltd.

"Bauhaus Stairway" by Oskar Schlemmer. *Reprinted with the permission of The Museum of Modern Art, New York.*

"Animals" by Rufino Tamayo. *Reprinted with the permission of The Museum of Modern Art, New York.*

"The Football Players" ("Les Jouers de Football") by Henri Rousseau. *Reprinted with the permission of The Solomon R. Guggenheim Museum, New York.*

"Dempsey and Firpo" by George Bellows. *Reprinted with the permission of The Whitney Museum of American Art.*

"The Dark Figure" by Federico Castellon. *Reprinted with the permission of The Whitney Museum of American Art.*

Table 1—"Summary of Maimonides Results on Tendency for Dreams to Be Judged More Like Target Than Like Nontargets in Target Pool". *Reprinted with permission from American Psychologist* (1985), *40*: 1219–1230. Copyright © 1985 by the American Psychological Association. Reprinted with permission.

NOTES ON CONTRIBUTORS

Nathalie Charraud is a psychoanalyst, a member of the École de la Cause Freudienne, and of AMP (World Association of Psychoanalysis). She teaches at Rennes II University.

Chris Cherry taught philosophy at Glasgow University and then at the University of Kent, where he is shortly to retire from his Readership. He was Master of Eliot College at Kent for some years. He has published extensively in many areas of philosophy, in particular ethics, philosophy of mind and philosophy of religion. He has long been interested in parapsychology and the paranormal, with a particular interest in near-death studies and the philosophy of survival.

Edward Emery Ph.D. is a Training and Supervising Analyst at the Westchester Institute for Training in Psychoanalysis and Psychotherapy in Bedford Hills, New York and is in private practice in Northampton, Massachusetts.

Jean-Claude Maleval is a psychoanalyst, a member of the École de la Cause Freudienne, and of the Association Mondiale de Psychanalyse. He is Professor of Psychopathology at Rennes II University and author of several works including *Folies Hystériques et Psychoses Dissociatives* (1981); *Logique du Délire* (1997); and *La Forclusion de Nom-du-Père* (2000).

M. Lietaert Peerbolte was a Dutch psychoanalyst, a member of the International Psychoanalytic Association, and author of several works including *Psychic Energy in Prenatal Dynamics, Parapsychology, Peak-Experiences.*

J. Marvin Spiegelman Ph.D. graduated as an analyst at the C. G. Jung Institute in Zürich in 1959. He has taught at the University of Colorado, the Hebrew University in Jerusalem, and for extended periods at UCLA, USC and Pacifica Graduate Institute. He has published extensively in the fields of psychotherapy, psychology and religion and has been practicing in the Los Angeles area since 1959.

Nick Totton is a psychotherapist and trainer working in Leeds, UK, a member of the European Association for Body Psychotherapy, and in a prospective member group of the Independent Practitioners Association. He is the author of several books, including *The Water in the Glass: Body and Mind in Psychoanalysis* (1998), and editor of *Psychotherapy and Politics International.*

Montague Ullman Ph.D. is past president of the Society of Medical Psychoanalysts, a Charter Fellow of the American Academy of Psychoanalysis, past president of the American Society for Psychical Research, past president of the Parapsychological Association, and a Life Fellow of the American Psychiatric Association. He is currently Clinical Professor Emeritus, Department of Psychiatry, Albert Einstein College of Medicine, Yeshiva University and has published extensively in this field.

Michael Whan MA is an analytical psychologist. He is a member of the Independent Group of Analytical Psychologists, the Association of Independent Psychotherapists, The Confederation of Analytical Psychologists, an external trainer for Re-Vision, Centre for Integrative Psychosynthesis, and the external moderator for the Amida Trust. He has published articles in numerous journals and contributed a chapter to *Drawing The Soul: Schemas and Models in Psychoanalysis* (2000). He is also a member of the Ecopsychology group of Psychotherapists and Counsellors for Social Responsibility, the Society for Psychical Research, and the Scientific and Medical Network.

Introduction

> "All this is still uncertain and full of unsolved riddles; but there is no reason to be frightened by it"
>
> Freud, 1933, p. 55

Psychoanalysis has by necessity an extreme tolerance for the unknown. At times this can, paradoxically, amount to ignoring it. One example is the attitude of analysts to the apparent fact that, as Freud put it:

> mental processes in one person ... can be transferred to another person through empty space without employing the familiar methods of communication by means of words and signs. [Freud, 1933, p. 39]

Counter-transference, projective identification, unconscious communication—all these terms and others are used as if they answered the question: what is going on here?

This book is based upon the premise that what is going on is often best described as telepathy: one example of the larger field of paranormal phenomena. Most of the contributors try to demonstrate, in different ways, that such phenomena are of direct relevance to psychoanalysis, and that they frequently impinge directly on its clinical practice—most obviously, though not exclusively, in the forms of telepathy and synchronicity. An activity which devotes itself to the twin tasks of sensing what a person is thinking and feeling, and uncovering obscure connections between things, can after all hardly fail to encounter telepathy and synchronicity if such phenomena are there to be encountered (these two terms, of course, frequently amount to alternative ways of describing the same events). Several of the contributors to this collection offer their own clinical experiences in support of Freud's and Jung's earlier findings that these phenomena are indeed present in the clinic.

A further feature of the paranormal is its profound relationship with the unconscious. It appears that most paranormal perceptions are in themselves unconscious, speaking the language of primary process, and manifesting in dreams and other involuntary channels. Not only that, but paranormal perceptions, even when they appear in consciousness, seem to be of a primary process nature, and intensely susceptible to the influence of phantasy and desire. When we enter the space of the paranormal, to some extent we abandon the laws of secondary process reality—including the distinction between objective and subjective truth. Hence there is a very real flavour of psychosis, which many investigators try with difficulty to domesticate and conceal.

Because of all this, the paranormal is hard to analyse, in both senses of the word. Like fairies and other such beings ("the folk that never sleep", as they were once called, a suitable name for primary process phenomena), the denizens of the paranormal are tricky, unreliable, deceptive; we can never quite get them where we want them.

Hidden things

In 1953, a collection of papers, edited by George Devereux, was published under the title *Psychoanalysis and the Occult* (Devereux, 1974). This current volume can be thought of as in many ways a sequel, update or response to Devereux's. All three of these relationships are complex, though; for example, the difference in titles reflects a difference in eras, on several levels, one of which is simply linguistic: the word "occult" has significantly changed its connotations over the half century since Devereux produced his anthology, and even more so since Freud used it in his unpublished 1921 paper, intended for analysts only, "Psychoanalysis and telepathy":

> It no longer seems possible to brush aside the study of so-called occult facts: of things which seem to vouchsafe the real existence of psychic forces other than the known forces of the human and animal psyche, or which reveal mental faculties in which, until now, we did not believe. [Freud, 1941, p. 177]

This word "occult" has had a very interesting history, one of the key moments in which was the controversy between Leibnitz and Isaac Newton over the theory of gravitation. According to Leibnitz, gravity, which acts at a distance, is an *occult* concept, in the sense that there is no physical mechanism specified by which the distance between two objects is crossed. Newton was, of course, an "occultist" as well as a scientist—or rather, perhaps, it is only in retrospect that certain elements of "science" can be separated out from the alchemy, numerology and Biblical studies which constituted other parts of his occultism; certainly it was out of this whole complex field of interests and concerns that he was prompted to consider calling his force of universal attraction not "gravity" but "amor".

Leibnitz was unable to tolerate a crucial intellectual move which Newton makes at least twice in his career: to *assume* exactly that which is problematic. Thus he assumes that an infinitesimal quantity can be treated as equivalent to zero, and then later reinstated as a quantity—and creates calculus; and he assumes that a force can operate at a distance, without specifying how—and creates gravitational theory. What seemed dizzily daring in Newton's lifetime becomes convention later on. But as we will see, there are several Leibnitzs in the field of psychoanalysis.

It is important, however, to note that few of the contributors to Devereux's volume apart from Freud himself actually use the word "occult". Most of them—certainly those more contemporary to 1953—use words like "paranormal", "parapsychology", or J. B. Rhine's coinage, now rather fallen out of use, "psi". This is also true of Devereux's own contributions, leading one to wonder whether "occult" was perhaps the publisher's idea rather than the editor's.

Strange and enduring silences

Apart from the title, the contributions to the two volumes are strikingly different. To begin with, Devereux had available to him six papers by Freud; mostly marginal and short, it is true, but still papers by the founder of psychoanalysis himself. Alongside these are ranged pieces by Helene Deutsch, Roheim, Burlingham, Hitschmann, Schilder—significant figures of institutional psychoanalysis, all prepared to engage deeply with the topic of paranormal phenomena. The situation today is drastically different: the paranormal is basically no longer discussed in the central psychoanalytic media, and certainly there are no major analytic figures—without disrespect to my distinguished contributors—who will own to a serious interest in the topic.

In 1946 Jules Eisenbud, one of the leading current writers on the paranormal and psychoanalysis, observed that:

> One of the most remarkable facts in the history of the psychoanalytic movement is the indifference with which Freud's publications on the subject of telepathy have been received. ... In the more than twenty years that have elapsed since Freud's first publication on the subject in 1922, scarcely more than a half dozen psychoanalytic authors have made clinical contributions to the field, and most of these have published single communications followed by strange and enduring silences. [Eisenbud, 1946, p. 32]

The late 1940s and early 1950s, however, saw a resurgence of interest in the subject, with numerous publications by Eisenbud, Ehrenwald, Fodor and others—none of them, by any stretch, central figures in the field of analysis, but between them building up a body of evidence and theory, and a general sense of seriousness regarding the topic, which culminated in Devereux's anthology. Thereafter—silence.

Hunting the warbler

What has created this dramatic shift? Charles Brenner offers a "participant's" account which is worth quoting at length.

> Interest in psi phenomena in analytic circles did not simply die away with the passage of time ... The manner of its disappearance

> makes an interesting story. In 1955 ... an article appeared in the International Journal [of Psychoanalysis] which offered an acceptable opportunity to speak up against extrasensory perception in the framework of psychoanalysis. The author of the article reported the following (Eisenbud, 1955).
>
> A patient ... so knowledgeable ... as to nearly qualify as a professional ornithologist, dreamed one night that he had seen a worm-eating warbler in New York's Central Park. According to the article, the patient knew that this was impossible because that particular migratory bird had never been seen in Central Park at the time ... Nonetheless the patient rose at 5 am, as New York bird watchers often do, went to the park, and saw a worm-eating warbler. ... His patient, [Eisenbud] said, unconsciously longed for a mother who, unlike his own mother, would always be available to gratify his every wish. His dream, therefore, was to be understood as a wish fulfillment. Like the tiny, worm-eating warbler of his dream, his mother would always be there, even when he knew it was impossible for her to be.
>
> ... A telephone call to the Audubon Society revealed that *helmitheros vermivorus,* familiarly known as the worm-eating warbler, had frequently been seen in Central Park at the season the patient had his dream. There was no psi phenomenon, no extrasensory perception involved at all. ... If one is correct in assuming that the patient knew of his analyst's interest in psi phenomena, it is clear that the whole episode bore a relation to the transference which was ignored ...
>
> Armed with my newly acquired knowledge of the habits of the worm-eating warbler, I wrote a short article ... It was duly published in the International Journal, together with a somewhat longer reply to it by the author of the original article. As far as I know, there has not been another ESP article in a reputable psychoanalytic journal from that day to this ... [Brenner, 1987, pp. 543–545]

"All of which," Brenner goes on to say with some satisfaction, "goes to show that authority, even the highest authority—in this case, Freud himself—is not as important as facts" (*ibid.*, p. 545). It is unfortunate therefore that Brenner's "facts" turn out to be as slippery as these things usually are: in the reply which Brenner mentions, Eisenbud produced a mass of ornithological evidence that the worm-eating warbler is—"in fact"—a vanishingly rare visitor to Central Park.

Apart from the intrinsically entertaining spectacle of two analysts arguing in tremendous detail over the habits of the worm-eating warbler, we can learn from this story that the disappearance of the paranormal from psychoanalytic discourse was certainly *not* for any evidential or theoretical reasons. Eisenbud gives at least as good as he gets in the argument with Brenner, theoretically as well as factually. He points out very cogently that even if the bird was considerably less rare than it appeared to be:

> by no means would the ... psi hypothesis be eliminated ... By way of analogy, let us imagine that a man receives a message from an unknown source stating that a certain rare book can be found at a given book mart. The man goes to this place and within a few minutes comes upon the book in question. He feels extremely grateful to his unknown benefactor, since to the best of his belief there are only two copies of this book in existence. Later he learns that there are actually five—or ten, or twenty, it matters little. It would be quite wrong for him to conclude now that there was no relationship between the message he had received and his discovery of the now only comparatively rare book. [Eisenbud, 1957, p. 55]

The pressure of exact authority

Despite Eisenbud's strong rebuttal, however, Brenner is more or less right to claim that at this point the paranormal largely disappears from analytic journals. The real reason seems to be a change in the analytic world view, well-represented in Brenner's own conclusion:

> I have a private rule of thumb in such matters: When a thing is impossible, it cannot be so. Like all rules of thumb, it is not infallible. Some things that are impossible turn out to be so, but they are the rare exceptions. In my opinion the rule holds good for psi phenomena. [Brenner, 1987, p. 545]

Just as the Church told Galileo, and Leibnitz told Newton, the thing is impossible and therefore need not be considered. This shift in attitude towards the paranormal can be correlated with much larger shift in the culture of psychoanalysis after World War II: a shift towards respectability and conventionality, and away from the sort of alignment with the weird and marginal which Freud, much as he deplored it, could not at the time dislodge.

> The numerous suggestions made to us by occultists that we should collaborate with them show that they would like to treat us as half belonging to them, and that they count on our support against the pressure of exact authority. Nor, on the other hand, has psychoanalysis any interest in going our of its way to defend that authority, for it itself stands in opposition to everything that is conventionally restricted, well-established and generally accepted ... Alliance and cooperation between analysts and occultists might thus appear both plausible and promising. [Freud, 1921, p. 178]

Freud sets up this idea only to knock it down: occultists, he argues, are fundamentally religious believers, whereas analysts are essentially sceptics. "In view of this difference between their mental attitudes, cooperation between analysts and occultists offers small prospect of gain" (*ibid.*, p. 179).

As I discuss in my own chapter of this book, Freud's own views on the paranormal were complex and nuanced, and went through many vicissitudes. Thus in 1911 Freud had told Ferenczi, the great analytic enthusiast of the paranormal:

> Jung writes that we must also conquer occultism and requests permission to undertake a campaign in the realm of mysticism. I see that the both of you can't be restrained. ... these are dangerous expeditions, and I can't go along there. [Falzeder & Brabant, 1992, p. 216]

This passage was Freud's comment on the letter from Jung which gives this book its title and epigraph. Not long afterwards, however, Freud is enthusiastic about publishing a book by Ferenczi on his thought transference experiments: "I like it very much ... study everything you need and write the volume for me, publication of which I will expedite as quickly as possible" (Falzeder & Brabant, 1992, p. 380).

For some years Freud's feelings veered back and forth in this way, with the negative side largely fuelled by concerns over the impact on the credibility of psychoanalysis of explicit support for the paranormal. Hence, although in 1924 Freud was highly enthusiastic about Gilbert Murray's experiments on telepathy—"I confess that the impression of these reports was so strong that I am prepared to give up my opposition to the existence of thought transference ... I would even be prepared to lend support to the cause of telepathy through psychoanalysis" (Falzeder & Brabant, 2000, p. 205, note 3); and although in March the next year Freud, Ferenczi, and Freud's daughter Anna conducted their own "rather successful" experiments in thought transference in March 1925 (*op. cit.*, p. 207); on March 20th Freud still insists that Ferenczi should not present his experiments to the Psychoanalytic Congress:

> I advise you against it. Don't do it. ... With it you are throwing a bomb into the psychoanalytic edifice, which will certainly not fail to explode. But we are in agreement in not wanting to hasten this perhaps unavoidable disturbance in development. [*op. cit.*, p. 209]

And of course the major figure trying to hold Freud back from any public commitment to the paranormal was Ernest Jones, who saw it all as nonsense, and preferred to think that Freud's belief was not real:

> The extent to which a given superstitious belief is accepted by the mind is usually one of degree, and it is often very hard to ascertain to what extent a person "really" gives credence to it. It is a common experience to get the reply when someone is questioned on the point: "No, I don't really believe it, but all the same it is very odd". [Jones, 1957, p. 406]

Freud himself tried to fob Jones off with the complex and unconvincing claim that:

> my adherence to telepathy is my private affair, like my Jewishness, my passion for smoking, and other things, and the theme of telepathy—inessential for psychoanalysis. [Gay, 1995, p. 445]

In 1921, Freud provided our second epigraph by writing to the psychical researcher Hereward Carrington that, "If I had my life to live over again I should devote myself to psychical research rather than to psychoanalysis" (Jones, 1957, p. 392). In 1929, Freud denied having made any such statement, but with grim satisfaction Ernest Jones proved otherwise: "In the eight years that had passed he had blotted out the memory of that very astonishing and unexpected passage" (*ibid.*). As Denis Farrell, one of the very few modern analysts to address the topic, observes:

> When one thinks that it was possible for a man as courageous and as intellectually honest as Freud was to be dissuaded and to dissuade himself from presenting his data, then the faint-heartedness of others of us in the face of such a challenge is, after all, easy to understand. As I struggled myself to recall and retain and record my own observations, I learned about this from firsthand experience. [Farrell, 1983, p. 80]

What follows

This anthology was originally to be edited by Duncan Barford, who found the title, and assembled some of the contributions. Unfortunately pressure of time made it impossible for him to complete the task, and I was asked to take it up. Perhaps the saddest lack in the volume as it appears is the absence of any contribution from Duncan himself. The material we do have, though, seems to me worthy to be compared with Devereux's book. It spans a wider range of psychoanalytic approaches than *Psychoanalysis and the Occult*, including not only orthodox Freudian work, but also contributions from the Lacanian, Jungian, and Reichian traditions.

It opens with two pieces which form a direct link with the earlier efflorescence of analytic work on the paranormal. Dr Montague Ullman was already publishing on this subject in the 1950s, and we are privileged to have a new paper from him, which combines quantitative research into dream telepathy—his field of special interest—with some powerful general points about why psychoanalysis needs to study the paranormal. He also shares some personal experiences of the paranormal which help us to understand why he has devoted much of his life to studying this field.

The second paper, by the Dutch analyst M. Lietaert Peerbolte, is an edited section from his book *Psychic Energy*, originally published in the 1970s and long out of print. The lack of attention which the book has received was no doubt exacerbated by the atrocious quality of the translation into English (this has been improved here whenever it was possible to ascertain what was intended). However, *Psychic Energy* was never likely to be taken up by the mainstream: it combines three topics calculated to raise hackles—the paranormal, birth and pre-birth trauma, and physical (rather than mental) sex. However, Peerbolte's treatment of telepathic dreams is both interesting and punctiliously orthodox; it gives a rare and fascinating opportunity to read a strict classical Freudian at work. Like Freud, Peerbolte emphasizes that telepathic phenomena are subject to the laws of primary process. In particular, he argues that telepathy occurs in psychoanalysis at meaningful and predictable points, in response to the analysand's wish.

Chris Cherry is not an analyst, but a philosopher. He contributes a philosophical discussion both of the concept of the paranormal itself, and of some psychoanalytic ideas about it. Cherry points out some of the paradoxes of the topic: notably, that "paranormal phenomena both cry out for and yet resist explanation. [Yet] finding an acceptable explanation—a psychoanalytic one, perhaps—for a paranormal event ... is tantamount to declaring that the event in question isn't paranormal after all." One of the chapter's great virtues is its insistence that the paranormal is *irreducible*—not just inexplicable at this moment, but inherently beyond explanation.

Michael Whan's paper is the first of two chapters from Jungian analysts. It offers a detailed account of Jung's theory of synchronicity, illustrated through the clinical experiences of both Jung and Whan himself. Following on from Cherry, Whan stresses the importance of tolerating "unknownness", and not assuaging our anxiety with spurious categories. He argues that "the parapsychological ... belongs to the very heart of psychological practice". Marvin Spiegelman, the other Jungian contributor, takes up the same theme from a rather different angle, focusing on the role of synchronicity in the analytic relationship, as a transference/counter-transference phenomenon. He brings in the experience of what is known as "embodied counter-transference", including subtle energy phenomena. Spiegelman's breadth and depth of experience parallel Montague Ullman's, and his contribution is equally valuable.

Sandwiched between these two Jungian pieces is the sole contribution which takes a wholly sceptical view towards the topic of the paranormal. Maleval and Charraud, two Parisian Lacanian analysts, look at the massive American (and not only American) phenomenon of UFO contactee stories; and argue that the material is demonstrably psychotic in nature. They are concerned mainly to use the work of John Mack, who has treated and written about many UFO contactees, as an example of what they see as the prime distinction between psychotherapy and psychoanalysis—essentially, an ethical one:

> A treatment can only claim to be psychoanalytic when the one directing it holds the ethical position of object *a*, which leads him to want nothing for the analysand, and to do without the resources of the discourse of the Master.

Hence their discussion of the paranormal is part of a campaign for a certain form of analytic treatment. For Maleval and Charraud, "In one sense, all forms of psychotherapy make aliens exist. It is only by introducing ethics to clinical practice that these fantasmagoria might fade away, and allow the truth of the subject to emerge."

Malaval and Charraud accuse John Mack of supporting "the inclusion of the therapist's subjectivity in the treatment". The same criticism could clearly be made of most "Anglo-Saxon" psychoanalysis (as Lacanians call it); it does indeed provide an opening for the paranormal, which, as I argue in my own chapter, is very often linked to the "experience of transparency between subjects". Most of the contributors to this volume probably fall within the scope of Maleval and Charraud's critique; but Edward Emery, who describes "the haunting of the intersubjective", in a powerful piece drawing on the important but neglected work of Abraham and Torok, offers a different model of the analytic relationship which is in some ways parallel to that of Maleval and Charraud:

> Contrary to the current emphasis on the analyst as a person, on their realness, their generative counter-transferences, their love for their patient, their ability to engage and make contact, I believe that the "aliveness" that is transformational for the haunted patient is initially not the aliveness of the analyst's productivity (whether phallic or maternal) nor of their "experience" so much as it is the "aliveness" in the analyst's silence.

The book concludes with my own chapter, starting out from the position of an adherent of the Reichian psychoanalytic heresy, and arguing that we should conceive of the paranormal—specifically, telepathy—as an *embodied* rather than a disembodied phenomenon. I try to connect the paranormal and the uncanny to the Lacanian "real", and hence to suggest reasons for the terror which the paranormal often sparks. In making these arguments I bring our attention back to Freud's own work on the topic: a fitting place, perhaps, to end the book.

A little bird told me

One unanticipated theme shared by several authors here—possibly even a synchronicity[1]—is the role of non-human creatures, animals, insects and birds, in our experience of the paranormal. Spiegelman suggests that "the prevalence of animals in such synchronistic events ... may attest to this phenomenon having an instinctual basis". Peerbolte, in particular, suggests a specific connection between birds and telepathy, pointing out how in fairy stories, birds are often used as a means of communication with those in captivity or far away.

All of which adds a particular poignancy to the story of the worm-eating warbler, and the way in which ornithological arguments about its presence or otherwise in Central Park became the vehicle for a battle over the presence or otherwise of the paranormal within psychoanalytic discourse! To repeat a point made earlier: psychoanalysis tends to assume the problematic—the communication of material outside the normally recognized channels—in a way which amounts to ignoring what is strange and exciting about this situation. In some ways it would be both more honest and more interesting to replace statements about communicative counter-transference, projective identification, analytic intuition, etc. with: "A little bird told me".

The lost battalion

It has become something of a tradition—begun by Freud—for writers on this topic either to conceal their own opinions about the paranormal, or to express high-minded agnosticism. I would like to break this tradition, and make it clear that I have had frequent experiences of paranormal events which render the question of "belief" superfluous. Telepathy, in particular, seems to me so basic to human existence that it is hard to imagine society being possible without it (while at the same time certain aspects of social reality depend upon its denial).

For these reasons, I very much support Montague Ullman's point about the "lost battalion" of psychotherapeutic and analytic clients who "instead of a fair-minded openness to the reality of telepathy, ... are met with a bias that confirms their fear of self-disclosure". This is particularly true in situations where the telepathic experience involves both client and therapist—but is denied or ignored by the therapist, a denial justified by arguments about neutrality, but based in reality, perhaps, simply on fear. The space of the paranormal can indeed be frightening. But psychoanalysis specializes in entering and tolerating frightening spaces. Why should this one be an exception?

Note

1. Another interesting synchronicity is Cherry's "accidental" use of the analogy of the horse which doesn't eat, employed in another context by Freud himself.

References

Brenner, C. (1987). Notes on psychoanalysis by a participant observer: a personal chronicle. *Journal of the American Psychoanalytic Association, 35*: 539–556.

Devereux, G. (Ed.) (1974). *Psychoanalysis and the Occult*. London: Souvenir Press.

Eisenbud, J. (1946). Telepathy and problems of psychoanalysis. *Psychoanalytic Quarterly, 15*: 32–87.

Eisenbud, J. (1955). On the use of the psi hypothesis in psycho-analysis. *International Journal of Psycho-Analysis, 36*: 370–374.

Eisenbud, J. (1957). Comments on Dr. Brenner's "Facts, Coincidence, and the Psi Hypothesis". *International Journal of Psycho-Analysis, 38*: 54–56.

Falzeder, E., & Brabant, E. (Eds) (1992). *The Correspondence of Sigmund Freud and Sandor Ferenczi, Volume 1: 1908–1914*. Cambridge, Massachusetts: Belknap/Harvard University Press.

Falzeder, E., & Brabant, E. (Eds) (2000). *The Correspondence of Sigmund Freud and Sandor Ferenczi, Volume 3: 1920–1933*. Cambridge, Massachusetts: Belknap/Harvard University Press.

Farrell, D. (1983). Freud's "thought-transference", repression, and the future of psychoanalysis. *International Journal of Psycho-Analysis, 64*: 71–81.

Freud, S. (1922). Dreams and telepathy. *S.E., 18*. London: Hogarth Press.

Freud, S. (1933). *New Introductory Lectures on Psychoanalysis. S.E., 22*.

Freud, S. (1941[1921]). Psychoanalysis and telepathy. *S.E., 18*.

Gay, P. (1995[1989]). *Freud: A Life For Our Time*. London: Papermac.

Jones, E. (1957). *Sigmund Freud: His Life and Work. Volume III: The Last Phase*. London: Hogarth.

McGuire, W. (Ed.) (1991). *The Freud/Jung Letters* (Abridged Edition). London: Penguin.

CHAPTER ONE

Dream telepathy: experimental and clinical findings

Montague Ullman

Over the course of my life I have had close encounters of four kinds with the paranormal or what has come to be known as psi phenomena.[1] In 1932, at the age of sixteen, I happened on the subject of what was then called "psychic phenomena". Impressed with how many great names were associated with the study of mediumship (William James, J. W. Crookes, Sir Oliver Lodge), several college friends and I embarked upon seances of our own at weekly intervals and lasting almost two years. The striking physical effects we encountered left their mark on each of us over the many years we remained in touch.[2]

That was encounter number one. It left me with a lifelong interest in the "paranormal" and an openness to it. Encounter number two was more fleeting and personal and lacked the consensual quality of my youthful experiences. It took the form of very occasional dreams that seemed to me to be either telepathic or precognitive. Here is one such dream that Jung might have considered a good example of synchronicity:[3]

The setting was late in 1945. 1 had just returned from military duty overseas and was enrolled as a candidate in a psychoanalytic program. The dream occurred early in my own analysis. In it I was watching an opera and was surprised to see a classmate of mine, who I shall refer to as Nat, appearing as one of the dancers on stage. Nat was a big, heavyset man weighing well over two hundred pounds. I knew him only casually as a fellow student. He was older than most of us, probably around fifty. I reported the dream in my next analytic session. The phone rang just as I completed my account. As he usually did, my analyst picked up the phone but the conversation went on for an unusual length of time, accompanied by sounds of laughter reaching my ears. With obvious surprise he then related the content of the call: "That was Nat and he was excited about the fact that he had been accepted for a part in a ballet and had his first performance last night when he danced on the stage of the Metropolitan Opera House."

I had known Nat was in analysis with my analyst, but by no stretch of my imagination could I have conceived of him as a ballet dancer. As an acausal coincidence it was loaded with meaning for me. Prior to its occurrence and very early in my analysis I had revealed my interest in parapsychology. I did not know for sure but sensed this would not be greeted favourably by my analyst who I knew to be a Marxist. To touch lightly on the dynamics of what was going on at the time I had a need (neurotically so) for both his approval and to be seen as special. I had the uncomfortable feeling that the exposure of my interest in the paranormal would result in my being seen as special, but not in the way I wanted it to. What better way of demonstrating the soundness of this interest than by participating in a precognitive dream scenario where both of us were vying for the analyst's attention at the same time.

Encounter number three was clinical in nature and occurred sporadically in the course of my psychoanalytic practice which ranged from 1946 to 1961. The dreams of my patients were of interest to me, not only for their ability to expose the deepest emotional currents at play, but also because of the historical associations of altered states of consciousness, such as dreams, with the occurrence of psi effects. One of the earliest investigators was F. W. H. Myers whose classic study (1903) explored the connection of psychic events to what he referred to as the subliminal level of awareness.

It was Freud (1963) who embellished this simple model with his speculations concerning the dynamic import of telepathic communications in their relevance to current conflicts, and the way in which unconscious processing left its imprint on the telepathic message. Surprisingly enough, or perhaps not, these early speculations of Freud were picked up by only a few of his followers, notably Stekel (1921),[4] until the forties when a number of psychiatric contributions appeared. These focused on the psychological factors conducive to the occurrence of psi effects. Most came through in the dreams of patients and did so under conditions which highlighted problematic aspects of the transference.

Certain criteria emerged which proved useful in identifying a dream as presumptively telepathic:

1. The corresponding elements between dream and reality should be:
   a) Unusual, i.e. not ordinarily occurring in dreams, or in the dreams of the particular patient.
   b) Non-inferential, i.e. elements the patient could not ordinarily infer from his knowledge of the therapist or his experience with him.
   c) Intrusive. This is included not as an absolute criterion, but when it does occur it is generally a reliable indicator of a paranormal event. It refers to the quality of standing apart and appearing as strange, unfamiliar or intrusive to the dreamer.
2. The relationship between the events in the therapist's life and the telepathic mirroring of them in the patient's dream should occur in close temporal relationship, usually a matter of several days.
3. The criterion of psychological meaning. The correspondence provides a unique strategy of defence employed by patients under conditions where the knowledge gained in this way reflects problematic aspects arising in the course of therapy.

The circumstances under which telepathic events appear in dreams have been variously described. Almost all writers emphasized the role of transferential and counter-transferential factors. As a result of either irrational needs on the part of the patient or the sensing of some negative quality in the therapist, the patient may, through the telepathic manoeuvre, succeed in exposing a particularly vulnerable area in the therapist. Servadio (1956) emphasized the patient's frustration and the blockage of communication. He saw sleep as favouring telepathic transmission by virtue of its regressive release of archaic mechanisms. Eisenbud (1970) was among the first to demonstrate the therapeutic usefulness of actively working with the telepathy hypothesis. Ehrenwald (1955) wrote extensively both on the criteria as well as the possible role of paranormal factors in the major psychoses. Ullman (1980) noted some of the characterologic and communication difficulties of the consistent telepathic dreamers.

Telepathic dreams occurred sporadically in my practice under varied circumstances. They came about when my own agenda interfered with effective contact (my counter-transference) or when the patient resorted to the telepathic manoeuvre in the interest of her own transferential needs. Both may be involved, as was the case with one patient who consistently responded to my personal and somewhat distracting need to have case material whenever I was about to write or lecture on the subject of telepathic dreams, while at the same time she established her own special status as a telepathic dreamer. Used manipulatively in this way, her secret knowledge was made known to the therapist while being in a position to disclaim any responsibility.

The inhibited, obsessively organized individual who tends to use language in the service of distancing mechanisms rather than facilitating contact is more likely to fall back on this manoeuvre. Telepathy appears as one way of maintaining contact at critical points in the management of contradictory needs for distance and inviolability and at the same time serving the inextinguishable need for closeness and safety.

In the following example, a dream containing unusual dream elements corresponded to a real event in my life. In this instance, the dream and the real-life event occurred on the same night (Ullman, 1980). A forty-two-year-old female patient, a seamstress, reported the following dream:

> I was at home with my boyfriend John. There was a bottle on the table containing part alcohol and part cream. It was sort of a white foamy stuff. John wanted to drink it. I said, "No, you can drink it later." I looked at the label. It read "Appealing Nausea." I meant to drink it when we went to bed, although we seemed to be in bed at the time.

She then reported another dream fragment from that same night:

> I had a small leopard. It was very dangerous. I wrapped him up and put him in a large bowl. Mother told me to take him out or he would die.

On the evening of the night the patient had these dreams, my wife and I attended a lecture at the New York Academy of Medicine on the subject of animal neuroses. The speaker presented a movie showing how cats can be made to develop an addiction to alcohol. Once the addiction developed and the alcoholic cat was offered the choice of a dish of milk or a dish of half-milk, half-alcohol the cat showed a preference for the alcohol–milk mixture.

"Tracer" elements such as the half-alcohol, half-cream mixture and the small feline creature suggest the possibility of telepathy. To establish the likelihood of this, one has to invoke the criterion of psychological meaning based on an elaboration of the underlying dynamics. The analysis of the dream did support the telepathy hypothesis. The scene in the movie, witnessed by the therapist, provided visual metaphors that appropriately expressed dynamics that were surfacing at the time in therapy. These included her feelings about the omnipotence of the therapist in relation to her, suggested by her identification with the animal being manipulated by the experimenter; her own despair about change, suggested by her identification with a leopard, an animal that cannot change its spots; and her ambivalence about relinquishing control and revealing the more sensual side of her character, suggested by her intent to drink an alcohol mixture aptly labelled "Appealing Nausea" at bedtime, while also being wary about it.

My first three encounters, while personally very meaningful, were essentially anecdotal in nature. Not undertaken in a spirit of scientific inquiry, there was no rigorous effort to rule out other possible causes, or chance itself. Such experiences carry conviction for the one involved, but have generally been of no great interest to science. Many well documented instances of this nature have been collecting dust for years in the files of the British and the American Societies for Psychical Research.

In consideration of this reality, the next logical step was for me to consider the possibility of an experimental approach. In 1960, in the course of my last year in practice, I received a grant from the

Parapsychology Foundation to conduct a pilot study to apply the then recent discovery of the connection of rapid eye movements (REM) to dreaming and how the possibility of near total recall of the dreams of the night lent itself to a dream telepathy experiment. The results were of enough interest to influence my decision in 1961 to terminate private practice and accept a full-time hospital appointment, making it possible for me to set up a sleep laboratory in the hope of establishing a quantitative result under conditions where all other possible causes were excluded.

Methodology

The formal studies were initiated at the Maimonides Medical Center in Brooklyn, New York in 1964 under the direction of Dr Stanley Krippner. The subjects were young adults selected on the basis of their ability to recall dreams and their interest in the experiment.[5] The subject's sleep was monitored electroencephalographically and he was awakened at the estimated end of each REM period to report his dream. An agent or sender spent the night in a separate room attempting to telepathically influence the subject's dreams by concentrating on the selected target picture at intervals throughout the night, and particularly when signalled that a REM period for the subject had begun. The target, generally an art print, was randomly selected by the agent from a pool of targets in opaque, sealed containers after the subject was in bed. Only the agent was aware of the target chosen for the particular night and he remained in his room throughout the night acoustically isolated from both subject and experimenter. The dream protocols were transcribed from the taped reports. Copies of them, along with copies of the targets used for any given experimental series, were given to three independent judges who assessed correspondences on a blind basis.

The specific hypothesis under consideration stated that a S's (subject's) dream protocol for any given experimental night would reflect the influence of telepathy by the appearance in the S's dream of correspondences to the target material viewed by the agent. Twelve 5 × 8 prints of famous paintings were selected as experimental targets. On a given night one of these was randomly selected and opened by an agent in a room at a distance from the subject. The latter remained in the sleep room throughout the night. His or her sleep and REM pattern were monitored by an eight-channel Medcraft Model D EEG in the adjacent control room. All verbal communication between the S and E (experimenter) was mediated through an intercom system and recorded on tape. Twelve different subjects were used in the first study, each sleeping one night in the laboratory. In the morning associative data from the S was added to the record of the dream reports. At a later point the transcripts made from the tapes were sent to three independent outside judges who had not been connected with the experimental procedure in any way. The judges also received the twelve potential target pictures and were asked to rank the targets in order of their closeness to each individual dream protocol, first for the dream material alone and then for the dream plus the associative data. The judges were also asked to express a confidence rating for each rank. The subject judged his own dreams against the targets in a similar way.

The means of the judges' ranks and ratings were entered on twelve-by-twelve tables and subjected to a two-way analysis of variance (for targets and nights) according to the Scheffe method. The rankings made by the Ss were handled similarly. The rankings were also evaluated by binomial expansion, with hits including ranks of #1 through #6 and misses including ranks from #7 to #12. The ranking of the subject was significant at the 0.05 level when evaluated by the binomial expansion method.

The approach varied somewhat as illustrated in the following studies.

I. The first screening study

For this study, twelve volunteer Subjects (Ss) spend one night each at the laboratory. Two staff members, one male and one female, alternated as Agents (As), attempting to influence Ss' dreams by means of telepathy. Target materials were famous art prints, randomly selected for each night once Ss had gone to bed. On the following morning, Ss were asked to match their dream recall against the entire collection of target pictures, selecting the art print which most closely corresponded to their dreams and ranking the others in descending order of correspondence. Three outside Judges (Js) followed a similar procedure; statistically significant data emerged from Ss' rankings and from one of the J's evaluations.

II. The first Erwin study

Dr Erwin, whose target–dream correspondences were the most direct in Series I, was paired with the male A from the screening study for a seven-night series.

III. The second screening study

Twelve different Ss and two As were utilized in another twelve-night series.

IV. The Posin study

Dr R. Posin, who participated in Series III, was paired with the A she had worked with during her night in the laboratory.

V. The Grayeb study

T. Grayeb, another S from Series III, was selected for this sixteen-night study. Without the knowledge of S, A concentrated on a target during eight nights of the study; for the other eight nights there was neither an agent nor a target. The condition was determined randomly once S had gone to bed.

VI. The second Erwin study

Dr W. Erwin was again paired with the A from Series II for an eight-night study. The art print was accompanied by a box of "multi-sensory" materials on each night to enhance the emotionality of the target. For example, Daumier's painting, *Advice to a Young Artist*, was accompanied by a canvas and paints to enable A to "act out" the artist's role. No S evaluation was accomplished for this study.

VII. The Van de Castle study

Dr R. Van de Castle, an S who had produced several direct target–dream correspondences in a telepathy study at another laboratory, was allowed to select his own A from the laboratory staff during the eight-night series. He selected a total of three As: one for a single night, one for two nights, and one for five nights. At the completion of this study, I had the opportunity to explore in greater depth the dreams he had with themes of aggression and sex, which had a greater telepathic impact. This would be in line with the evidence from both anecdotal and clinical services that paranormal events are linked to affective processes.

Results

After a careful examination of our methodology and data Child (1985) summarized the statistical results of the entire range of experiments performed on paranormal dreaming (several on precognitive dreaming were included) at the Maimonides Medical Center (see Table 1).*

Table 1
Summary of Maimonides Results on Tendency for Dreams to Be Judged More Like Target Than Like Nontargets in Target Pool

	Judges' score		Subjects' score		*z* or *t* resulting from judgments		
Series	Hit	Miss	Hit	Miss	Judges	Subjects	Sources
GESP: Dreams monitored and recorded throughout night; agent "transmitting" during each REM period							
A. 1st screening	7	5	10	2	$z = 0.71$[b]	*$z = 1.33$*[b]	Ullman, Krippner, & Feldstein (1966)
B. 1st Erwin	5	2	6	1	$z = 2.53$[b]	$z = 1.90$[b]	Ullman et al. (1966)
C. 2nd screening	4	8	9	3	$z = -.25$[b]	*$z = 1.17$*[b]	Ullman (1969)
D. Posin	6	2	6	2	$z = 1.05$[c]	$z = 1.05$[c]	Ullman (1969)
E. Grayeb	3	5	5	3	$z = -.63$[c]	$z = 0.63$[c]	Ullman, Krippner, & Vaughan (1973)
F. 2nd Erwin	8	0			$t = 4.93$[a]		Ullman & Krippner (1969)
G. Van de Castle	6	2	8	0	$t = 2.81$[a]	*$t = 2.74$*[a]	Krippner & Ullman (1970)
H. Pilot sessions	53	14	42	22	*$z = 4.20$*[b]	*$z = 2.21$*[b]	Ullman et al. (1973)
Precognition: Dreams monitored and recorded throughout night; target experience next day							
I. 1st Bessent	7	1			$t = 2.81$[a]		Krippner, Ullman, & Honorton (1971)
J. 2nd Bessent	7	1			$t = 2.27$[a]		Krippner, Honorton, & Ullman (1972)
K. Pilot sessions	2	0			$z = 0.67$[c]		Ullman et al. (1973)
GESP: Dreams monitored and recorded throughout night; agent active only at beginning or sporadically							
L. Sensory bombardment	8	0	4	4	*$z = 3.11$*[b]	*$z = 0.00$*[c]	Krippner, Honorton, Ullman, Masters, & Houston (1971)
M. Grateful Dead	7	5	8	4	$z = 0.61$[c]	$z = 0.81$[c]	Krippner, Honorton, & Ullman (1973)
Clairvoyance: Dreams monitored and recorded throughout night; concealed target known to no one							
N. Pilot sessions	5	3	4	5	*$z = 0.98$*[b]	$z = 0.00$[b]	Ullman et al. (1973)
GESP: Single dreams							
O. Vaughan, Harris, Parise	105	98	74	79	$z = 0.63$[c]	$z = -.32$[c]	Honorton, Krippner, & Ullman (1972)

Note. GESP = general extrasensory perception. Italics identify results obtained with procedures that preserve independence of judgments in a series. For some series, the published source does not use the uniform measures entered in this table, and mimeographed laboratory reports were also consulted. Superscipts indicate which measure was available, in order of priority.
[a] Ratings. [b] Rankings. [c] Score (count of hits and misses).

*Reproduced from Child (1985) with permission from the American Psychological Association.

Including in his assessment a critique of the various efforts at replication, he concluded:

> What is clear is that the tendency toward hits rather than misses cannot reasonably be ascribed to chance. There is some systematic—that is, nonrandom—source of anomalous resemblance of dreams to targets. [Child, 1985, p. 122]

> The experiments at the Maimonides Medical Center on the possibility of ESP in dreams clearly merit careful attention from psychologists who, for whatever reason, are interested in the question of ESP. To firm believers in the impossibility of ESP, they pose a challenge to skill in detecting experimental flaws or to the understanding of other sources of error. To those who can conceive that ESP might be possible, they convey suggestions about some of the conditions influencing its appearance or absence and about techniques for investigating it. [Child, 1985, p. 128]

Form

There is empirical evidence suggesting that, in some instances at least, forms contained in the target material come through more clearly and recognizably than the content itself. This applies to complex targets as well as simple targets where the form itself is the predominant feature.

There are two experimental techniques which may have a possible bearing upon the perceptual aspect of telepathic effects as this relates to similarities based on form. Each of these techniques limits information input, but in different ways. Tachistoscopic presentations limit exposure in time. Work with the stabilized retinal image limits information ordinarily collected and maintained through the play of eye movements about an object under fixation.

There have been a number of experiments beginning with the awakened interest in the Pötzel phenomenon demonstrating that cues occurring outside of conscious awareness can produce perceptual illusions as well as influence cognitive problem-solving activity. Ericksen (1958) suggests that what occurs following the subthreshold presentation of a stimulus is not a registering of the stimulus at an unconscious level, but simply a fragmentary partial perceptual response. It takes the activated state of dreaming to bring to bear upon this unidentifiable percept a number of response systems, which then clothe it with an identity approximating the original stimulus. What is occurring is the very reverse of the usual dynamic explanation in terms of unconscious perception, repression, and reappearance through the channels of censorship and dream work. The appearance in the dream is based not on a lowered threshold for unconscious perception, but rather on a lowered threshold during the REM state for the activation of a number of relevant response systems which have the additive effect of establishing at least some of the features of the original stimulus.

Klein (1959) agrees that for discrimination to occur there must be some degree of partial registration in awareness. He does insist that subception is a real effect, that fragments or aspects of the image register in this way and that they can be recovered directly through intentional recall and indirectly through associations and dreams. An interesting effect noted in subception studies is the alteration in figure ground relations with the loss of the ability to make that particular distinction. Tachistoscopic display of the Rubin double profile results in two opposing shapes confronting each other. Of importance from the standpoint of telepathy, as we shall see, is that in the face of experimental cut-off of information the object is fragmented, shapes are abstracted and autistic processes shape the percept.

Similar effects are noted in connection with the work of Evans (1967a,b) in his observations on fragmentation phenomena associated with binocular stabilization. He notes that under conditions of stabilization when a pattern disappears it does so in parts and the parts drop out in a non-random fashion. He talks of levels in the hierarchy of the visual system and suggests, as an explanation of the fragmentation phenomena, that when the information supply is limited, as in stabilization experiments, not all levels of the hierarchy are activated. As a consequence only parts of the pattern are seen corresponding to the level of the hierarchy reached. Evans also notes the characteristic stabilization fragments after repeated tachistoscopic exposures (*Figure 1*).

The fragmentation of images noted by Warcollier (1938) (*Figures 2–4*) and Sinclair (1930) (*Figures 5–7*), in their efforts to effect transfer of information at a distance, resembles in remarkable ways the fragmentary percepts obtained through the two experimental

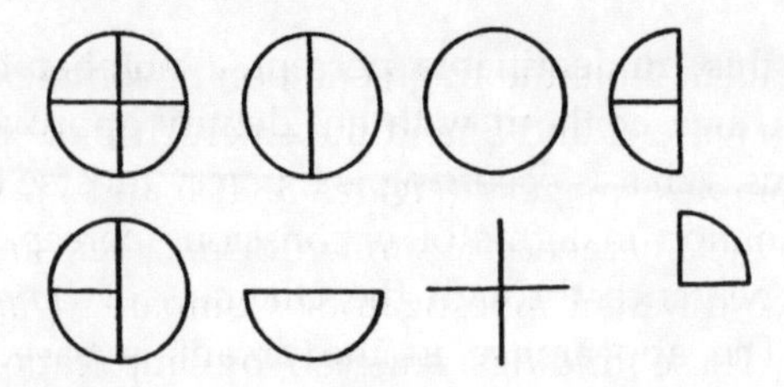

Figure 1. Typical fragmentations of a stabilized image (Evans, 1967a).

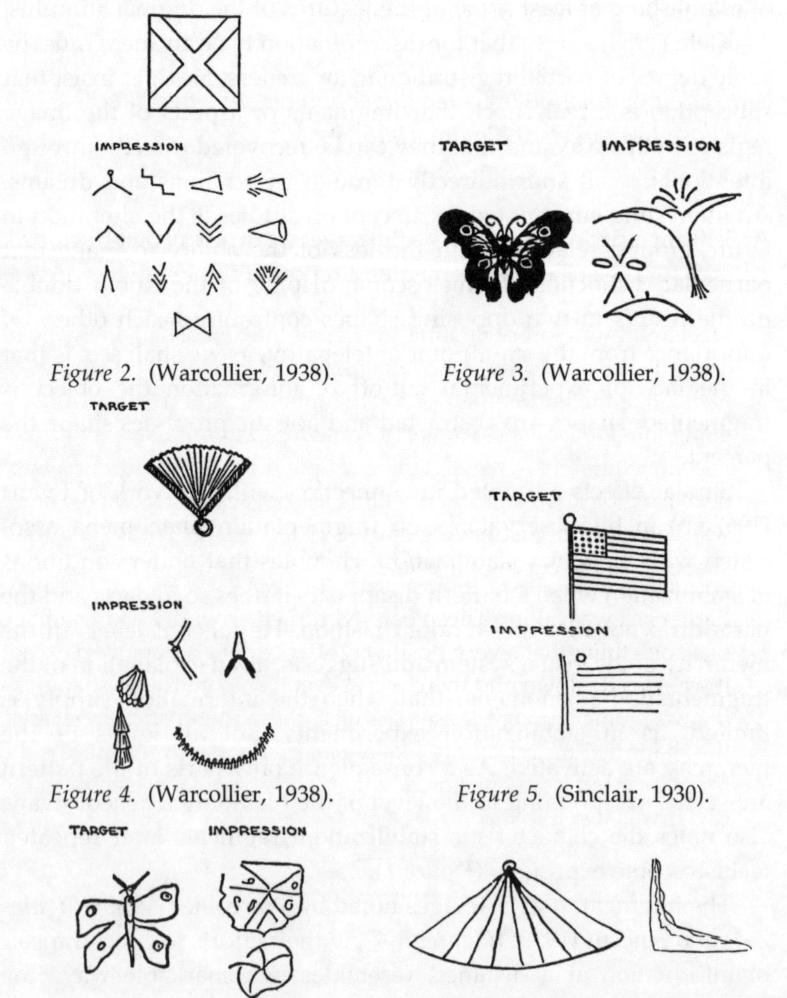

Figure 2. (Warcollier, 1938). *Figure 3.* (Warcollier, 1938).

Figure 4. (Warcollier, 1938). *Figure 5.* (Sinclair, 1930).

Figure 6. (Sinclair, 1930). *Figure 7.* (Sinclair, 1930, p. 149).

strategies described. Note the fragmentation of complex forms into simpler forms (*Figures* 2 and 5) and the emergence of simple forms out of more complex imagery (*Figures* 3, 4, 6 and 7). It is also of interest to note the emergence of similar forms when similar targets are used by two different investigators. Compare *Figures* 3 and 6, and 4 and 7. These findings suggest, by implication, that the neurophysiological pathways involved in the processing of telepathic transfer may be the same as in normal visual perception.

In our own experimental work correspondences in form were noted under a variety of circumstances.

A. Explicit correlation between target and dream when simple forms were used as targets (Ullman, 1966)[6]

Example 1

At 3:40 am a circle was drawn as the target by experimenter (*Figure 8*). At 3:53 am the subject awakened and reported the following dream:

> I feel as if I was sort of floating to sleep at the time. I had an image of a, oh, it wasn't really like a dream, it was sort of like being on a *round*, like the bottom half of a large tube, such as if you would be going into the Holland Tunnel or something, sort of like a road. As I was travelling, there seemed to be people there but it didn't seem to be like a typical dream, sort of falling asleep. I caught an image and I was conscious of just having started to fall asleep. I was on a road shaped like the curve of a trough.
>
> Earlier as I was falling asleep before I turned around, I had an image of a something that's very positively shaped, like a door stop except it was upside down and there were several smooth round shapes, as if I was going through these passages, these round smooth shapes, the shape as I meant it only like a *rounded* doorstop, sort of like the fin of a car but it was upside down and it wasn't connected with the car. It was just like that.

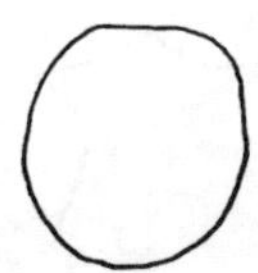

Figure 8. Example 1—circle.

Example 2

This example used the same subject and was on the same night as Example 1. At 4:30 am angular shapes were drawn by experimenter (*Figure 9*). At 6:30 am the subject reported the following dream:

> I had a number of dreams in sequence. But I don't remember them well. One was, we were standing around, some people were standing around, and they had in their hands *canes* shaped like hockey sticks, used upside down, the curved part up. But they were shaped more like *free form* than plain hockey sticks. And there was in the dream two of my wife's cousins—a married couple. We see them about twice a year and in the dream I was kind of indifferent to them or critical of them because of some opinions they had. And you made a comment, "Why are you so critical?" And I had other dreams I can't recall, there were a series of them. You sort of woke me up after I had them. I mean you asked me about the dreams after they had gone on for some time in the past. As a matter of fact, I remember waking up after the one with the hockey sticks and wondering why you didn't ask me whether I had been dreaming. I went back to sleep. That's all I can think of.

Inquiry the following morning produced this additional information:

> [You mentioned hockey sticks?] Yes, I guess it was like a party, people were there and they had *canes*, but very nicely shaped canes like hockey sticks, they weren't hockey sticks actually but about the same size, long and the shape was very good for them. Now I think I know ... before I went to sleep I was thinking of the fact that Leah and I were invited to a banquet at the Waldorf given by this international society for the welfare of cripples, maybe that's why

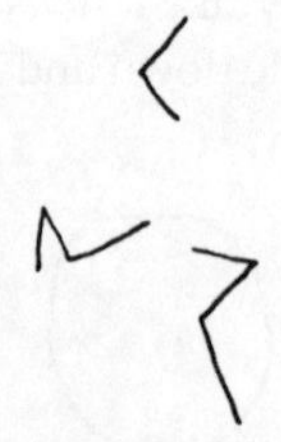

Figure 9. Example 2—angular shapes.

this came, and of course I don't like the idea of having to go formal and we were planning to go camping around that time but it seemed we were invited as guests. The hockey sticks were not all exactly the same shape. It has to do with disability, at the same time in spite of the disabilities these people get around pretty well.

B. Explicit correlation between dream and formal aspects of target when more complex target material was used

Example 3

The target picture showed a monk squatting before what the agent initially took to be a square blue patch of stone. Later, on closer examination, this appeared to be a garden. Along one border there was a diamond-shaped pattern in the pavement (*Figure 10*).

4:20 am:

I was approaching a masonry wall with the stones put together very neatly. Someone else and I are seated in a cab of some large

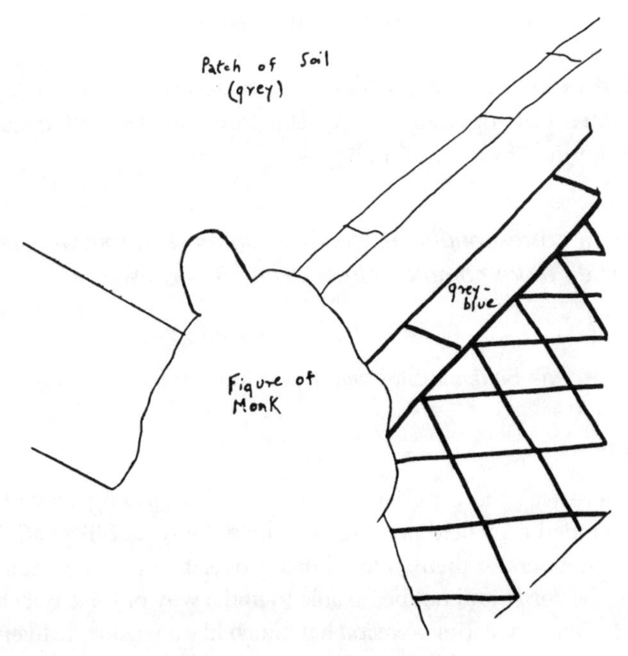

Figure 10. Example 3—monk.

> vehicle—it might be a tractor. We're coming up to this wall. I was with someone else. We were travelling in what seemed like the front of some very big vehicle parallel to the large wall. We came to a small *diamond-shaped hole* in the wall. One of us remarked "Look at that." The wall was gray.

5:24 am:

> There was a figure of a *diamond*, a *diamond* shape was in it.

5:35 am:

> We were in Alaska, my wife and I were together. It was about 7:00 o'clock in the morning and I said to her, "Well, it's very unlikely that you'll ever see the sun this low in the horizon again at such an hour." And she said, "Yes, I noticed that." It wasn't at all cold. We were walking along in what seemed to be a forest with only what seemed to be very few trees until we came to one large, very large tree, with thick branches, no leaves. It was at the time when it didn't seem to be cold, and Lillian pointed out to me that on the trunk of the tree there was a large *diamond*, like a trapezoid, that had been cut out of the centre of the trunk of the tree.

It should be noted that the first dream described a masonry wall with stones put together neatly. The three subsequent dreams all make reference to diamond shapes.

C. Implicit correspondences between dream and formal aspects of target when more complex target material was used

Example 4

The target was *Bauhaus Stairway* by Oskar Schlemmer (*Figure 11*).

Dream no. 1:

> ... there was the experience of *mounds*. The feeling was of being surrounded on a field, a monstrous field, by sort of like *anthills*, but large numbers of them, and climbing over them. and around them back and forth. and not being able to find a way out. Then it changes to a feeling of wearing a *conical* hat, much like a wizard ... Everything was spinning around *counterclockwise*, whirling, whirling, turning,

Figure 11. Oskar Schlemmer, *Bauhaus Stairway*, 1932. Oil on canvas, $63\frac{7}{8} \times 45$. Collection The Museum of Modern Art, New York. Gift of Philip Johnson.

and it's going in the same direction, and in some respects I was forcing consciously, deliberately, helping myself in the process, as if I was doing a spin ...

Dream no. 2:

> ... I remember describing to you sensations ... and these were being in some sort *of* tunnel, some sort *of* windy, open plain, climbing up to a hill ... I thought *of* ... *Mt. Appelier*. I think this was the first thing I had related, where I had felt I was going up a road, driving my car of some sort and looking back and forth, but still going upward, you know, ascending this mountain ... They weren't exactly anthills. Initially, they started off as bumps, sort of like ... a fez, but they were small and rounded off on top instead of squared *off* like a fez. It's like the little pies children make with a pail.
>
> [The experimenter then asked "Please make a guess at what you think the target for the night was."]
>
> [Subject] One of the elements that pervaded almost everything was this conical shape—pointed, conical, mountainlike, conical, hat-like cones ... I'd say some sort of form element, conical in shape ... It's the one thing that seems to unify all of the fantasy, and all of the dreams.

Example 5

The target was "The Dark Figure"—a painting by Castellon (*Figure 12*). This painting portrays four people, one of them garbed in a sombre, dark-brown gown. There are four round hoops above the figures; the hoops are held in the air by distorted children's hands. In the background is a red brick wall.

First dream report:

> ... For some reason I've been thinking of a *barrel* ... you know, *spinning* around ... There was some kind of activity or motion going on. The barrel was spinning ... like spinning in a circle ... It was like spinning. A top. Clockwise, left to right ... *Dark Brown* wooden colour ... A red wheel spinning around.

Second dream report:

> I thought I saw lights and these lights were arranged in almost a *circular* fashion ... You have a circle again and there was some movement there ...

Figure 12. Frederico Castellon, *The Dark Figure*, 1938. Oil on canvas, $17 \times 26\frac{1}{8}$ Collection Whitney Museum of American Art, New York.

Sixth dream report:

> ... there was a photograph I was looking at and in this photograph there was a bunch of people standing, and out front there were four people in *costumes* whose picture we were taking ... They were just posing ... and looked pretty ridiculous ...

Post-sleep interview:

> ... All I remember at first, I think, was these wooden barrels, maybe three or four ... There was the *iron rim* going around the middle to hold the slats together, and ... going around and around, spinning like a *top* ... I also remember something about pale greenish-white lights ... They formed kind of like an arch as though they started to spiral or circle ... swirling like whirlpools ... This photograph was a rather big one and it had these young guys in costumes ... Two summers ago when I went to that camp for retarded children, they asked me to put on skits and costumes ... There is a lot of circling and spiralling effects in my dreams, so any combination of effects like those I would look for in the target.

Example 6

The target was the painting *Football Players* by Henri Rousseau (*Figure 13*).

First dream:

> *Semicircular*. In the first one, I'm sort of near a balcony, only I'm inside the building and the balcony comes back into the building in

Figure 13. Football Players, by Henri Rousseau, 1908.
The Solomon R. Guggenheim Museum Collection.

a semicircular way. I suppose the balcony itself outside the doorway is some kind of straight routine type of balcony structure, but I'm inside the buildings (if you want to call it that), but it's more like a courtyard, and there's like a railing coming inside from the balcony along the floor of this stone courtyard, and I had the feeling as though it had vines on it or something. As you approached the balcony to look out, it seems to look over something like the mall in Washington—toward like the Washington Monument.

And then the second image I got was again standing in a kind of courtyard looking toward a sort of Roman courtyard—it's more of—it's a European kind of building, with a sort of terrace jutting out from the bottom of the building again, a *semicircular* quality like statues in a *semicircle*; the two ends of the *semicircle* are toward me and the *semicircle* goes back away from me, and there's like a fountain in the centre. That's all. Those two things came to me. Sort of half-dreaming, half-asleep way.

Second dream:

A floor in Bloomingdales where the houseware stuff is, and there's like empty book shelves on the left side of the room, on one of these—and these shelves are like painted black, and the wall behind the shelf (the whole thing) is like a black shadow box; and on it is this lone object shaped like a *cylinder*, sort of like a cheese box, only small, about five or six inches in diameter, and it's red lacquer, and it's spinning like a top—only it's not really—it's *rotating* around … and now I remember that the *semicircle* of the balcony did the same thing, and also the inverted *semicircle* of the statues in the other thing.

Third dream:

Oh, I think of *summer camp*. I remember … that you have to be able to tip over a canoe and right it again, something like that. These were obstacle tests.

Fourth dream:

I was peeling an onion and talking to somebody … But before that, I was dreaming about my mother as a little girl standing in the doorway of a *Victorian parlor*, facing a niche of some sort, and this

> arch doorway was all surrounded with some kind of filigree-like curtains, or some twig design that they thought was very artistic around 1903 or 1904 or so. [Rousseau painted *Football Players* in 1908.]

Fifth dream: No obvious references.

Sixth dream:

> Myself and two other kids ... Anyway, we were swimming in a swimming pool ... The scene shifts and it has something to do with the *headmaster* of a prep school, so I suppose that the swimming pool was at the prep school.

Excerpts from subject's associations:

> There was an *awful lot of movement* ... I think it was kind of a counterclockwise motion—circular, revolving motion ... There was even a merry-go-round in it somewhere.

The points of formal correspondence rest on the repeated reference to semicircular quality, the arrangement of statues in a semicircle and a form that is spinning like a top (cf. the football). Other interesting areas of correspondence involve the reference to a camp or prep school and the Victorian setting.

D. Correspondence based on both form (square framework) and content (Madison Square Garden, boxing)

Example 7

The target selected and shown in *Figure 14* was *Dempsey and Firpo* by Bellows. This target portrays two boxers and a referee in a rectangular boxing ring. One of the boxers has been knocked through the ropes into the audience.

Excerpts from subject's first dream report:

> ... something about posts ... Just posts standing up from the ground, and nothing else ... There's some kind of a feeling of moving ... Ah, something about *Madison Square Garden* and a boxing fight. An angular shape, as if all these things that I see were

Figure 14. Dempsey and Firpo, 1924, George Bellows.
Oil on canvas, $51 \times 63\frac{1}{4}$ in.
Collection Whitney Museum of American Art New York.

in a rectangular framework. There's an angular shape coming down toward the right, the lower right, as if you were seeing a filming that took up a whole block ... That angular right hand corner of the picture is connected with *Madison Square boxing fight* ... I had to go to *Madison Square Garden* to pick up tickets to a boxing fight, and there were a lot of tough punks—people connected with the fight—around the place and I had a hard time finding the people who were supposed to have the tickets for me, and a guard was in front of the gate to the office where these people were and I had to talk with this guard. I could have had an argument with him, but instead we got along and talked about it, and finally he let me through the gate into the inner office and I finally got the tickets.

Excerpts from subject's second dream report:

The machine is a strange shape. It's got two squares and stands about as high as a man and it's got two squares, as if cube forms connected by a vertical shaft ... I can't associate that shape with

> anything I know. It's strange, too, I'm unclear if there are two or three figures in the dream because there seems to be the presence of other people ... These people seem to have met in a social situation but they were there for some other purpose anyway, and they came together, but when they came together it was apparently the only reason that they came together. Now it seems to be clearer. There's another figure. It seems more clear that there's one older figure of an old man and two younger ones that I can remember, and there certainly is an awareness of a third person.

Excerpts from subject's third dream report:

> A hexagonal cube appeared. It's a cube with a number of sides. I don't know exactly how many, but something like six or eight ...

Excerpts from subject's fourth dream report: No obvious correspondence.

Excerpts from subject's associational material:

> Well, the thing that came to my mind was as if this picture took place in a *square frame* ... I went to *Madison Square Garden* with some money to pick up tickets which had been ordered by someone in the office, and again there was this huge building—this was just the association to *Madison Square Building* or *Garden*—there was this huge building and there were all these wrestling and *boxing posters* around, and a bunch of kookie-looking people—most of them sort of looked like they could have been wrestlers, or *old fighters* or something—in line wanting to get tickets to these events, and I went upstairs and went to this thing called the *Boxing Club* or something where you get tickets ... I think if you hadn't brought it up, I think I might have forgotten about that Madison Square Garden.

This was an interesting synchronicity involving a past event (having gone to Madison Square Garden) and the choice of target for that night.

E. Correspondence based on emotional impact

The randomly selected target, "*Animals*" by Tamayo, is shown in *Figure 15*. The painting depicts two dogs with flashing teeth eating

Figure 15. Animals, 1941, Rufino Tamayo. Oil on canvas, $30\frac{1}{8} \times 40$ in. Collection, The Museum of Modern Art, New York. Inter-American Fund.

pieces of meat. A huge black rock can be seen in the background. The points of correspondence between dream and target picture are noted in the following excerpts.

Excerpts from S's second dream report:

> ... the name of the dream was "Black Wood, Vermont" or something like that ... Well, there's this group of people, and they have an idea that they're picked out for something special ... and that these other people were threatening enemies ...

Excerpts from S's third dream report:

> I was at this banquet ... and I was *eating* something like rib steak. And this friend of mine was there ... and people were talking about how she wasn't very good to invite for *dinner* because she was very conscious of other people getting more to eat than she got—like, especially, *meat*—because in Israel they don't have so much meat ... That was the most important part of the dream, that *dinner* ... It was

> probably Freudian like all my other dreams—you know, *eating*, and all that stuff, and a banquet ... Well, there was another friend of mine, also in this dream. Somebody that I teach with, and she was eyeing everybody to make sure that everybody wasn't getting more than she was, too. And I was chewing a piece of ... *rib steak*. And I was sitting at the table eating meat, and people were telling me that this Israeli friend of mine was not nice to invite to a banquet because she was always afraid she wasn't getting enough ... I was invited because I'm polite and not demanding, but I just tried to keep my mouth shut in the dream. I tried not to say anything about her, even though in a way I was glad that she was finally being found out ... And the second one ... was about Vermont, Black Rock, Vermont ... Yesterday, I was at the beach, and I was sitting on one of the rocks ... and I felt like that mermaid from Black Rock ...

The content of dreams

Elsewhere (Ullman, 1973, 1986; Tolaas, 1986) it has been suggested that the screening of content for appropriateness for inclusion in the dreaming experience can be understood on the basis of a vigilance hypothesis. This view suggests that dream consciousness is an elaborate form of orienting activity designed to attend to, process and respond to certain aspects of residual experience, with an endpoint being reached in either the continuation of the sleeping state or its interruption and consequent transformation to awakening.

The affective residue which makes its presence felt in the dream operates reflexively or automatically as a scanning mechanism. Ranging over the entire longitudinal history of the person, it exerts a polarizing influence, drawing to itself and mobilizing aspects of past experiences that are related to it in emotionally meaningful ways. In a different context, Dewan (1969) has called this "emotional tagging" and has identified it as a device facilitating memory storage and consolidation. Here it is viewed as an energizing or mobilizing effect necessary to help the sleeping organism to fully assess the meaning and implications of the novel or disturbing stimulus and through the participation of a monitoring process either allow the sleep cycle to remain intact or to result in arousal.

The concept of vigilance in relation to dreaming suggests a survival function. The intrinsic emotional honesty of dream imagery is the means that serves this purpose. Just as other animals survive in the wild by being in accurate touch with their physical environment, we humans have to be in truthful touch with our human environment. We are a single species and our ultimate survival as a species is dependent on maintaining a level of genuine interconnectedness that can overcome the forces that lead to fragmentation. Dreams call to our attention anything in our waking life that either strengthens or undermines our ties to others or to unresolved residues from our past that shape our lives. Dreams have an advantage over waking life, in that whatever our unconscious has to say to us it can say it without pandering to our waking ego.

In connection with the issue of connectivity that I have found the writing of the late David Bohm (1987) on wholeness to be relevant, particularly his concept of the implicate order which consists of a seamless ground of interconnectedness that in turn gives rise to the discreteness of the manifest or explicate order. He likens the seeming discreteness of macroscopic entities to standing waves forming out of a fluid medium. From subatomic particles on up there is an intimate and durable relation to the implicate order that sustains them.

The dream's focus on interconnectedness suggests that the imagistic mode of the dream is closer to the implicate order than the discursive mode of waking consciousness (Ullman, 1987). The initial transformation takes place when what is unconscious (implicit) assumes the form of the sensorially apprehended images (explicit) that appear in the dream.

While dreaming, experience is organized along lines of emotional contiguity rather than temporal and spatial contiguity. The affective scanning that takes place while dreaming can, on occasion, bridge a spatial gap and provide us with information independent of any known communication channel. Emotional contiguity, under conditions we know very little about, appears capable of integrating transpersonal as well as personal content into the dream. Anecdotal accounts have for a long time pointed in this direction and the circumstances under which they occur strongly suggest that in matters of life and death the vigilant scanning of one's emotional environment reaches out across spatial boundaries in a manner that has yet to be explained.

Correspondences

In the experimental work the correspondences noted could be classified as follows:

I. Correspondences based on form

  A. Direct or explicit correspondences

    1. With simple forms as targets (*Figures 2–4, 7* and *8*)

    2. Abstracting simple forms from more complex targets (*Figures 5* and *6*)

  B. Indirect or implicit correspondences (*Figures 11–13*)

II. Correspondences based on emotional response (*Figure 14*)

Psychiatric implications

When the individual by virtue of limiting psychological or emotional factors fails to maintain a sense of effective participation in the here-and-now, psi effects occasionally occur. In my experience patients who were more fragile and vulnerable in regard to their hold on reality had more often and more striking paranormal experiences. In 1949 1 wrote:

> … Very ill individuals teetering on the brink but not yet over on the psychotic side often indicate remarkable psi ability in the course of analysis. … once psychosis, or the complete loss of effective relationships with other people sets in, the indications at present are that at least in the experimental situation psi functioning is not remarkable, nor is it in the clinical situation in my own experience … [T]he consistent clinical fact [is] that psychotics in their fantasies make elaborate pretensions at psi ability, sometimes quite openly, sometimes in a more disguised form. [Ullman, 1949]

In the light of this formulation paranormal ability comes into being as a last desperate level of relatedness when personality factors interfere with more effective contact. Once the individual has withdrawn from the struggle to maintain his sense of relatedness, fantasy takes over and there are delusions of telepathy rather than any genuine demonstrable paranormal ability. At a practical level there are clear cut technical and instrumental gains when there is explicit recognition of the telepathy hypothesis and its possible application in the therapeutic situation. Anyone sensitive to the occurrence of such effects would be in a position to recognize and handle counter-transferential difficulties more promptly and more honestly. The work of Jourard (1971) shows that self-disclosure is a powerful factor in accounting for the level of disclosure offered by others. Psi events make it possible to engage in a deeper level of mutual disclosure when such disclosure is relevant to the therapeutic situation. Eisenbud's accounts are of particular interest in this connection with the freedom he felt in disclosing his own interest in telepathy and the way that interest influenced the transferential dynamics not only with a patient (*telepathy à deux*) but at times with a third patient as well (*telepathy à trois*) (Eisenbud, 1970).

After a somewhat dormant period with regard to psychoanalytic interest in dream telepathy, a recent paper by Bass (2001) took note of the various ways collusion occurred between the unconscious of the patient and the unconscious of the analyst, amounting at times to presumptuously telepathic exchanges. He calls attention to the possible relevance of this to two basic concepts of quantum mechanics. The first is that observations made at a quantum level are, in some still mysterious way, dependent upon the arrangements made for the observation. One cannot objectively separate what is observed from the observer. The second draws upon the possible relation of telepathic transfer to the now established fact of nonlocality. When two similar atomic particles are once "entangled" and then separated, they undergo simultaneous and corresponding changes when a feature of one particle, e.g. spin, is altered. No known force can generate that instantaneously.[7]

There is one, perhaps somewhat tangential but nevertheless relevant, aspect to the work on telepathy. Those of us who have taken a public position espousing the reality of psi events are aware of a lost battalion of people who have had telepathic dreams that seemed both genuine and relevant to current issues in their lives and which left them confused and concerned often to the point where they questioned their own sanity. To share it with others would risk rebuff. People don't ordinarily go around having experiences like this. I have known of situations where the distress was severe enough for the individual to seek psychiatric help and were faced with the psychiatrists' failure to discern or consider the difference between a genuine telepathic experience and the claim of telepathic powers as a symptom of schizophrenia (so noted in the diagnostic criteria of schizophrenia in the American Psychiatric Association, *DSM III*). Instead of a fair-minded openness to the reality of telepathy, they are met with a bias that confirms their fear of self-disclosure. Caught in this bind, such individuals ultimately gravitate toward fringe groups in search of the support they need. One hopes that greater knowledge and a deeper understanding on the part of the therapist of the nature and reality of psi will someday save these individuals from the pain and distress of a frustrated search for help and at the same time broaden the horizon of the helping profession itself.

Notes

1. Psi is a term used to denote the main areas of parapsychological research, namely, telepathy, clairvoyance, precognition, and psychokinesis.
2. For a detailed account of these events, see Ullman (1993, 1994a,b, 1995).
3. Jung used this term to refer to acausal meaningful coincidences linking external events to personal meaning.
4. Jung had an early and lifelong interest in the paranormal.
5. For a complete account of these studies, see Ullman *et al.* (1989).
6. Examples 1, 2 and 3 are from the pilot studies referred to earlier.
7. For a discussion of the possible relevance of quantum concepts such as complementarity, the uncertainty principle, the relation of the observer and observed and non-locality to dreaming consciousness and telepathy, see Ullman (1999).

References

Bass, A. (2001). It takes one to know one. *Psychoanalytic Dialogues, 11*: 683–701.

Bohm, D. (1987). *Wholeness and the Implicate Order*. London: Routledge & Kegan Paul.

Child, I. L. (1985). Psychology and anomalous observation: The question of ESP in dreams. *American Psychologist, 40*: 1219–1220.

Dewan, E. M. (1969). *The Programming (P) Hypothesis for REMs, Res. Rep., Air Force*. Bedford, Mass.: Cambridge Research Laboratories.

Ehrenwald, J. (1955). *New Dimensions of Deep Analysis*. New York: Grune & Stratton.

Eisenbud, J. (1970). *Psi and Psychoanalysis*. New York: Grune & Stratton.

Eriksen, C. W. (1958). Unconscious processes. In: M. R. Jones (Ed.), *Nebraska Symposium on Motivation* (p. 169). Lincoln: University of Nebraska Press.

Evans, C. R. (1967a). Fragmentation phenomena associated with binocular stabilization. *British Journal of Physiol. Optics, 24*: 242–248.

Evans, C. R. (1967b). Further studies of pattern perception and a stabilised retinal image: The use of prolonged after-images to achieve perfect stabilisation. *British Journal of Psychology, 58*: 315–327.

Freud, S. (1963). *Sigmund Freud: Studies in Parapsychology*, P. Rief (Ed.). New York: Collier Books.

Jourard, S. M. (1971). *Self-disclosure, an Experimental Analysis of the Transparent Self*. New York: Wiley.

Klein, G. S. (1959). Consciousness in psychoanalytic theory: Some implications for current research in perception. *Journal of the American Psychoanalytical Association, 7*: 5–34.

Myers, F. W. H. (1903). *Personality and its Survival of Bodily Death*. London: Longmans, Green.

Servadio, E. A. (1956). Transference and thought transference. *International Journal of Psychoanalysis, 37*: 392–395.

Sinclair, U. (1930). *Mental Radio*. New York: Albert and Charles Boni.

Stekel, W. (1921). *Der Telepathiche Traum*. Berlin: JohannesBaum Verlag.

Tolaas, J. (1986). Vigilance theory and psi. Part I: Ethological and phylogenetic aspects. *The Journal of the American Society for Psychical Research, 80*: 357–391.

Ullman, M. (1949). On the nature of psi processes. *Journal of Parapsychology, 13*: 59–62.

Ullman, M. (1966). An experimental study of the telepathic dream. *Corrective Psychiat. Journal Soc. Therapy, 12*: 115–139.

Ullman, M. (1973). A theory of vigilance and dreaming. In: V. Zikmund (Ed.), *The Oculomotor System and Brain Function* (pp. 452–456). London: Butterworths.

Ullman, M. (1980). Parapsychology. In: H. I. Kaplan, A. M. Freedman & B. J. Saddock (Eds.), *Comprehensive Textbook of Psychiatry* (3rd edn). Baltimore: Williams and Wilkins.

Ullman, M. (1986). Vigilance theory and psi. Part II: Physiological, psychological and parapsychological aspects. *The Journal of the American Society for Psychical Research, 80*: 375–391.

Ullman, M. (1987). Wholeness and dreaming. In: B. S. Hiley & F. David Peat (Eds.), *Quantum Implications*. London: Routledge & Kegan Paul.

Ullman, M. (1993). The Bindelof story, Part I. *Exceptional Human Experiences, 11*: 17–28.

Ullman, M. (1994a). The Bindelof story, Part II. *Exceptional Human Experiences, 12*: 2531.

Ullman, M. (1994b). The Bindelof story, Part III. *Exceptional Human Experiences, 12*: 208–221.

Ullman, M. (1995). The Bindelof story, Part IV. *Exceptional Human Experiences, 13*: 1–12.

Ullman, M. (1999). Dreaming consciousness: More than a bit player in the search for answers to the mind/body problem. *Journal of Scientific Exploration, 13*: 91–112.

Ullman, M., Krippner, S., & Felstein, S. (1966). Experimentally induced telepathic dreams: Two studies using EEG-REM monitoring technique. *International Journal of Neuropsychiatry, 24*: 420–437.

Ullman, M., & Krippner, S. (1969). A laboratory approach to the nocturnal dimension of paranormal experience: Report of a confirmatory study using the REM monitoring technique. *Biological Psychiatry, 2*: 259–270.

Ullman, M., & Krippner, S. (1970). Telepathy and dreams: A controlled experiment with EEG-REM monitoring. *Journal of Nervous and Mental Disorders, 151*: 394–403.

Ullman, M., Krippner, S., & Vaughan, A. (1989). *Dream Telepathy: Experiments in Nocturnal ESP* (2nd edn). Jefferson, N.C.: McFarland.

Warcollier, R. (1938). *Experiments in Telepathy*. New York: Harper and Brothers.

CHAPTER TWO

Parapsychology and psychoanalysis

M. Lietaert Peerbolte

Case I

My studies in parapsychology from a psychoanalytical point of view commenced in 1936. They owed their origin to the fact that in the course of a treatment a female patient produced a dream with a distinctly telepathic character. The circumstances were, briefly, as follows. A week before she had the specific dream, the patient, acting in a transference state, begged her psychiatrist to requite her love (more will be heard about her masculine role presently). The cautious refusal of this request threw the patient into a deplorable mental state in which she alternately hoped to succeed in her attempts and was driven back again to her sense of inferiority that she had before the transference. In this state she had the following dream.

Dream 1

> I am in bed with Dr L. P. in a side-room. Another patient enters, a woman wearing a brown hat trimmed with a feather. The latter is holding a child in her arms, while leading another one by the hand.

> This woman remarks: "In the hall were two blue ewers full of water which were upset by one of the children." You thought: "All that lot of water in the corridor!" But you remained polite. The patient sat down, next to the side of the bed. The children were placed in a basket, and there they turned into kittens. You said to the children: "Stroke my chin, and tell me what you feel." I then left the room on purpose in order to leave you alone with the patient and, in the corridor, tied a violet-coloured ribbon round my hair.

The analytical protocol of this dream, written out on November 2nd, reads as follows:

> *Side-room*: "Long, narrow side-room. I don't know where. In bed with you."
>
> *Woman*: "Dark woman. The worst thing about it was that you treated the children so nicely."
>
> *Violet-coloured ribbon*: "Formerly I used to wear ribbons in my hair but never violet-coloured ones. One has a youthful look with a ribbon in one's hair. I did it on purpose, for then one looks childlike."
>
> *Ewers*: "We used to have them at home; my brother once fell into one of them. He cut his head, and all the water flowed over the floor. But the main issue was that you were much vexed and yet behaved so nicely."
>
> *Jealous*: "I was already jealous at the age of three. You are jealous yourself, I am sure of it. Anyway, you cannot keep many things concealed."
>
> *Kittens*: "You, with your face standing over those pussies. I was very jealous."

On the 4th of November the patient entered my consulting room much excited, and at once asked me if I had become a father. Answering in the affirmative—labour had begun in the evening of October 31st and the child was born on November 1st—I at the same time asked her how she had become aware of that fact. She answered that on November 3rd she had had a mental flash, "while thinking at the same time: 'My vexation will have reached its peak when the doctor gets a child', I suddenly had the impression: 'Oh, but he has one already'."

Spontaneously she then said that she now understands her dream. The upsetting of the ewers means a birth, and at once the dream is clear to her, i.e. telepathically she had felt the *partus*.

Elsewhere I have elucidated the genuinely telepathic character of the dream in great detail. I therefore think that it is sufficient here to point out that it was quite impossible for the patient to gain knowledge in a normal way of this confinement, whilst, moreover, the coincidence in the timing of the dream with the occurring birth (both happened in the same night) is too close to deny the dream's telepathic nature. In the meantime my interest was roused to the highest degree.

The protocol made out on the 6th of November runs as follows:

> *Violet-coloured*: "I put the ribbon too low, and it was of an inferior quality like that used for flower-baskets. I sometimes wear a ribbon when I am ill. Of late, I seemingly am so very calm. I am living again in a membrane. But as a matter of fact, I am so rebellious. I do not know what to do if I have to remain alone; I should like to give my own body a good thrashing."

In the course of the treatment finally the following data appeared:

> *Woman in a brown hat*: "A female friend of mine who is being divorced."
>
> *Side-room*: "I slept there when a child. Gas-light was still in use then, which I was not allowed to turn out myself. When I felt very bad, I turned up the gas. Mother was mortally afraid; she came every moment to have a look. I thought: By and by I'll do it, though. Two years ago I did so, and now I should like to do it once more."
>
> *Basket*: "At home we had a pussy-basket with one or more pussies in it."
>
> *Stroke my chin*: "You do this yourself when you feel you are mistaken."
>
> *Tell what you feel*: "When I was a little child, I liked to see my father shave in the evening. When he had shaved himself very clean, I was allowed to stroke his chin, it felt deliciously soft, and it smelled nice. Usually, he gave me a whisk over my face with the shaving-brush. Then I got angry and hit him. I should like to be such a child again."

If we proceed to interpret the dream in the usual way, we shall, briefly, remark the following items. The patient is back again in her childhood (lies in her bed in her little room, the side-room). In this child state she commits incest with her psychiatrist (father-image). She is prevented from doing so by a rival, a woman in the same circumstances as herself (her female friend who was getting divorced). The two children she cannot place. The blue ewers take her back to childhood. The childish envy she had of her little brother is expressed by saying: "he cut his head". Another example is the following dream:

> My brother is 16 years old. He was a little girl instead of a little boy. I felt sorry for him and said to mother that I never remarked it before. Mother said, she had never noticed it; and the boys at school did not notice it either.

Finally, the second part of the dream we are discussing here is likewise reducible to a child state (even the ribbon in her hair points in the direction of this wish). Hence, in analytical terms, in this dream we are dealing with a strong incestuous desire, and consequently the patient is still connected to the oedipal phase. Since this desire cannot be satisfied, she again feels herself enclosed in a "membrane", just as she was in another dream that will be communicated later. Moreover, accepting the telepathic nature of this dream, it is justifiable to regard the friend who is going to be divorced as a substitute for my wife, and the rival is clearly a mother-image. If we bear in mind that this dream was produced during the transference phase when she could not gratify her incestuous desire, it will become apparent that the moment, too, at which the dream occurred was fully determined, not only from a parapsychological point of view but also from an analytical one. Finally, the combination of a wish for incest and the transference back to a child state is likewise clear. The trouble which she suffered in childhood was always the product of the incest taboo (from this viewpoint, her desire then and now to turn on the gas can be understood).

A few questions have not yet been answered satisfactorily. First, it did not become clear why the woman described in the dream should be a mother-image. In fact, one would rather be inclined to deduce from the patient's associations that this woman represented the patient herself. From the friend being likewise divorced we construe theoretically the link with the psychiatrist's wife in two directions: (a) it is possible that this dream-vision contains the wish to be this wife herself, i.e. the friend who is going to be divorced and who is herself, too, is the psychiatrist's wife; (b) it is also possible that here the wish is that the psychiatrist's wife will be divorced, and so the meaning is that the friend (that is to say, the psychiatrist's wife) is getting a divorce. Probably both tendencies are represented in the same dream–vision.

Secondly, the patient had no ideas who the two children might be. Are we here concerned with a child state? The patient's parents had two children, a little brother and herself. In this case the missing link for the establishment of the mother-image would be present after all.

From the above it is evident, therefore, that this dream may be explained in two ways: (1) as a reaction to a certain disillusion in an active transference phase; (2) as a telepathic dream reflecting an occurrence happening to the analyst. The fact that a dream may allow two interpretations was the reason that I took up the further study of dreams showing a pronounced parapsychological character. As, however, my studies made it evident that parapsychological phenomena are closely related to a person's mental structure, I deem it expedient to explain the psychical structure of this patient by looking at further dreams from the analysis.

Dream II

> A small fire breaks out in a glass bowl containing a fish and a small bird. The fire terrified the two animals to death but nevertheless they do not leap out of the bowl which has a narrow opening. Someone took the bird out; it was dazed but flew away after some time. The fish had been out of the water, and was at the point of dying. It had very large eyes. Somebody poured water over its head.

The associations connected with this dream are:

> *Glass bowl*: "I am enclosed in a membrane which I cannot pierce. I am living in a mist."

Fish: "Astrologically speaking, I am a Pisces."

Bird: "Birds fly. It must be delicious to do whatever one pleases. The bird was kept a prisoner in that bowl."

Fish and bird: "What I should like to be, and what in reality I am. To others I seem cool and cold, that is the fish; I was born in the sign of the Fishes; birds are free in the air."

Large eyes: "They protrude from the head; as a child I had large eyes."

Small fire: "Annihilation."

In the first place, the bird points to her wish to be free. As a matter of fact, she is very jealous of her husband who, after the divorce, would lead his own life, a free man, whilst she herself, feeling her desires, is not free to do whatever she wishes. Considered in this way, this dream is a faithful reflection of her former marriage: the bird, the husband; the fish, herself, suffering from the unhappy marriage. Someone took the fish out of the bowl, meaning that a divorce is concluded (the divorce was only obtained after her legal adviser had strongly recommended it to her), and the bird is the husband flying away. Meanwhile, she herself, the fish, is at death's door; it is lying for a long time in a dry spot (sexual abstinence).

The water poured over the fish's head refers to the psychotherapeutic treatment during which, at the moment her dream was produced, her transference had barely begun and she had the secret wish to satisfy her sexual desires with the analyst. The entire tragedy taking place in a glass bowl having a narrow opening, out of which neither the little bird nor the fish could escape, distinctly typifies her infantile attitude towards life, in which she represents matrimony as an affair *in utero*. The patient, indeed, also produced dreams in which this infantile attitude is more strongly emphasized, and from which her strong maternal link becomes prominent.

Thus, while on the one hand the small fire symbolizes her ended marriage, on the other hand it represents as well her sexual desire. Owing to enforced abstinence her old Oedipus complex was strongly activated, for the maternal link expressed by the symbol of the glass bowl has a distinctly negative note, the mother being the person who prevents the desired incest. In her neurosis this motif plays a prominent part, and again and again this mother-image apparently keeps her a captive and inhibits the desired incest (incorporated in the neurotic symptoms).

The patient, kept prisoner by the mother-image, is threatened, however, by being consumed, annihilated by abstinence. (There is a fish in the glass bowl. The fish and the bird symbolize two sides of her, i.e. the fish, cool and cold as she seems to be; the bird, free as she would like to be.)

It is striking that the fish is often a masculine symbol. If she could be a bird, then she would be a woman (free), while as a fish, she fulfils a masculine role (which among other things is expressed in the telepathic dream; in the fact that she thinks that her brother had to be a girl, and that she must be a boy; and also in her jealousy towards her former husband).

This situation is centred in a perfectly negative Oedipus complex by which, after the failure of incest (mother will not let me free), there appears a strong tendency to identify herself with her father (fish), while the bird is kept a captive. This negative relation towards the father-image, deduced from the first motif, now appears to be clear from the very first dream she produced in the course of the treatment.

Dream III

> I was afraid. I awoke pouring with perspiration. I had to go by tram from A to B. I had a five pound note in my hand. The tram was full of gypsies. I sat beside a man who could not keep his hands off me. I went and stood next to the driver on the platform. The same thing happened again. I had to change the banknote. They wanted to take it from me. I jumped out and got into another tramcar. But there, too, the same thing happened all over again. Then I wanted to walk to B. I had no money. At a hotel I hailed a taxi to drive me to B. The driver said: "One shilling, because it is you". Another driver demanded ten shillings, kept stopping the taxi along the road, and again did not leave me alone.

While this dream speaks for itself, we may now expect that, under the influence of the bird-motif, she must have a negative relation toward her mother. The following dreams clearly express this relation.

Dream IV

My mother said: "A young man came to me at the door with a mug of water. He wanted to predict the future, and would do it from the water." I asked her what she had done. She had taken a key and hit him on the head with it. I was very angry.

Dream V

In a little garden; my mother was sitting on a chair. Somebody came home, wearing trousers and having long hair. A long coat on to hide the trousers. I looked at him. That somebody took on a threatening attitude. I said: "Alright, I know all about it; I will not talk about it." Then I pulled down my mother by the neck to kill her. [Her wish to be a boy arose after the unsuccessful incest]

Dream VI

With a man in bed, naked. Mother lay between us, a bit lower down. I did not know what to do with my hands. If I kept them down by my side, I touched him. That was not permitted, for mother was lying next to him. Both were visibly embarrassed.

Dream VII

I was with you at home, not here, but in a strange house. The treatment was over. I had still to steal something from your house that neither you nor your wife was allowed to know about. I did not go out, I hid somewhere. Then I saw your wife standing at the door. She had shown out a patient. In your wife I recognized Mrs A. Then I slept. Awoke with my hands above my head, somebody was holding me by the wrists. I became afraid. That somebody was standing behind me. I wanted to free myself and looked around. It was you. Oh no, this I can trust, that is nice. You said: "Sleep in peace." Then you were in an adjoining room, there was a gentleman with you. You began to pay draughts or chess. I heard the pieces falling with a clatter on to the table. You said: "Oh no, that is true." And then you came to me and gave me a couple of succulent plants. I slipped, lost my shoe; I knew that it was under water. Somebody was walking beside me, a woman. I said: "My shoe is falling into the water." She said: "No, it will lie there." I would not lose it.

It appears, therefore, that the patient, in her endeavour to positively experience incest during treatment, produced the telepathic dream at a moment when the positive phase was in danger of failing. This positive phase is symbolized in the form of the bird in her dream. At the moment the castration-motif is touched upon in the treatment, the bird flies a little in the air, and the dream attains a telepathic character.

The bird-motif, as a symbol, has been so heavily weighted with all kinds of meaning in the literature that I intend going into it in a special study. Here, however, I will confine myself to pointing out the role of birds in fairy-tales where they are very often used as invisible messengers to keep in touch with somebody who, for example, is being held in captivity. I personally am inclined to ascribe a telepathic character to that bird-motif.

However, it should not be lost sight of that it is just the hatred toward the mother as a castrator which keeps forming the unexpressed undertone in the whole situation, owing to which the situation really "stands in the sign of the fish". Thus, on the one hand we perceive telepathic contact taking place by means of the bird-motif, while on the other hand it operates just at the moment when the bird is again kept in captivity, because the fish, which had been in the background, suddenly appears at the instant that the positive heterosexual libido current is in danger. The two alternating motifs, bird and fish, form together a compulsive reiteration, and at the moment of conversion of the bird into the fish, the parapsychological phenomenon made its appearance.

Although not expressed in the analysis, I still have to see the psychic layer in her case through a primeval castration-complex (mother has left me). A mother fixation arose which is strengthened by the mother forbidding incest in the following phase, while the antagonist of the castration, i.e. the longing for care and a feeding mother, leads up to a negative Oedipus-state (fish-motif).

The following dream shows the same development.

Dream VIII

A bedroom, a double bed and a single bed. I had slept in a bed in another room, and was chased out by somebody. Then I went to my parents' bedroom, and entered without knocking. The double bed

> was empty, father and mother were lying in intimacy in the single bed. Father covered up when I entered. I behaved as if I had not seen anything, and went on tiptoe to the double bed. I was going to lie in it. When I wanted to get into the bed, father and mother were lying in it. I still had no place to lie in. Father got up, went to the washing-stand, and ejaculated. "Fine", I thought, "I have prevented you. You have had no fun." Then I awoke.

* * *

Case III

Whereas in the case of patient A [above] the repetition compulsion could be seen as situated at the oedipal (genital) level, although it was supposed that in her case it was more properly localized in the oral phase, this oral localization plainly presents itself in the case of patient B [in Case II, omitted]. Since the telepathic contact would thus be connected with a repetition compulsion in the oral stage, the investigation was immediately continued by studying other parapsychological case-material.

In the first place I turned my attention to a series of dreams of an allegedly paranormal nature published by J. M. J. Kooy (1934). From a scientific point of view it would be highly desirable to be able to give two separate interpretations of all dreams of such a series, that is to say, a parapsychological one, and a psychoanalytical one. In reality, however, there are limits to our powers of interpretation, e.g. I was not able to explain all dreams in an analytical sense. Matters would have been different if the dreamer had been in analytical treatment. Therefore, I had to select dreams I could interpret without too much difficulty. In the paper quoted we are informed first that the dreamer had had precognitive dreams before the series described. Although those dreams do not belong to the experimental series, I think it right to record them here because they place us at once in the very midst of the problem. This parapsychological anamnestic introduction runs as follows:

> The earlier precognitive dreams were principally connected with a very important event in my life, i.e. my father's death. About March, 1932 (I cannot remember the exact date), I awoke on a certain

morning in my room at R. in a very dejected state of mind. In a state between sleeping and waking, I clearly saw my room, the window and the brass knobs on the railing of my bed's foot. Suddenly, time seemed to make a leap, my father (at the time in good health and energetically active, as far as appearances went) was dead; and consequently I was alone in the world. The strong support of my life had now dropped out, and I had therefore to take measures to shift for myself. My dejected state of mind did not last for long, for, though the surroundings remained identical, the melancholy passed off, and with a sigh of relief I remembered the real situation, i.e. my father was still alive. But I could not dismiss the memory of that depressive internal experience. Some weeks afterwards, when in England on a business-trip, I saw in my hotel-room in London a bed with brass knobs, while the room also had a window at the foot of the bed. In spite of myself, a feeling of uneasiness pervaded me. I had arranged with my father that he would send me instructions by cable but the telegram did not arrive till very late that evening. Only when I had received the telegram did I feel safe in my hotel-room, being sure that no bad news could be sprung on me. During another night at Q (I cannot remember exactly which), I again had an impressive and very sad dream. In the midst of a wood I saw a large chapel (a kind of church sometimes found in Roman Catholic cemeteries). I heard bells ringing violently, I saw graves and on them the image of a broken column. The next instant I was eating pancakes together with my mother, sister and betrothed in some place or other. My father was not present. This dream, too, long obsessed me like a total nightmare.

Afterwards, at the beginning of my father's illness, and shortly before his operation, I once more had a sort of vision in which I saw myself walking in the garden (of the paternal home at Bosch en Duin) and conversing with someone, saying that my father had died. On that occasion I had the sensation of an illness, in which death should be considered a deliverance rather than a terror. I felt dejected but nevertheless relieved. All those gloomy dreams which, judging from ordinary appearances, seemed utterly fantastic, unfortunately appeared to have been very serious predictions. On the first of June, my father and I visited the town of Leyden to look at the electrical installations of a roll-bascule bridge we had built there. The next day, I was informed from my parents' house at Bosch en Duin that my father, on account of an indisposition, had stayed at home, a quite unusual thing for him to do. On the third day he underwent an operation, after which he so far recovered that he intended to resume his work, and this he did full of energy However, on 12 September, 1932, he died of carcinoma of the intestines after a rather painful illness, so that we felt his passing away as a relief for him. As a curious detail I would like to add that the physician's name who was present at my father's death was Pannekoek ("Pancake"). Long before my father's illness, my mother, too, had had alarming dreams, in which she saw my father going away in a train or ship, etc ...

All the above quoted dreams are by no means insignificant from an analytical viewpoint. First, the dreamer seemed to have leant heavily on his father whom he regarded as his main support. An oedipal state is indicated, emphasized by the information that the mother also had precognitive dreams bearing on the father. The suggestion is obvious that, on the one hand, the dreamer, leaning on the father, is tied to him. The father, energetically active, takes the lead in their mutual work. On the other hand, however, the startling information about the mother is a hint to the analyst to keep an open mind as to the incestuous background of the whole situation. It is also remarkable that the father's death is predicted, among other things, by a broken column (the penis of the father has been smashed); afterwards the dreamer with his mother, sister, and betrothed eat pancakes (the dreamer is now his father's successor—"now I am eating him": oral sadistic triumph, totem-meal?). So the parapsychological anamnesis is in some ways an analytical introduction at the same time.

In the controlled series, dreams regarding funerals and fatal accidents appear to be predominating in a remarkable way. The very first dream of this series is a precognitive one referring to a funeral procession, related by the dreamer as follows:

> In a flash a funeral procession appeared, and I noted in French (in consequence of the auditory hallucination which I had at the moment of the flash): *Colonne funebre, caveau tire a cheval d'abord*. In order to minimize as much as possible the chance of meeting a funeral procession, I resolved, as I was already staying at Bosch en Duin that Friday afternoon, to stay at home the following Saturday morning. It seemed most improbable to me that on Saturday

afternoon I should come across a funeral procession in these surroundings. But when posting a letter that afternoon, at a quarter past two, I was astonished to come across a funeral procession on the road. The procession, however, was not composed of coaches drawn by horses but of a motor-hearse with five mourning-cars. Consequently the prediction was not fully realized, for precognition and future event were only partially similar.

Here is another instance:

(March 9th, noted when I awoke in the morning). Father lost his life by crashing in an airplane. Mother spoke about all the things father would have done when still alive: travelling together, etc. I, however, doubted whether the accident had been a mortal one. Conclusion (also noted down immediately): a KLM airplane or one from Soesterberg will soon be wrecked. In the evening of March 9th I perused the paper in order to see if such an accident had occurred but found no mention of it. The morning paper of March 10th, however, contained the following item: "a military airplane [from Soesterberg, a military airfield] crashed at Venlo. Pilot and mechanic injured, also one of the onlookers". The accident happened in the afternoon of March 9th, 1933.

The dream quoted above is interesting, because it emphasizes the father's death as well as the precognitive element. One might raise the question whether the dreamer possesses paranormal faculties in connection with his father's death. The fact that so many of his dreams bear on death should then be interpreted as a phenomenon of generalization. But if we look into the matter closely, we can see the death-motif alternating sometimes with coffin-motifs. The latter motif is evident in the dream now to be quoted:

Dream-note August 9th: I meet with Mr de Bie who is dusting a drawing-office or a loft. A moment afterwards, I am sucking water out of the ground with a kind of funnel in a wide plane such as the Wieringermeerpolder [one of the first parts of the Zuyderzee to be drained]. While I was performing this queer work, the nozzle of the funnel comes into contact with a box. I, then, see the box lying at my feet in a cavity (a trench). The box has the shape of a flattened

> parallelepipedon (hence that of an ordinary packing case). Curious to know its contents I prize off the lid of the box, and find a corpse.
>
> This Mr de Bie (whom I saw in the dream) had some business to do in the drawing-office of a firm in whose service I was as an engineer during some years. In the morning of August 9th mother asked me if I wanted to read a short article written by Professor Nijland in the paper about a spot on Saturn. I unfolded the newspaper in order to read the article pointed out but all at once another paragraph caught my eye—"Horrible Murder", the headline ran, and I read that the corpse of the packing-case maker de Bie had been found in a trench. Regarding the odd sucking of water out of the ground by means of a funnel, this apparently refers to the system of drainage applied in the Wieringermeer polder [Zuyderzee], in which trenches play such a prominent part. For nearly three months I had been employed in the Wieringermeer as a field-engineer, experimenting with a heavy diesel-tractor, used for drawing heavy trench-ploughs (which dug trenches in a single run). During the whole time of my employment we were digging trenches, kilometre after kilometre. No wonder that in the dream trenches, draining and Wieringermeer appeared.

So the dreamer is sucking water out of the ground on an extensive plain with a kind of funnel. Analytically this can hardly mean anything else but the sucking at the mother, the extensive plain itself often being a female symbol, whilst the sucking of water by means of a funnel, in my opinion, permits of no other interpretation (if necessary, one can take for an accessory motive some libido of the urethral phase, in consideration of the water). "Performing that strange work I contact a box with the nozzle of the funnel." Keeping in mind the fact that a box is always a female symbol, there cannot exist the slightest doubt that the nozzle is a symbol for the penis. Moreover, the incestuous motive in question is accentuated by the information that the dreamer prises open the box and, of course, finds a corpse, i.e. the punishment for the incest is castration (death). It is remarkable that the funnel itself represents the mouth, the nozzle of the funnel, on the contrary, the penis.

In the dream sucking and sexual intercourse (also the manner in which he found the box in a trench suggests this same motif) are simultaneously represented in a symbolic form, i.e. the funnel sucks, the nozzle strikes a box. Both oral and genital libido appear to be tied to the mother. Moreover, it is noteworthy that the box is a coffin. This motive gives to the mother-image a very definite colouring, i.e. on the one hand, the mother kills me, on the other, I wish the mother were dead. There is no doubt that an analysis of the dreamer himself would throw more light on the content of this dream, yet I believe myself justified in concluding, basing myself on the three dreams discussed here and their interpretation, that a castration-complex is present. In connection with it there exists a sadomasochistic fixation to the mother (she will castrate me, and I hate her), and also to the father (fear of his death and "I should like him to be dead but I don't dare to kill him": the totem-meal after his death = "when he is dead, I shall be his successor").

This fear of castration seems to be closely connected with precognitive dreaming about mortal accidents. Thus we find in these dreams the same relation between parapsychological and psychoanalytical data as in cases I and II. This coincidence of a paranormal contact with a fixation of libido appears to occur so regularly (see also the instances mentioned below) that in my opinion the paranormal contact is most probably of a libidinous nature. In the dreams discussed above we see (and the same holds good for the cases still to be discussed) a coinciding of paranormal impressions with the manifestation of unconscious conflicts, depending on unconscious fixations of libido. Though at first sight, the conclusion that libido may have a paranormal character may be somewhat surprising, yet it can be rendered plausible from a theoretical point of view by bearing in mind that we are aware of libido only insofar as it is mentally perceived by us. For instance, a person who comes for analysis has very little consciousness of his libidinous ties: they are not perceived. The analysis gradually increases the degree of perception. So it might be possible that just as many persons cannot perceive their normal libidinous fixations, so also those whose libido can be perceived by the aid of an analysis do so only to a certain degree, and are unable to perceive another form of libido, exactly like the novice analysand (resistance).

* * *

As I have already observed, one renders oneself liable to be accused of arbitrariness if, out of a series of dreams, one selects and classifies only four, leaving the rest undiscussed. Against this reproach I can, besides my incompetence to analyse any of the remaining dreams, put forward two arguments: (1) in the series there are a number of dreams which, in my opinion, do not show clear evidence of the cropping up of a Dunne-effect [i.e. precognition—Ed.]; (2) the most impressive dreams, as a matter of fact, always express a fear of death and accidents. Obviously, one is inclined to analyse especially the dreams bearing on death. Hence, I believe myself justified, notwithstanding the selection made, in finding in the dreams discussed here an indication that the paranormal is a form of libido, and that it depends only on the degree of perception whether one is conscious of this form or not. Moreover, paranormal libido seems to coincide with a mother-complex.

* * *

Case V

Patient E is a boy, eighteen years old. To gain a good insight into this case it is necessary to keep in mind some details contained in the anamnesis given by his mother. The latter is about fifty-seven years old and the daughter of a well-to-do solicitor. She received a good education. She is said to have been rich when young. Her youth was characterized by an adoration of her father, and a dislike of her mother. She was at college for some years, but did not complete her studies. In her college period she went into society a good deal and received several proposals of marriage. However, she declined all such offers, her suitors being too dull for her taste. After her years at college, she devoted much of her time to social work and became a member of the Labour Party. In that work she believed she had found her ideal. She then became acquainted with her future husband, a man thirteen years younger than herself and coming from the working class. Never intending to marry him, she offered to bear the expenses of his studies. He accepted this offer, provided that she would marry him. She decided to accept this condition. A child was born of this marriage, the son who is the subject of this case-study.

Before long the marriage proved to be a failure. The father did not finish his studies, though the mother herself helped him with

Latin, Greek, etc. The jobs he got through his wife's intervention rapidly succeeded one another, because in not a single case did his work give satisfaction. At the end of five years of marriage, they were divorced, and it appeared that the fortune she had brought with her in marriage had dwindled to next to nothing. The mother wished to keep the small remnant of her fortune for herself, in order to help her son. She declared she had never felt any love for her husband. After her divorce, she had to fend for herself, and to date she is extremely poor.

Her entire life is devoted to her son who is said to have been a difficult child from his very infancy. The father would have nothing to do with him, and prevented the mother from occupying herself a great deal with him. This was the reason that at the age of two-and-a-half-years the boy still could not speak a single word. The mother then was advised to talk more with the child. At the age of three he was already quick-tempered, but kind-hearted, indulgent to others, but tyrannical to his mother. At school he was an indifferent pupil, though according to his teacher he could have done better.

At the age of twelve he grew afraid of thieves, thunder-storms, etc. Ever since that time he became suspicious. He was insolent, picked quarrels everywhere, and grew arrogant. Then he turned into a lover of music (as was his mother), played the piano, and even started to compose pieces himself. He was considered a genius by all persons with whom he daily came into contact (all of them belonging to the working classes). Somewhat later on his mother, although she denied it, also saw in him a great artist. His mother described his later years, when he was about sixteen years old, as follows: "He openly says: 'I am a great artist, everyone has to be at my service'. He is insolent, offensive, and lazy. He sings, writes and reads in bed. 'Let me have my own way,' he exclaims, 'no matter what the consequences are going to be. I don't care whether I am killed, or commit suicide or am reduced to poverty.'"

During the last two years the situation at home became almost unbearable. He was insolent, aggressive, especially so in his dealings with his mother, who sustained many bruises. Suddenly he would stand motionless for minutes at a time, completely absent in mind. When his mother addressed him when in such a state, he would bluster out: "I am thinking." He is constantly under the impression that his mother is spying upon him. He now but rarely visits the Academy of Music where he gets his lessons. He passes his time composing at home. He prefers to compose modern music, for which a good knowledge of harmonics seems to be superfluous, and also he writes poetry at home. In general, he never gets to bed before two or three am. In the daytime he prefers improvising while lying in bed.

It is also of interest that, besides this clinical anamnesis, the mother also supplied some parapsychological data. She told me that it was a remarkable fact that from his early youth a telepathic contact had existed between her son and herself, causing both of them to dream simultaneously in reference to the same theme. She added that the phenomenon did not seem at all strange to her, for from infancy she had possessed this gift. At my request she gave a circumstantial parapsychological anamnesis concerning herself, but of little value as dreams she had produced in the past could not be evidenced any more. Still, I feel it wise to quote some of those dreams here. One of her synchronic, or double dreams, was described by her in these words:

> I dreamed that I was a snake and crawled, writhing, from my bed on to the floor, then came to a bed, raised my head and saw Piet (her son) lying in the bed. Then I awoke. In my dream I did not intend to do him any harm, I only looked at him. He awoke weeping and said: "Just now mother was lying, as usual in her bed, and now I dream that a snake crawled from beneath the blankets."

A second synchronic dream—as related to me by the mother—is as follows:

> I was standing on the bank of the Amstel [a river flowing through Amsterdam] but it was not the Amstel but a kind of sea, water was flowing over the quay. Two soldiers seized me. We struggled with one another, for they wished to throw me into the water. I saw the hat I was wearing floating on the water. When I woke up I was dimly aware of the fact that Piet had been present in the shape of a little boy. The next morning Piet said: "I dreamed about soldiers and water, and your hat was floating on the water."

Further the mother related that she and her son often say and think the same thing simultaneously. For instance, the mother goes to fetch from her writing desk some photographs of Piet in his youth, in order to show them to Piet's physician. She is standing near her desk with the keys already in her hand, and without having informed her son of what she intended to do. Suddenly, he is standing in front of her, crying out with flashing eyes: "Where are my photographs? Hand them over!"

Though none of these events can be recorded in an evidential manner, still, I felt that it would be of some importance to ask the son, during treatment, if he remembered any dreams he had had simultaneously with his mother. Having told me, by way of preamble, that these dreams "bore on the relation between other images of my mother and my own one" (by this he unconsciously meant incest, as emerged in the treatment), he answered that he remembered a dream where:

> I had a definite rhythm in my head. I was playing with bricks. Wanting to feel the rhythm as a living sound, I marked it by beating with a brick on the floor. Mama was in bed, asleep. The aura of the surroundings had a glaring reddish-yellow colour. I beat out the rhythm more and more insistently, and steadily louder. Mama implored me in a horribly plaintive, heart-rending voice to stop it. But I continued more and more violently. Then she hid her face beneath the blankets, and became hysterical. I steadily went on knocking on the floor, looking at her all the time. There was something weird beneath the blankets. I had a feeling of anxiety and hate, a big, writhing, venomous black snake made a hissing sound. I was frightened to death.

This dream occurred simultaneously with the mother's snake-dream. The patient did not remember other dreams.

I thought it advisable to have the son removed from the family circle, and managed to board him with other people, coming to an agreement with the mother that she was not to seek any further contact with him. After a six-month dispute I finally succeeded in persuading mother and son to do as I wished. During this time when mother and son lived separately and had no contact with one another, to my certain knowledge, they both related their dreams to me. The mother was not very liberal in telling me her dreams; the greater part of them she had already forgotten. Nevertheless, a few of them were related to me. One of those dreams I quote below:

> My son cried softly: "Dear old thing, do you advise me to go to the little church?" I answered: "Do as you please." I supposed he would go first to the bathing establishment.

In this dream she expresses the expectation that her son, too, will shortly dream about a little church. Indeed, two nights later the son had the following dream:

> Village with a church. There appeared a light in the sky, a large white figure having a human shape with an expressionless head, a war cripple. In it I saw much of myself: depravity, hate, dismay, anxiety, confusion. The apparition was afraid of its own destructive power, just as I had been. Just fancy that others would get to know to what extent these vices had developed in me; that would mean rank misery. The village seemed to be good-natured but as a matter of fact the atmosphere was heavily charged.

In my opinion it is quite evident that the two dreams are closely related. It is also probable that the analysis is clear at once. *The little church*—the mother; the mother thinks the son too dirty, he therefore has to take a bath first. On the other hand, the son undergoes the incest with hate and fear, as in the snake dream. It should be noted in this connection that during treatment he repeatedly expressed the opinion that his mother had immoral intentions in respect to himself. I personally believe this opinion to be unfounded. Still, this does not in any way diminish its psychological value. Furthermore, it was remarkable that during treatment the mother regularly made disguised attempts to get into contact with her son, whilst the latter complained that his mother was again interfering with him (the mother's attempts to take up contact were unknown to the son as long I did not inform him about them). On the other hand, the son ostentatiously made attempts to contact his mother who, however, in the meantime had moved into another house, the address of which the son did not know. The mother then complained in a letter to me that the son was saying everywhere that he preferred her to be dead. These two opposite sides of the incest coin followed one another regularly. Indirectly this proved that the telepathic contact was still continuing (for an important part the treatment consisted in bringing the extremely strong fixation into consciousness).

Finally, I would like to note that this boy, at the age of seven years, sometimes had the sensation of lying in a coffin, whilst everything around him was dead; only his soul was living. He said literally: "I lived in a confined space, in which I almost choked."

The telepathic contact between mother and son in this case is, taking the dreams into consideration, evidently to be attributed to incest desires. But the metamorphosis of the mother into a snake is most remarkable. I would like to interpret it as a penis-symbol by which the mother-complex is suddenly brought to the fore, together with the primeval castration-complex (for already at the very young age of a year-and-a-half he was afraid of shadows, cast upon the road by long palm-leaves).

The psychopathic character—I had to diagnose a schizoid psychopathy—the defective development of the ego, and the wish to return to the cradle, are in my opinion the principal causative elements bringing about this telepathic contact.

Discussion

In order to arrive at a thorough understanding of the entire problem brought forward here, it is indispensable to examine once again the so-called mother-complex. In the present paper the mother-complex is taken in a wider sense than is done in the Viennese Psychoanalytical School. In my opinion this castration-complex rather contains the feeling of being deserted by the mother, betrayal, the loss of trustworthy support. From this point of view, the envy felt by the elder child towards the baby would have to be interpreted as a reactivation of this complex. That is to say that the elder child misses the support and care now given to the baby. This causes it to become jealous. I feel that I am justified in broadening the original notion because it gradually has become clear that the oedipal castration-complex cannot be maintained in the original Viennese meaning either, at least not in all cases.

In the data discussed above, the following successive phases of the complex are observable from the viewpoint of psychological development. First, after having formed a mother-complex the child has a repetition compulsion with two components, i.e. (a) "I wish to be supported and taken care of"; and (b) "I have been betrayed". This antagonism toward the mother is maintained till the father appears on the scene. Then, normally, the antagonism, using the heterosexual relation to the mother as a conductor, is transferred to the father. This transfer creates on the one side a homosexual component (the support and care desired from the father), on the other side the oedipal castration-complex. Hence, in the Oedipus phase the original primeval castration-complex is given up for the erotic relation to the mother. If the effort to obtain care and support from the father fails, regression back to the mother takes place (the castrated baby clutches at his mother's petticoats.).

The success of the transference to the father depends on two factors: (1) the strength of the primeval betrayal (depending on the mother–child relationship); and (2) the father–child relationship: father repels. The first case we term a fixation to the primeval castration-complex, the second a regression.

* * *

Summarizing the case-material discussed here, it becomes evident that patient A has an unconscious wish to commit incest with the analyst. The attempt fails, and the antagonistic tendency, the castration-complex, comes into action. In the telepathic dreams this reactivation manifests itself by the feeling of envy for the new female patient. As an answer to the question of why this patient has a functioning, hence, a strengthened incest tendency, we can only presume that her castration-complex (the mother is her castrator) possesses a real pre-oedipal character (mother-complex). In order to avoid this anxiety she wishes for actual incest (if it succeeded, the castration-complex could be overcome). She is a prisoner in a demonic circle, the repetition compulsion. At the moment the positive antagonistic tendency yields to the reactivated negative one, the paranormal phenomenon appears.

The psychic structure of patient B [Case II omitted above] is clearly under the influence of the mother-complex. The mother must give him a piccolo; the elephant (father) is an animal that has to rock and feed him. The aggressiveness resulting from the oedipal attitude towards the father is entirely subordinated to the mother-complex. The antagonistic tendencies of the repetition compulsion consist in the wish to be cared for and the betrayal. At the moment the positive tendency gives place to the negative one, the telepathic contact manifests itself.

In Case III some dreams point to an oedipal fixation (this is most evident in the second dream, i.e. the dreamer is eating pancakes). Upon closer investigation the repetition compulsion appears to be located on the oral level, that is, a wish for support and a feeling of being deserted, betrayed. This motive of betrayal appears in the "de Bie dream", in which both the oedipal and the oral fixations show themselves in the funnel-symbol, and in the dream in which the physician deserted the dreamer (something that really happened), in consequence of which a Dunne-effect appeared in the dream, which is so thoroughly mixed up with the real betrayal that this dream can only partly be regarded of a parapsychological nature.

In Case IV [omitted above] we have to restrict ourselves to the conclusion that on the oedipal level a fixation exists to the mother-image, whereas the telepathic relation manifests itself at the moment that the prohibition, pronounced by the father (castrator), is activated by an advice of the physician.

Case V appears to have a strong incest-motif, an unconscious incest by both mother and son (cf. the dream about the church). It is a remarkable thing that the mother dreams this desire without any restriction, with the exception, however, that the son has first to go to the bathing-establishment, whilst in the son's corresponding dream the incest wish has a very nasty flavour (hate, anxiety). Of course, one presumes that this Oedipus complex is related to the mother-complex, as is demonstrated in the dream about the snake. The hate and anxiety seem finally to be essentially directed toward the phallic mother. We may suppose that the support-motif on the oral level, combined with the incest-motif on the oedipal level, form together the positive antagonistic tendency, whereas the negative one consists in the oral and genital castration-complex. The telepathic contact is contained in this antagonism (the appearance of this at the moment the positive antagonist is replaced by the negative one is not so typical as in other case materials).

Although, because of the difference in depth of the various analyses, the case materials are heterogeneous in many respects, a common factor can still be observed. Be it a happy event, a desired one, or a sad event, the parapsychological phenomenon, always considered from a psychoanalytical viewpoint, not only proves to be connected with a positive wish but to be induced, in fact, by the negative antagonistic tendency, the castration-complex in its various levels.

In the discussion of the case material above, I have already anticipated the explanation of the phenomenon. As soon as libido, acting in a definite direction, runs the risk of being counteracted, a first reaction to such a threat will be an intensification of the original libidinous impulse. Whereas in our case material the counteracting factor (to be regarded a castration-complex) is always so strong that the positive tendency is pushed into the background, the intensification of the latter will last only for a short time. It seems that the moment of intensified libido is the most suitable for telepathic contact.

One should not lose sight of the fact that the original libido in all discussed cases depends on a fixation, either in the Oedipus-level or in the oral one. In other terms, the telepathic contact appears at the very moment that the fixed libido exerts its utmost strength to conquer the threat of castration (overcompensation). Consequently, the case materials raise the question whether through greater intensity a quality of libido manifests itself which we might term *paranormal* (cosmic). By its means a person might be able to become cognizant of facts in a paranormal way, i.e. perceiving without the use of the sensory channels.

This provisional conclusion has to be further investigated in two directions, i.e. a parapsychological and a psychoanalytical one. From a parapsychological point of view we can state that the paranormal phenomenon is closely connected with the moment of repetition compulsion, when one tendency is repulsed by another. Hence, at the point of the encounter of two antagonistic tendencies a heightened sensitivity to cosmic impulses makes its appearance (parapsychologists often assume that such impulses are going on all the time, and that the degree of perception only depends on individual sensitivity).

From a psychoanalytic viewpoint, however, this connection is not evident: it is very strange that libido should be sensitive to cosmic impulses. Everything becomes still more strange if we can irrefutably prove that in a part of our case material the real antagonistic tendencies of the repetition compulsion are to be found at the oral level, that is to say that the sensitivity in question is fixed to the oral castration-complex.

When describing the case material, I already anticipated the explanation of this sensitivity of the libido by pointing out that we are conscious of libido only insofar as we perceive it. The establishment of the relation of "cosmic libido" to the oral castration-complex compels us to take a further step. If we wish to uphold the libido theory, we are, in my opinion, forced to suppose that this cosmic libido was already present before this castration-complex came into existence. If this be the case, it is easy to explain why certain phenomena appear together with a reactivated oral castration-complex. For every situation of fear brings with it an increased psychic tension, because extra energy is concentrated upon the threatened point (cf. Freud, *Beyond the Pleasure Principle*). Consequently, the reactivated oral castration-complex also causes a concentration of libido, whereby the libido that receives cosmic impulses (in short, "cosmic libido") is augmented. Hence, it can emanate more energetically than usual.

The supposition of the existence of an independent cosmic libido in the auto-erotic stage requires some explanation. As far as I am aware, no practical data are available concerning such a cosmic potency of libido in the first year of life. ... It seems that the child in the auto-erotic stage has some cosmic experience. There is no ego, hence no object, the child seems to be one with its surroundings. Considering that this cosmic experience disappears along with the development of the ego—whereas with the patients from whom the preceding case-materials were taken we have to do with an ego which tolerates many id endeavours as ego-syntonic (that is, personalities of a more psychopathic nature)—we may see in all this an indication that part of the cosmic libido from the auto-erotic stage has been retained, precisely in those individuals where, in connection with oral castration, the development of the ego is less complete because of an excessive search for support.

If the above is taken into consideration, one need not wonder that this cosmic libido is connected with the child's surroundings during the first year, and, after many years under the guidance of the oral castration-complex, is also connected with things other than its closest environment. All the types of libido known to date follow this path of the incessant creation of new substitutes (transferences). One can even go so far as to argue that it is no wonder that the mother-image becomes Mother Earth, i.e. cosmic libido, attached to the mother, coming via this fixation into contact with the earth and receiving impulses from it.

References

Freud, S. (1920). *Beyond the Pleasure Principle. P.F.L., 11, S.E., 18.*

Kooy, J. M. J. (1934). Introspective research on the Dunne effect. *Tijdschrift voor Parapsychologie, 6*: 144–169.

CHAPTER THREE

Explicability, psychoanalysis and the paranormal

Chris Cherry

Introduction

Speaking of what he takes to be Freud's view that anxiety is always a repetition in some way of the anxiety we felt at birth, Wittgenstein draws attention to one reason for the "marked attraction" of psychoanalytic exploration. Freud himself regularly emphasizes that people are *disinclined* to accept explanations he provides in analysis. However, "if the explanation is one which people are disinclined to accept, it is highly probable that it is also one which they are *inclined* to accept" (Wittgenstein, 1966, p. 43). And again: "There is a strong tendency to say: 'We can't get round the fact that this dream is really such and such.' It may be the fact that the explanation is extremely repellent that drives you to adopt it" (*ibid.*, p. 24).[1] People are conflicted: they both want and don't want to accept the sort of thing psychoanalytic explanation offers.

We can add two further reasons for the "marked attraction" of psychoanalytic explanation. The first is its unstoppability, annexing just about everything in its path, the seemingly unexceptionable and everyday included. The second is the way in which it leads us to see things in initially unfamiliar ways: everything is what it is and something else as well.

With parapsychology and the paranormal the corresponding attraction is the *weirdness* of the phenomena treated. Here we find a corresponding confliction: people want and yet don't want explanations to be found for what is ostensibly paranormal. (I intend the weird to be a far broader category than the one Freud labels "the uncanny",[2] including but not exhausting it. There is nothing uncanny about, for example, micro-pk experimentation, where testers try to produce physical effects merely by willing that they should occur. However, the results are sometimes decidedly weird.)

As in the case of psychoanalysis, we can give two further reasons, again involving issues of explanation, for why parapsychology is seductive. First, paranormal phenomena both cry out for and yet resist explanation. And secondly, finding an acceptable explanation—a psychoanalytic one, perhaps—for a paranormal event, such as a telepathic exchange or a poltergeist display, is tantamount to declaring that the event in question isn't paranormal after all. So the idea of the paranormal is, as it were, provisional, and the claim that it applies to this or that is always under threat: the subject matter of parapsychology is, we might say, chronically defeasible.

In the next section I shall concentrate mainly on parapsychology and the paranormal, elaborating and illustrating the brief remarks above. In the third Section I shall do much the same for psychoanalysis, and contrast the approaches of the two disciplines. In both sections I hope some cross-fertilizing will emerge. In the fourth Section I shall discuss some aspects of the relationship between the paranormal and the uncanny.

Parapsychology and the paranormal

I said above that people's characteristic attitude towards the paranormal and its study is split, divided, rather like an attitude of love–hate, perhaps. For they want, and indeed expect, "normal" explanations of one kind or another to swallow up—explain *away*—whatever is ostensibly paranormal, while at the same time hoping none will be found. (It is this ambivalence which gives the theory and practice of parapsychology a bad name, making it seem to appeal to what Plato, with other things in mind, describes as the least rational and worthy part of the soul.[3]) Now, anyone who does not merely expect normal explanations to be forthcoming but who holds that they *must* be—who believes in the omnipotence of naturalistic explanation—is committed to the view that either one of two alternative accounts can always be given of any and every ostensibly paranormal phenomenon: either there was no such phenomenon and what really happened was something not remotely paranormal, or else the phenomenon occurred just as described, but is as such perfectly explicable, whether now or at some time in the future. I want to explore, and ultimately reject, this scepticism.

The paranormal is no more a space, or arena, within which certain kinds of things are supposed to happen than is the unconscious; and no more an alternative world with its own idiosyncratic and sporadic regularities—or irregularities—than is the magical. It is rather a label applied, by those who believe in them, to events, or states of mind, or capacities, or powers which possess very curious properties. It is unnecessary to attempt an exhaustive classification of ostensible phenomena, and so I list below only those kinds directly relevant to what follows.[4]

1. ESP (extrasensory perception): non-sensory perception or perception beyond the normal senses.
   (a) Telepathy (aka thought transference): contact or communication between mind and mind.
   (b) Clairvoyance, clairaudience, clairsentience: contact between mind and object or event.
   (c) Precognition: paranormal knowledge of the future in dream or waking state: sometimes predictive, sometimes premonitory.
   (d) Retrocognition: paranormal knowledge or perception of past events.
   (e) Paranormal memory: reincarnation experiences and the like.

2. Apparitional phenomena
   (a) Apparitions of the living.
   (b) Apparitions of the dying or recently dead: crisis apparitions.
   (c) Apparitions of those long dead: haunting apparitions.

3. Miscellaneous physical phenomena
   (a) Psychokinesis (PK): "mind over matter".
   (b) Levitations, apports, materializations. etc.

4. Altered states of consciousness
   (a) Mediumistic, trance, and possession states.
   (b) Lucid dreams: awareness and control of dream content.
   (c) Out-of-body experiences (OOBEs): "astral projection", "travelling clairvoyance".
   (d) Near-death experiences (NDEs).
   (e) Mystical experiences, including variants of a, b, c and d with religious content.

What is distinctive about the above (and other related) categories? Well, they are assuredly not merely *abnormal*, anomalous or statistically deviant. A June snowfall in Kent, a jackpot win on the lottery, an asteroid colliding with earth, a kitten born with five legs—these are abnormal, but not paranormal. Either we can explain them readily enough in terms of current scientific knowledge allied with probability theory, or else we are justifiably confident that they are explicable in terms of readily conceptualizable extensions, or refinements, of that knowledge. It is true that the abnormal is an exotic and intriguing category sometimes confused by the superstitious with the paranormal.[5] But the point I have made can be generalized to cover the less glamorous but far more extensive area of the as yet *unexplained*. The fact that there is a great deal we cannot now explain doesn't, typically, incline us to suppose that the bulk of it is *inexplicable*. That is to say, we expect that what we are comfortable to identify as advances in the neurosciences or genetics or astrophysics will provide perfectly sound answers to questions which currently trouble us. We believe that sufficient causal accounts of recognizably scientific sorts will one day be given to almost all of what is at present unexplained. And we further believe that almost all that remains unexplained is so because we are not clever enough to explain it.

Does this rational optimism leave any room for the paranormal? That is to say, are we ever entitled to suppose that certain kinds of event, if they occur as described, are not merely unexplained but *in principle* inexplicable? I believe we are; and I believe further that we can be certain that some instances of these kinds have occurred and continue to occur. In short, I believe, though cautiously and selectively, in the paranormal. This belief, however, as I remarked above, is chronically defeasible; for it is conceivable that in respect of any such instance it might sooner or later be shown that it *didn't* occur, or didn't occur as *described*. I shall return to this in a moment.

To call something paranormal, then, is not to assign to it a special kind of provenance or explanation, but rather to declare that no explanation could conceivably be assigned to it.[6] The strength and scope of this claim are not commonly appreciated. In the Society for Psychical Research's *Glossary of Terms*, "Paranormal" is defined as a "term applied to any phenomenon which in one or more respects exceeds the limits of what is deemed physically possible on current scientific assumptions ..." (Thalbourne, 1982, p. 50). This is too generous a definition, tending to confuse the unexplained with the inexplicable. I propose the following, tougher one:

> A paranormal event is one with respect to which we do not have the first idea where to begin looking for an explanation, and with respect to which any explanation ultimately adduced would have to fall outside anything we might imaginably identify as common sense or science.

This definition broadly accords with C. D. Broad's account (Broad, 1962, pp. 3–6) of the paranormal as that which transgresses, or bypasses, one or more "basic limiting principles". These are principles which are assumed without question in any rational explanatory endeavour. They are not *themselves* principles of common sense or science, but principles which underpin and structure common sense and science. As such, they constitute what is to count as rational enquiry into the world around us. They are presuppositions, not just of understanding how and why things happen, but of controlling the way they happen and indeed making them happen. The most foundational of these basic limiting principles are the following four:

(1) principles setting conceptual limits to the ways in which knowledge may be acquired;
(2) principles setting limits to the action of mind on matter;
(3) principles affirming the dependence of mind on brain; and

(4) principles affirming the ubiquity and direction of causality and of cause and effect.

Every seemingly paranormal occurrence is described in terms which apparently transgress (or bypass) one or more of these principles. It now becomes clear in which sense, and why, the paranormal is inexplicable: anything accountable an explanation must invoke, no matter how tacitly, principles to which paranormal phenomena just cannot be subject, and so explaining something must thereby defeat its claims to paranormality. Explanatory respectability is incompatible with paranormality, and hence discovering an explanation for a seemingly paranormal occurrence entails redescribing that occurrence so that it no longer looks as if it violates basic limiting principles: either it didn't happen or if it did it could not have been what it seemed to be.

Now, there are several possible responses to this. One is to deny that to be genuinely paranormal an event *has to* violate basic limiting principles. A second is to deny that there are, in effect, any such principles constitutive of scientific—and commonsensical—rationality. A third is to insist, whilst accepting the definitional and constitutive features of limiting principles, that nothing answering to the paranormal ever happens, for the conditions it has to meet price it out of the market. The first two responses collapse, from different directions, the distinction between the everyday causal fabric of our world on the one hand and the apparent episodic puncturing of that fabric on the other. The first does so by reducing the paranormal to the warp and weft of the fabric, the second by stretching the fabric to encompass anything and everything that can possibly happen.[7] The first has the consequence that anything which strikes a person as impressive or arresting may, if he or she pleases, be called paranormal; the second the consequence that the most fundamental certitudes of common sense and scientific method are provisional only, and revisable as and when necessary to accommodate any and every blip.

It will be obvious by now that the first response is unhelpful and evasive. The second is counter-intuitive. So as not to beg questions we can readily invent occurrences, which, if they happened as described, couldn't intelligibly or plausibly be given routine explanations of a scientific or common sense sort. Imagine, for instance, a self-sustaining horse, or a person who rises in the air and hovers unsupported above the ground:

> A horse, which has been normally born and reared, is now deprived of all nourishment ... instead of dying ... goes on thriving ... A series of thorough examinations reveals no abnormality in the horse's condition: its digestive system is always found to be working and to be at every moment in more or less the state it would have been in if the horse had eaten a meal an hour or two before.

Or again:

> Suppose you find nothing, nothing on me and nothing in the room or above, below, or around it. You cannot think it is the effect of an antigravity device (even if there be sense in that idea) because there just is no device. And you know that, excluding phenomena like tornadoes, it is impossible for a physical body in free air to behave thus in the absence of a special device.[8]

These two invented examples illustrate something very important. They suggest that in seeking an explanation of what seems to happen no one would dream of proposing that abundantly well attested laws about the need living creatures have for nourishment, or about mass and gravitational pull, are after all muddled, inadequate, misunderstood or sometimes just false, and someday may be refined and better understood. That is to say, certain foundational laws stand firm, are non-negotiable: calling them into question is not an option. So explaining in cases of this kind is quite unlike explaining sickle cell anaemia or black holes, where it is assumed from the start that what is sought is a physical explanation covering the phenomena in question. We *know* that nothing—no amount of tinkering with laws we are quite certain about—could conceivably accommodate such cases. Instead, explaining them could only mean something like showing that the horse is not really self-sustaining, or that the hoverer wasn't *really* hovering unsupported. (We would then be able to describe what actually happened, and perhaps explain further why it was that people got it wrong and so misdescribed the situation.) My illustrations suggested, however, no such explanation could be found—but then, they were imaginary.

The second response, then, was that it is always in principle possible to find explanations accommodating whatever may happen, no matter how bizarre, for no foundational law or limiting principle is immune to revision, extension or replacement. I have argued that this is wrong. In my examples, laws and principles stand firm, as they must, and so as they are described the events simply do transgress (or bypass) them. All an explanation could aspire to would be to establish misdescriptions. In contrast with the second, the third response accepts this, agreeing that the self-sustaining horse and hovering man are indeed transgressive; but, significantly, they are fantasies. They couldn't, precisely because they are transgressive, ever really happen. Something *else* must have happened, and showing what that was is the would-be explainer's business. Thus, both responses deny the possibility of the transgressive, the second because laws and principles are infinitely flexible and can absorb whatever comes along, the third because they are rigid and omni-prescriptive, and won't allow the transgressive to occur.

I believe that the third as well as the second response is wrong. That is, I believe that the concept of transgression is both coherent and instantiated: that there are events which, if they occur, must be described as violating foundational laws and basic limiting principles; and that we have no rational alternatives to accepting that events of this sort do sometimes occur. So we are justified in claiming both that the idea of a paranormal event is intelligible and that such events can and do occur very much as they are reported: they are neither explicable nor explainable away.

I shall end this section with two paranormal illustrations. Both have in common the rationality, stability, and veracity of the protagonists, the corroborative nature of their testimonies and the subsequent painstaking and independent examination of the reports. All attempts to provide naturalistic explanations in terms of trickery, deception, hallucination, and confusion appear to fail.

The first case is arguably the best documented haunting recorded in the copious literature on apparitions. The haunting, known as the Cheltenham Hauntings, was by an apparition of a tall woman dressed in black at the home in Cheltenham of the Despard family (Mackenzie, 1982, Chap. III). There were innumerable regular sightings over several years by, it is estimated, at least seventeen people. Some twenty further people heard the ghost, but did not see her. Rosina Despard, the Despard's eldest daughter, who at nineteen was studying to be a doctor, kept a detailed and meticulous record of her sightings, often shared by others; and this appeared in the *Proceedings of the Society for Psychical Research* whilst the haunting was still taking place. Her subsequent report of the first time she saw the apparition will give the reader some idea of the perceptive, careful, and wholly unsensational nature of her account:

> The figure was that of a tall lady, dressed in black of a soft woollen material, judging from the slight sound in moving. The face was hidden in a handkerchief held in the right hand. This is all I noticed then; but on further occasions, when I was able to observe her more closely, I saw the upper part of the left hand side of the forehead, and a little more of the hair above. Her left hand was nearly hidden by her sleeve and a fold of her dress ... [T]he whole impression was that of a lady in widow's weeds. [MacKenzie, 1982, p. 43]

Although there has been some controversy about the putative identity of the apparition it is usually taken, by those who had known her, to be Imogen Swinhoe, the second wife of the previous occupant of the house.

No remotely satisfactory analysis of haunting apparitions has been offered. The three principal features of the Cheltenham Hauntings which inspire confidence are the regularity of collective sightings, the plausible identification of the apparition with someone who, when alive, had lived in the Despards' house, and the exceptionally full account given by the central protagonist. Many recorded cases have these features, of course, but they are normally less prominent and often less coherently formulated. Taken together they strongly suggest that if ghosts are hallucinations they are *veridical* hallucinations. (Broad calls them "veridical quasi-hallucinations".)

The second is a case of precognition. In October 1966 a huge coal tip slid down a mountain-side on to the mining village of Aberfan. Pantglas Junior School was partially buried and 128 school children died. A psychiatrist who worked with the bereaved after the disaster recorded twenty-four cases of ostensible precognitive knowledge of the event, many (but not all) on the part of children who described to parents in remarkable detail what was about to happen to them and their friends. This is what ten-year-old Eryl Jones told her mother a fortnight before the disaster:

> "Mummy, I am not going to die." Her mother replied: "Why do you talk of dying, and you so young: do you want a lollipop?" "No", she said, "but I shall be with Peter and June" [school mates]. The day before the disaster she said to her mother: "Mummy, let me tell you about my dream last night ... You *must* listen. I dreamt I went back to school and there was no school there. Something black had come down over it." [Grattan-Guinness, 1982, p. 149]

In the communal grave Eryl was buried with Peter on one side and June on the other.

These two cases are unrepresentative of very many others only in that they are exceptionally well documented, attested, and (as far as these things are possible) confirmed. Each violates at least one basic limiting principle of the four summarized above. On balance, I believe, it would be *irrational* to deny in respect of any one of them that things happened very much as reported: they are neither explicable nor explainable away. They may of course possess readily explicable, even mundane, features which incline, or enable, people to have paranormal experiences, or which furnish a context apt to trigger paranormal occurrences; and this is something I shall return to. More immediately, however, I want to turn to psychoanalytic explanation.

Psychoanalysis and the paranormal

At the beginning I remarked that psychoanalytic explanation typically leads us to see things in a new and often unexpected light. If we assent to a psychoanalytic explanation of a motive, or a piece of behaviour, or a relationship, or an emotion, we are brought to perceive it differently and—much the same thing put in another way—to describe it differently. Now, superficially, this is true of successful explanations of the paranormal. For if we accept a causal, naturalistic explanation of an ostensibly clairvoyant or telepathic episode, we thereby come to perceive what has now been explained as different from what we formerly supposed (and perhaps hoped) it to be. We take it to have been demonstrated that the episode wasn't paranormal after all, and that what *really* went on was something else. The reason for this rewriting is, as we have seen, that paranormal phenomena are incompatible with any explanation whatsoever—except perhaps one in terms of kindred paranormal phenomena, as clairvoyance may be explicable in terms of telepathy, or communication from a deceased person in terms of ESP between living persons.

But our initial description of why we behaved in a certain fashion isn't abandoned and replaced by an acceptable psychoanalytic account, because it suffers defeat in the way in which an initial paranormal description suffers defeat. For one thing, parts of that initial description survive—after all, we still *behaved* in that fashion. For another, the psychoanalytic account is, in the end, an alternative interpretation which we may take or leave: it doesn't *have to* drive out the account originally offered by the agent and informed observers. In the third place, and most importantly, it is far from clear why the kind of explanatory account, favoured by many psychoanalysts, should possess the logical (by contrast with the psychological) powers it manifestly does. Why, for instance, should a causal, aetiological explanation of a belief encourage one to agree that the belief explained isn't after all the belief one supposed oneself to hold? Here again, the answer is clear in the case of paranormal phenomena and beliefs in their veridicality. To assent to a causal explanatory account is to discard one couched in terms of the paranormal, because the paranormal is acausal, inexplicable in the sense I have noted. But nothing like this is true of what the analyst seeks to explain.

Even so, the psychoanalyst's drive to redescribe, whatever its credentials, might be expected to find a ready target in talk of the paranormal. I shall start with a case in point, impressive, not so much because its treatment is obviously successful, as because it helps us clarify, and perhaps resolve, the issues I have raised.

In an article entitled "Occult processes occurring during psychoanalysis" Helene Deutsch sets out to explore the bearing upon ostensible telepathic communication of the "occult processes" of "unconscious mental life". Of the two cases of apparent telepathy she recounts that with the more markedly telepathic (or perhaps clairvoyant) elements is of a patient who in a dream apprehends that it is about to be Deutsch's eighth wedding anniversary.

Deutsch tells us she had taken great professional care not to disclose the event even though she had been "intensively preoccupied" with it. She explains the telepathic encounter ingeniously, in terms of unconscious projective identification between patient and analyst (the patient's mother playing a significant part), the whole emanating from "infantile affective factors":

> If this identity is recognized by the sensorium, the process [telepathic communication] acquires the appearance of an "occult phenomenon", because the perception emanating from within is immediately projected into the external world. This process differs from the process underlying projection in hallucinations only insofar that its content is actually identical with the real content of the field upon which the idea is projected. The receiving medium knows nothing of the complicated internal processes which preceded this event. The medium believes in the reality value of his projections just as the psychotic believes in that of his hallucinations. The difference between the two lies in the fact that the environment recognizes the reality value of the medium's projections, because objective reality and the content of the projection which had been structured by reality happen to be congruent. [Deutsch, 1953, p. 144]

It is unnecessary to go deeply into the "complicated internal processes" in terms of which Deutsch purports to analyze telepathic experience. (Though it is worth drawing attention to an unexpected parallel with Hume's associationist analysis of the "secondary passions" in Book II of his *Treatise*.) The question which needs putting is, rather, what Deutsch thinks she has established. On the face of it, she seems to suppose that she has explained *away* telepathic communication by adducing a complex of natural (though largely unconscious) causes which, once accepted, drive out any notion of paranormality: "[A]nalytic experience ... indicates that 'occult phenomena' are a manifestation of a greatly strengthened intuition, which is rooted in the unconscious affective process of identification" (*ibid.*). Telepathy is unconscious, or preconscious, heightened empathy, striking but perfectly explicable. This view is also Marion Milner's:

> I believe in the existence of telepathy in its literal sense of empathetic communication, so that I think games of telecard-reading, etc are a

> bit off beam. When your idea finds its thinker I fancy the unconscious is sensitized to a kind of mental climate which comes through and is translated into conceptions. [Milner, 1988, p. 270]

If we suppose, as perhaps we should, that Deutsch's intention is to demonstrate that the anniversary case is not one with paranormal features then she probably succeeds, partly because it never really convinces. But she is not of course interested in any one single case but in ostensible telepathic powers *überhaupt*, and it is easy to find cases for which her sort of explanatory account just would not work. Consider the following case, which combines telepathic with other transgressive features:

> At Fiesole ... I was giving my little children their dinner at half-past one o'clock. It was a fine hot day. As I was in the act of serving macaroni and milk ... the wall opposite me seemed to open, and I saw my mother lying dead on her bed in her little house (in England). Some flowers were at her side and on her breast ... and the coffin was there. It was so real that I could scarcely believe that the wall was really brick and mortar, and not a transparent window ... Owing to a family quarrel, I had left England without telling my people where I was going ... I was so distressed at the vision that I wrote ... By return of post came the statement that [my mother] had died. At the hour I saw her she was removed from her home to Kensal Green Cemetery. [Myers, 1903, pp. 355–356]

There is no intelligible way in which the empathetic mechanisms posited by Deutsch could be made to accommodate cases of this sort. (It doesn't help her to propose that the episode is best taken as an instance of clairvoyant viewing. If that is so her account fares even worse.)

There is, however, another way of interpreting Deutsch's intentions. Her concern might be not so much to redescribe in scientific terms one—and by implication any—kind of paranormality, but to describe the sorts of circumstances, including emotional states, which predispose towards paranormal displays of one or another type. This is a far more interesting thought, and it is important to be clear about what it amounts to. It is no longer the thought that telepathy, let alone the paranormal at large, can be exhaustively explained in causal, scientific terms, but the thought that a specific set of circumstances, whether or not the ones she mentions, might facilitate or even be necessary to the exercise of paranormal capacities or the occurrence of paranormal events. If this is so, it certainly does not *mean* that the paranormal is identical with, or reducible to brain events any more than the beauty of a rainbow is to droplets of moisture held in suspension. It does not mean that the paranormal is reducible. What it does mean is that we can identify contexts or occasions where the paranormal is more likely to show itself. This is a less modest achievement than it looks, and I shall return to it later.

It is Deutsch's remarks towards the end of her paper which lead me to think she may entertain this new possibility. She concludes with the words:

> ... [A]nalytic experiences confirm that occult powers are to be sought in the depth of psychic life, and that psychoanalysis is destined to clarify this problem in the same manner in which it has previously clarified other "mysterious" happenings in the human psyche. [Deutsch, 1953, p. 146]

How, then, does psychoanalysis clarify? I have suggested earlier that it seeks to clarify, though I do not know how wittingly or self-consciously, by encouraging us to perceive and hence describe certain things, some of them routine and everyday, in seductively new ways. The old perceptions and descriptions come to appear obsolete or inadequate or even false. This mission to redescribe is, of course, theory-driven, and some hint of its power has already been given in the context of the paranormal. But *how* does it possess such power? This is a big question, and I shall approach it selectively.

The following well known passage is excerpted from Freud's *Moses and Monotheism*:

> The strong male was the master and father of the whole horde: unlimited in his power, which he used brutally. All females were his property, the wives and daughters in his own horde as well as perhaps those robbed from other hordes. The fate of the sons was a hard one; if they excited the father's jealousy they were killed or castrated or driven out ... The brothers who had been driven out lived together in a community clubbed together, overcame the father, and ... all partook of his body ... [Abbreviated from *Moses and Monotheism*, 1939, p. 81]

Freud ostensibly gives, and certainly intends to give, the reader a series of historical claims or hypotheses about the causal antecedents which he believes constitute the sufficient (and perhaps necessary) conditions of Judaeo–Christian belief and practice. At first sight, we are presented with two distinct, and distinctly characterized, sets of phenomena: on the one hand primaeval horde, incest, patricide, cannibalism, guilt feelings, and thirst for atonement, and so forth, and on the other the ritual practices and eschatology of Christian belief; and are invited to construe the events constituting the second set as the causal product of those constituting the first.

Freud, however, also believes that he has told us *what Christianity really is*. That, and why this is so are apparent from what he proceeds to do with his originating conditions. Although the doings of the primaeval horde are initially presented as nothing but the *causes* of Christian practice and belief, they are subsequently treated as what the practice and belief are *about*. The matter cannot after all be perceived in terms of twin sets of causally related episodes, for what begin life as specifications of causal antecedents end as meaning-specifications. We are expected to conclude that what the believer professes is in reality *identical* with what Freud the prehistorian chronicles. So the notion of a "complete explanation" in terms of originating causes derives, in cases of this kind, from casting candidate causes in the role of meanings: this is what Jews and Christians really believe, whatever they may imagine they believe. Religious belief is an encoded memory of primaeval horror, and what the theologian describes is in reality what Freud the prehistorian deciphers.

So Freud implies that psychoanalytically explaining how something originated is unmasking it. And when what demands explanation is a belief, assent to that explanation is assent to a more or less radical redescription of what is really believed. And not unexpectedly, what is really believed is usually nastier, for otherwise it would not have been disguised or repressed. Freud's account of occult mechanisms imposing an acceptable form on material which cannot be tolerated in an unworked state is a quite general one, but in my view most powerful when it is applied to belief—systems and ideologies—in particular, to religious belief, magical belief, and belief in the paranormal,[9] for it proposes a wholesale rewriting of the beliefs in point. But is it right and, more particularly, is it *explaining* anything? I think the answer to both questions is no, and that this negative is of the first importance for parapsychology and the paranormal. I shall try and show why fairly briefly.

The first thing to notice is that even though Freud talks constantly about cause and hypothesis, his pattern of explanation goes far beyond, and sometimes bypasses, what we would ordinarily deem causal explanation. Thus, I may establish the causes of a Kansas twister or of malaria or of a pile-up on the M25, but doing so doesn't in the least incline me (or anyone else) to *redescribe* what it is I have causally explained—unless of course I believe the phenomenon is paranormal and so without cause. Again, I may know the causes of my holding a certain belief—I may read it in a book, someone may have told me, or I may have experimented—without this piece of information encouraging me to recast or give up that belief. The matter of why I hold a given belief is distinct from the matter of whether I ought to hold it, of whether it is true or false. With Freud, however, things are assuredly not the same once I have accepted the causal story he tells: because of why I hold certain religious beliefs, those beliefs are not what they seem and must be replaced by something else. So what Freud does with his causal narratives goes far beyond what those narratives themselves entitle him to do. This must mean either that they are not causal narratives after all or that they are much else in addition. Their power must lie in the further uses to which they are put, and the mechanisms which put them to these uses.

But cannot their power lie in their special nature? Now it is indeed true that they often look special: for they tend to resemble their effects. For instance, the story of the primaeval horde and what ensued is, feature for feature, indeed very like Judaeo–Christian eschatology, a belief which it is supposed to causally explain. The resemblance between cause and effect is simply too good to be true. What has happened, it seems, is that Freud, dispositionally in thrall to the hermeneutics of suspicion (the expression is Ricoeur's), nominates as cause, and then elaborates as causal story, the impression produced upon him by religious belief and practice. The causal story is then declared the true object of belief. Interestingly, the procedure is not unlike what Freud calls "imitative" or "homeopathic" magic, after Frazer: "If I wish it to rain", he writes, "I have only to do something that looks like rain or is reminiscent of rain". (Totem and Taboo, 1913, p. 138). "Likewise, if I wish to explain something, I have only to think of something that looks like what I want to explain or is reminiscent of it". So we might call Freud's mode of *explanation* homeopathic or imitative.

I said above that I do not think imitative explanation is explanation proper. By this I mean that it is unlike explanation in the empirical sciences and by common sense. It is unclear, for instance, how one might test for truth or falsity this or that rewriting of a phenomenon or a belief, or assess its superiority in richness or clarity or comprehensiveness over what it seeks to replace. A general inclination to assent to it is perhaps a test of kinds, but this might just be because it sounds more fun, or more daring, than the original.

What we can say is that the mission of imitative explanation is to create new possibilities of seeing and understanding our relationships with each other and our impact on the world around us, irrespective of how far we accept them.[10] I earlier sought to establish that paranormal events, if they occur, are inexplicable for they have nothing we might identify as causes. Freud, and probably Deutsch, don't believe they do or can, occur, but are instead the product of unconscious causes and causal mechanisms. Here, of course, "cause" and "explanation" are used in their familiar, unreconstructed senses. What, however, would imitative explanation make of the paranormal and of the belief that it is sometimes substantiated? And how compelling would redescription be?

Although there is no hope of resolving such matters, they now, along with closely related issues raised in the previous section, can be brought into sharper focus by a brief comparison of the respective approaches explored—one implicitly, the others explicitly—in this chapter: the common sense sceptic who maintains that causal explanations can always be found for the paranormal, the analyst who believes that the paranormal can, and should, be recharacterized in more complex but categorially different terms, and the parapsychologist who is, to varying degrees, disposed to take the paranormal at its face value. Because it is familiar and abundantly documented the three viewpoints will be looked at in relation to the near-death experience.[11]

It is certain that many, and perhaps most, people who find themselves in life-threatening situations have remarkable experiences. It must be said, immediately, that there is confusion about the significance of the *occasion* and *context*, by contrast with the *content*, of such experiences. Must an experient actually be near to death, or merely imagine that he or she is about to die? And if the former, what counts as "near to death"? Must the state meet rigorous clinical criteria or will a more intuitive assessment do? Although these matters are very important it is enough to say here that near-death experiences (NDEs) typically occur on those occasions when competent observers are convinced (erroneously in the event) either that the subject is dead or else that death is imminent or certain as a consequence of trauma from, for instance, falling, drowning, road accident or cardiac arrest. We are allowed to be as vague as this because we already have the primary and obvious way of identifying experiences as near-death in terms of the characteristic and quite extraordinary content reported. For even though subjects—and more particularly those who write on the topic—diverge somewhat in their accounts of what a near-death experience is like, there nonetheless remains a remarkable degree of basic agreement.

It is common to distinguish five stages in a near-death experience: *peace*, *body separation* (*out of body experiences* and *autoscopy*); *entering the darkness* (or *the tunnel*); *seeing the light*; and *entering the light*. Each of these five stages may be further subdivided. It is particularly significant that experients often report phenomena such as *panoramic recall* (or *life review*); meeting and perhaps communicating with a "*being of light*"; and encountering and conversing with *deceased* friends and relatives. The stages tend to unfold in order, with the first being by far the most frequent, reported by sixty per cent of subjects, and the last the least so (ten–twelve per cent). All this, along with other features, seems to imply, at least to those who have had the full experience, a progressive disclosure of what it is—or will be—like to be dead.

Two important preliminary points must be stressed. First, there are many well attested instances of paranormal cognition occurring during, in particular, the second and fifth stages. Thus, subjects may, once they regain consciousness, be able to give detailed and accurate reports of what went on in their environment whilst to all intents and purposes they were profoundly unconscious, perhaps to the point of registering electro-cerebral silence. Again, some subjects claim to have encountered in the course of their experiences not merely deceased relatives and intimates, but deceased persons who *they could not have known at the time of the alleged encounter* were in fact dead, but who they had every reason to suppose were very much alive.

Secondly, those subjects who have experienced the fourth and fifth stages invariably describe their experience in mystical terms: ineffability, transcendence of time and space, neotic quality, "oceanic" feelings, and the like. Even if we are disinclined to treat talk of "out-of-the-body" as anything more than a phenomenological conceit, we are still left with a remarkably persuasive body of ostensibly paranormal perception and cognition correlated with, and perhaps grounded in, an altered state of consciousness. So even if much of what transpires in the earlier stages of a NDE may be explained in terms of endocrinological and cerebral changes produced by trauma, or of little-understood biological adaptive mechanisms, or even of birth-event mimicry, we are still left with much that is *prima facie* inexplicable. In what follows I shall focus on the last two stages of the experience, seeing and entering the light, labelling them a composite transcendent phase, though without intending to beg too many questions.

Jung's autobiographical account of the transcendent phase, experienced when he was semi-conscious following a severe heart attack, is at once moving and fairly typical; but it remains ultimately agnostic:

> It is impossible to convey the beauty and intensity of emotion during these visions. They were the most tremendous things I have ever experienced ... I can describe the experience only as the ecstasy of a nontemporal state in which present, past, and future are one. Everything that happens in time had been brought together into a concrete whole ... One is interwoven into an indescribable whole and yet observing it with complete objectivity. [Jung, 1962, p. 326]

A less artful but more specific report is this:

> Then suddenly, I saw my mother, who had died about nine years ago. And she was sitting—she always used to sit in her rocker, you know—she was smiling and she just sat there looking at me and she said to me in Hungarian [the language her mother had used while alive], "Well, we've been waiting for you. We've been expecting you. Your father's here and we're going to help you". All I felt was a tremendous kind of happiness, of pleasure, of comfort. And then

> somehow she took me by the hand and she took me somewhere [pause] and all I could see was marble all around me; it was marble. It looked like marble, but it was very beautiful. And I could hear beautiful music; I can't tell you what kind, because I never heard anything like it before. [cited in Ring, 1980, pp. 320–321]

Enough has been said to give the feel of a near-death experience. How might it fare when under different kinds of examination?

It will be recalled that to accept a naturalistic—scientific or common sense—explanation for an ostensibly paranormal phenomenon must necessarily drive out reference to paranormality. Of the several candidate categories of causal explanation on offer here I take the dying brain hypothesis, without pretending to do justice to its complexities. The most comprehensive dying brain apologist is Susan Blackmore (1993) who argues that *all* features of NDEs, ranging from their uniformity, coherence, and content across cultures and history to their apparent extrasensory dimensions, can be best accounted for in terms of the neurochemical condition in which the experients find themselves. Thus:

> The joy and peace are consistent [consistently present] because of the natural opiates released under stress. The tunnel, light and noises are consistent because they depend on the structure of the brain's cortex and what happens to it when it is deprived of oxygen or is affected by disinhibition and random activity ... The life review is consistent because the endorphins cause random activation and seizures in the temporal lobe and limbic system ... [T]he dying brain hypothesis explains why people seek paranormal evidence ... By understanding the role of the limbic system and temporal lobe it accounts for the experiences of familiarity, insight and déjà vu and for the increase psychic experience after the NDE. [Blackmore, 1993, pp. 262–263]

Blackmore supports her general hypothesis with a wealth of neuroscientific detail, but this cannot affect the logic of her argument, which rests in the end upon the kind of relations which obtain between physico–chemical events, mental representations and the outside world (always assuming there is one). This is a philosophical issue. Now, one of our basic limiting principles is that mental events cannot exist in dissociation from physical, that for any thought, perception or even sensation there must be a corresponding neurophysiological event which, when taken in conjunction with a number of other factors, is sufficient to cause a thought, perception or sensation. Among these other necessary factors are ordinary entities in the external world which in one mode or other impinge upon the subject's central nervous system. It is, however, possible for a subject to have a seemingly veridical experience *as of* a colour, sound or substantial physical object when none is causally present, or when what is causally on offer has little or no customary connection with what is experienced—and, it might be added, believed to be present. In cases of this kind—of delusion, hallucination, and dreaming, for instance—we suppose the experience to be subjective and self-generated, and the belief, if it is one, to be false or at best only fortuitously true. We are able and entitled to suppose this because we know, on public and independent grounds, that there just is nothing "out there" which answers to the experience.

Independent tests further equip us to identify the kinds of physical and mental conditions regularly associated with perceptions and beliefs which are not reality-grounded and have no external object. We know when not to take seriously what the dreamer, dement, and schizophrenic claim (see e.g. Serdahely, 1992). It cannot, however, be quite like this for a near-death experient; for there just is no independent test, and it is this that makes the reports so exciting. We may not *assume* that the reports are false (or worse) by virtue of the damaged condition in which the subjects find themselves without begging the question at issue. What we may do is argue that the characteristic near-death condition is sufficiently similar to conditions which we know, on independent grounds, are apt to generate delusions and false beliefs to encourage us to doubt the veridicality of near-death claims. The jury is, I think, out on the matter of sufficient similarity; but even if it were possible to establish such a degree of similarity it would still be premature to dismiss the truth of near-death reports. They display a unique phenomenology which at present we lack any satisfactory means of testing for truth.

It is worth making two further points before passing on to the psychoanalyst. First, there is considerable evidence that at any rate many near-death experients have not anomalous or degraded brain activity, but no activity whatsoever; and a silent brain is not the same as a dysfunctional one. For one thing, it transgresses, as the latter doesn't, a basic limiting principle: mind in the absence of active matter. Secondly, the well-evidenced paranormal cognition and perception we find in many NDEs remains recalcitrant to the sufficient similarity argument: we don't find similarly enhanced capacities in other pathological conditions. The two points are related: if cerebral silence and paranormal skills are found together in the near-death subject it may be that the former serves to liberate or promote the latter. I shall come back to this in a moment.

This is a good point at which to turn to psychoanalytic explanation. Because some of what I have said above holds good for any kind of NDE explanation, including the psychoanalytic, I can be brief. The analyst, it will be recalled, appeals to different sets of candidate causes from the scientific sceptic, and then takes them a step further by invoking mechanisms which transform them from causal accompaniments of near-death (and indeed other) experiences into redescriptions of what these experiences, and their reports, are really of and about. Therein lies their power to seduce. It takes little ingenuity to devise an account (though I don't know of one) formally parallel to Freud's narrative of the primal happening, but couched in terms of psychoanalytic mechanisms and processes, which successfully encode fears, wants, and uncertainties in a more felicitous form. We may either adopt or resist, for there is no possible truth test other than a readiness to say (and feel): yes, this is how it *must be*. But many don't succumb; and as I have suggested there is a less intuitive truth test for claims based upon NDEs: they check out. If they are not after-the-event fabrications they *must be* paranormally founded.

There is, however, a rather different direction psychoanalytic concerns may incline us to take. In common with the earlier redescribing mission, it is little interested in issues of truth and falsity. The value of the NDE, it argues, lies not in any representation of realities (for probably there is none), but rather in its psychotherapeutic effects. And it is certainly true that subjects can find the experiences life-transforming, whatever their beliefs and attitudes. A great deal has been written about this dimension, and I mention only one of the more recent and coherent discussions. Its claims are comparatively modest: NDEs are one form of first-personal narrative which contribute to ensuring "that our relationship to tales of rebirth, of transcendence of death, remain vital and relevant" (Kellehear, 1996, p. 254). Kellehear quotes with approval the observation that "when one judges a symbol, one cannot say whether it is true or false, but only whether it is vital or weak".

Now, the analytic insistence that what really matters about NDEs is that they serve as an intensely personal reminder of lost things is not contemptible, but it is only a part of the story. They serve in this way just because most experients *are* led to make substantial truth claims about what they have experienced: a necessary condition of their psychotherapeutic efficacy is precisely that NDEs are believed by many who have them to be much more than that. It is for philosophy to determine if there actually is anything more by bringing into focus again the epistemic concerns which risk being marginalized. I end this section with a suggestion about how this might be done.

The notion that physiological or chemical eccentricity *necessarily* undermines or invalidates perceptual and cognitive judgement must be resisted. To be sure, those who are for one or another reason in deviant states of consciousness—or unconsciousness—are apt to make radically deviant claims. But instead of treating that deviance as a mark of incoherence, might we not leave open the possibility that it is, on occasion, a mark of privileged access to truths not otherwise in reach? This of course is to stand on its head a covert assumption of natural scientist and analyst alike: the assumption that the aberrant is the untrustworthy—or worse. And we might entertain a further thought: mightn't one mode of privilege be paranormal access to realities? If so, what at first looked very much like impairment may in the end impress as empowerment. This, however, is the beginning of another story.[12]

The paranormal and the uncanny

Freud's marvellous essay (Freud, 1985)[13] on the uncanny deserves acknowledgement and brief discussion—brief because in effect it leads us *away* from paranormal concerns towards those with horror and the occult, ideas which (despite much confusion) are linked only sporadically and incidentally to that of paranormality. For this reason I shall concentrate mainly on what Freud has to say about

Hoffman's tale *The Sandman* (Hoffman, 1988). My concluding thesis will be the negative one that the uncanny and the paranormal belong to very different realms of discourse.

In this celebrated story Hoffman has a student, Nathaniel, fall in love with a beautiful doll, Olympia, whom he has spied upon as she sits at a window across the street from his lodgings. We are meant to suppose that Nathaniel mistakes an automaton for a human being (and so a person). The mistake is the result of an elaborate but obscure deception on the part of the doll's designer, Professor Spalanzani. Nathaniel is disabused quite by accident when he overhears a quarrel between Spalanzani, who made Olympia's clockwork, and the sinister Coppelius, who contributed the eyes (real eyes, it seems).

His fellow students are not sure what to make of Olympia. They find her behaviour oddly disturbing, it is true, but it is far from clear that they are not likewise duped. Siegmund remarks that:

> [S]he has appeared to us in a strange way rigid and soulless ... She might be called beautiful if her eyes were not so completely lifeless. I could even say sightless. She walks with a curiously measured gait; every movement seems as if controlled by clockwork. When she plays and sings it is with the unpleasant soulless regularity of a machine, and she dances in the same way. We have come to find Olympia quite uncanny; we would like to have nothing to do with her; it seems to us that she is only acting like a living creature, and yet there is some reason for that which we cannot fathom. [Hoffman, 1988, p. 116][14]

Well, is the situation uncanny? And if it is what makes it so? In his essay, Freud addresses himself to these questions. Jentsch,[15] to whom Freud refers, identifies as situations peculiarly likely to excite impressions of uncanniness those which illustrate, "doubts whether an apparently animate being is really alive; or conversely whether a lifeless object might not be in fact animate". Freud develops this observation in all manner of brilliant (though reckless) ways; but its application to *The Sandman* leaves him cold: "... Jentsch's point of intellectual uncertainty has nothing to do with the effect. Uncertainty whether an object is living or inanimate, which admittedly applied to the doll Olympia, is quite irrelevant ..." (Freud, 1919, pp. 219–230).

Up to a point Freud is right, at any rate about the source of uncanniness in this story (his own proposals are by the way). Yet he is careless. He shows only that "intellectual uncertainty" is unnecessary for exciting a sense of the uncanny. For all he says it might here—and elsewhere—suffice. And whom does Freud take to be uncertain? It cannot be Nathaniel, so perhaps it is Siegmund. More to the point, why on earth should Freud call uncertainties—and, presumably, certainties—of such an order "intellectual"? Isn't this just what they are not? What they are is, of course, conclusively *resolved* in the tale. The issue is settled once and for all the moment Nathaniel discovers that Olympia is not a thing of flesh and blood but an artefact made of wood: an *imitation*. One certitude replaces another.

No doubt it was the availability of such straightforward, conclusive resolution that led Freud to focus, dismissively, on the "intellectual" dimension. If so, he was over-hasty. For it is, rather, their easy resolution that makes Nathaniel's initial certainties at once evidently pathological and philosophically untroublesome. (He is thus both like and unlike Sack's visual agnosiac who famously mistook his wife for a hat: Sacks, 1986.[16]) Quite generally, resolution stifles a sense of the uncanny. For such a sense demands that doubts of the sort Jentsch identifies will never be satisfactorily resolved: that one will forever remain unsure if one's attitude and conduct towards the suspect entity are appropriate ... or grotesquely inappropriate. This means, of course, that no coherent posture will be assumed since higher-order anxieties will colour and subvert every transaction. Nothing of this sort is suggested in *The Sandman*.

So a degree of uncertainty whether something is living or inanimate must persist indefinitely. And yet it cannot be perceived as *irresolvable*. If it were, the suspicion that one might be mistaking the inanimate for the animate (and vice versa) would begin to look empty, and a contrast between what, on any existing conception, is appropriate and inappropriate to each would cease to have any clear sense. For it to be uncanny the uncertainty must be chronic. But it must be also accidental rather than essential. Here is an example:

> He observed this court with fascination: how different it was from the one that he had left in Florence! It radiated a sense of brute force that both attracted and repelled him. Through the smoke, he saw

> powerful jaws, with several teeth missing, vociferating, laughing and devouring; hands covered with lace and jewels, but greasy and scarred, closing over viands or other hands; ardent, but witless eyes resting on him with cruel insistence. Were these creatures entirely men, or were they all more or less the products of matings with bears, wolves, or some other beasts of the forest of the Vendée? Foxes' eyes, wild boars' muzzles, badgers' heads, hairy chests hung about with golden chains and pectoral crosses, a hundred surprising details—flared nostrils, pointed ears that could be made to move, and the squeals, wails and hisses that replaced words and laughter as the night wore on—yes, everything about the ball that suggested animal brutality and innocence. [Tournier, 1988, p. 79]

If we press this thought further we move into encounters not with inanimate things behaving in suggestively animate ways but with kinds which are unnatural because impossible: unthinkable human derivatives, the assorted *undead*. They belong nowhere, have no world to call theirs. Yet any description of their nature and capacities must begin by borrowing from the human (See Rice, 1977 and Margolis, 19xx). It is in this context that Freud's observations about "*(un)heimlichkeit*" are so penetrating. The *unhomely*—the eerie, weird, indeterminately fearsome—is, precisely, the uncanny. He quotes Schelling: "'Unheimlich' is the name for everything that ought to have remained secret and hidden but has come to light" (Freud, 19xx, p. 345. Freud explores the idea of *unheimlichkeit* on pp. 341–347).

Fictions of a related genre show us what it is like, and what our responses are like, when uncertainty is made *essential*. They deal in things which belong nowhere because they belong simultaneously to both animate and inanimate worlds, and move easily between the two; or—which is not so very different—deal in apparently animate objects brought into existence by impossible means. They do so by conjoining, in their subjects and their subjects' worlds, features which we accept as unproblematically animate (and perhaps sentient) with ones which are unproblematically neither. The rules of this game make resolution between the animate and the inanimate unthinkable, and discourage us from seeking any. Instead they propose new categories and so stimulate fantasies about categorically *novel* responses which are sure to be as hybrid and incoherent as their impossible fictional objects.

The best, and decidedly uncanny, example I know of the apparent "manufacture" of the animate is in Umberto Eco's *Foucault's Pendulum*:

> Among tropical plants were six glass ampoules in the shape of pears—or tears—hermetically sealed, filled with a pale-blue liquid. Inside each vessel floated a creature about twenty centimetres high: we recognised the gray-haired king, the queen, the Moor, the warrior, and the two adolescents crowned with laurel, one blue and one pink ... They swayed with a graceful swimming motion, as if water were their element. It was hard to determine whether they were models made of plastic or wax, or whether they were living beings, and the slight opacity of the liquid made it impossible to tell if the faint pulse that animated them was an optical illusion or reality. [Eco, 1989, p. 347]

Now, although ideas of the uncanny ("unhomely") and the paranormal sometimes intersect and combine—as in the case of certain hauntings like the recurrent Bluebell Hill phenomena in West Kent—the former are neither necessary nor sufficient for the latter. They pertain, so to say, to distinct psychological genres. In particular, the sense of a hard-wired insolubility is foreign to, and distracts from, the field of the paranormal. Unless it is an empty notion, it is what subsumes phenomena with respect to which we may be *certain* that nothing resembling an explanation could be found. And the conviction, right or wrong, that sometimes things are like this is akin not to a sense of the uncanny but to the "intellectual" stance which Jentsch and Freud identify.[17]

Notes

1. A classic example is the flowering branch episode in Freud's "The Interpretation of Dreams", where the dreamer's branch covered with red camellia-like flowers is made to become (among other things) a repressed ideation involving the phallus. For further discussion of this dream see Cioffi, 1998, p. 212 note.
2. Freud's great paper on the uncanny is discussed in the concluding section.
3. Plato's target is most forms of art and especially drama, which he believes engage our emotions and intellect in reprehensible and

dishonest ways, and seduce us away from truths which, on some level, we already know. I don't share this view of art, but understand how it can have plausibility when extended to parapsychology and an enthusiasm for the paranormal.

4. Thus, I omit several "respectable" paranormal categories, such as mediumistic phenomena, as well as more suspect ones like crop circles and abduction narratives which arguably manifest a pathology.
5. Abnormal phenomena are freaks, aberrations of nature sometimes called "Fortean" after Charles Fort, who collected and published cases. In what immediately follows I seek to meet head-on the common counter-argument that the paranormal is in essence an historical, relative notion by suggesting that there are things which simply *couldn't* be explained naturalistically or scientifically; and that it is rational to believe that such things sometimes happen.
6. Which is one reason why the greatest works in the parapsychological field are descriptive and classificatory, and rarely attempt to explain. They predicate "miraculous" works in much the same way, except that a provenance is commonly assigned. The following exercise might be set to students:

   > Several times a year crowds gather in the cathedral at Naples to witness the miraculous liquifaction of the "blood" of St Janarius. A phial is half-filled with a substance that looks like blood. During the ceremony the phial is repeatedly picked up and moved around to see if it has liquified. Liquefaction may take minutes, hours or even days and it will occur at any time of year, summer or winter. Which of the following provides the best hypothesis to explain this phenomenon?
   >
   > A This is a genuine miracle.
   > B The contents of the phial are photosensitive and liquefy on exposure to light.
   > C Liquefaction and solidification of the contents of the phial result from the growth of a micro-organism.
   > D The substance is thixotropic, changing from solid to liquid when mechanically disturbed.
   > E The substance is a hygroscopic, deliquescent solid, becoming liquid when it absorbs moisture from the air.
   >
   > There is no definitive, correct answer although current thinking favours explanation D.

   However, the miracle option is not an explanation (and probably not an hypothesis), as are the others, but rather what is left if and when the others (and perhaps yet more) have failed.
7. The position Hume found himself in his essay "Of miracles". Much that Hume says is relevant to the concept of the paranormal, but his discussion of testimony and veridicality would take us too far afield.

An ostensibly paranormal event is a profane analogue of a miracle, with the attributed divine provenance omitted; and Hume's analysis oscillates uncomfortably between miracles as violations of natural laws (cf. the first response) and miracles as merely "signs and wonders" (cf. the second response. I examine these issues in Cherry, 1974).

8. These illustrations are borrowed from Holland, 1982, and my own discussion of the logic of cases like this in Cherry, 1975. Holland left it unattributed; and I, too, was unaware that Freud uses the same illustration until the editor of the present collection drew my attention to *S.E., 11*, pp. 5–33. Weird ... or what?
9. By contrast, his *modus operandi* is most perspicuous when he treats the everyday and the discreet. The *locus classicus* is the *Psychopathology of Everyday Life*, but perhaps the most ingenious display is in Freud 1936, where Freud penetrates ever deeper into the process of amazement that the Acropolis "really *does* exist, just as we learnt at school!": Freud, 1901, p. 241, until he reaches what he takes it encode, an expression of filial piety elicited by the triste recognition that "one had got further than one's father ... as though to excel one's father was still something forbidden" (*op. cit.*, p. 247).
10. I have explored these and related issues more fully in Cherry, 1976, pp. 315–339, and Cherry, 1980, pp. 58–69, and drawn upon some of the ideas in these papers with which I still agree. For other work in similar vein to which I am almost certainly indebted, but with which I am not always in agreement, the reader is referred to Wittgenstein, 1966 and Cioffi, 1998. Wittgenstein thinks what I have called "imitative explanation" is in effect an invitation to adopt a new notation. The invitation is hard to resist, but our reason to accept it is not necessarily worthy.
11. Philosophy has, however, remained surprisingly silent, and I have tried elsewhere to redress the balance, variously focusing on fear of death and its palliatives, the evidence (or otherwise) for survival suggested by near-death experiences, and what it might be like to survive death.
12. One which I go some way to telling in Cherry, 1995. See also Cherry, 1984 and 1987.
13. Throughout this section I draw upon certain ideas in Cherry, 1991.
14. Grotesquely inappropriate transactions between human beings and artefacts are a significant theme in Fantastic and Surrealist literature and painting, and (like the present case) seem to be special applications of the idea of the inanimate becoming animate which is found everywhere in myth and fairytale. The audience attunes to the fantasy with an unerring sense of epistemic pitch.
15. Freud has in mind "a fertile but not exhaustive" paper of 1906 by Jentsch, "The psychology of the uncanny": Freud, 1919, p. 219.

16. Sacks says that his patient had special difficulty with the animate, which he "so absurdly misperceived" (Sacks, 1986, p. 20).
17. An excellent recent discussion of the possibilities or otherwise of "ostensibly infrangible" evidence for some kinds of paranormal events is to be found in Keen *et al.*, 1999.

References

Blackmore, S. (1993). *Dying to Live*. London: Prometheus Book.

Broad, C. D. (1953). *Religion, Philosophy and Psychical Research*. London: Routledge.

Broad, C. D. (1962). *Lectures on Psychical Research*. London: Routledge.

Cherry, C. (1974). Miracles and creation. *International Journal for Philosophy of Religion*, *4*: 234–245.

Cherry, C. (1975). On characterizing the extraordinary. *Ratio*, *xvii*: 52–64.

Cherry, C. (1976). Explanation and exploration by hypothesis. *Synthese*, *33*: 315–339.

Cherry, C. (1980). Meaning and the idol of origins. *The Philosophical Quarterly*, *35*: 58–69.

Cherry, C. (1984). Self, death and near-death. *International Journal for the Philosophy of Religion*, *16*: 3–11.

Cherry, C. (1987). Near-death experiences and the problem of evidence for survival after death. *Religious Studies*, *22*: 397–416.

Cherry, C. (1991). Machines as persons? In: D. Cockburn (Ed.), *Human Beings* (pp. 11–25). Cambridge: Cambridge University Press.

Cherry, C. (1995). Are near-death experiences really suggestive of life after death? In: D. Cohn-Sherbok (Ed.), *Beyond Death*. London: Macmillan.

Cioffi, F. (1998). *Wittgenstein on Freud and Frazer*. Cambridge: C.U.P.

Deutsch, H. (1953). Occult processes occurring during psychoanalysis. In: G. Devereux (Ed.), *Psychoanalysis and the Occult* (pp. 133–146). London: Souvenir Press.

Eco, U. (1989). *Foucault's Pendulum*. London: Secker and Warburg.

Freud, S. (1900). *The Interpretation of Dreams*. *S.E.*, *4&5*: 1–625.

Freud, S. (1901). *The Psychopathology of Everyday Life*. *S.E.*, *6*: 1–279.

Freud, S. (1913). *Totem and Taboo*. *S.E.*, *13*: 1–161.

Freud, S. (1919). The "uncanny". *S.E.*, *17*: 217–252.

Freud, S. (1936). A disturbance of memory on the Acropolis. *S.E.*, *22*: 239–248.

Freud, S. (1939). *Moses and Monotheism*. *S.E.*, *23*: 7–137.

Grattan-Guinness, I. (Ed.) (1982). *Psychical Research: A Guide to its History, Principles and Practice*. Wellingborough: Aquarian Press.
Hoffman, E. T. A. (1988). *Tales of Hoffman*. London: Penguin.
Holland, R. F. (1982). The miraculous. In: *Against Empiricism*. London: Blackwell.
Hume, D. (1956). *A Treatise of Human Nature, Volume 2*. London: Dent.
Jung, C. G. (1962). *Memories, Dreams, Reflections*. New York: Pantheon.
Keen, M., Ellison, A., & Fontana, D. (Eds.) (1999). The Scole Report. *Proceedings of the Society for Psychical Research, 58*, Part 220.
Kellehear, A. (1996). *Experiences Near Death*. Oxford: Oxford University Press.
MacKenzie, A. (1982). *Hauntings and Apparitions*. London: Heinemann.
Margolis, J. *Dracula the Man: An Essay on the Logic of Individuation*.
Milner, M. (1988). *The Suppressed Madness of Sane Men*. London: Routledge.
Myers, F. W. H. (1903). *Human Personality and its Survival of Bodily Death, Volume II*. London: Longmans Green.
Rice, A. (1977). *Interview with the Vampire*. London: Futura.
Ring, K. (1980). *Life at Death*. New York: Coward, McCann and Geohegan.
Sacks, O. (1986). *The Man Who Mistook His Wife for a Hat*. London: Pan.
Serdahely, W. J. (1992). Similarities between near-death experiences and multiple personality disorder. *Journal of Near Death Studies*, 2(1): 19–37.
Thalbourne, M. A. (1982). *A Glossary of Terms used in Parapsychology*. London: Heinemann.
Tournier, M. (1988). *Gilles and Jeanne*. London: Minerva.
Wittgenstein, L. (1966). Conversations on Freud. In. C. Barratt (Ed.), *Letters and Conversations*. Oxford: Basil Blackwell.

CHAPTER FOUR

Mercurius, archetype, and "transpsychic reality": C. G. Jung's parapsychology of spirit(s)

Michael Whan

> "Parapsychology plays a subtle part in psychology because it lurks everywhere behind the surface of things. But, as the facts are difficult to catch, their theoretical aspect is still more elusive on account of its transcendent character"
>
> C. G. Jung, 1973, pp. 378–379

> "At bottom the only courage that is demanded of us is to have the courage for the most strange, the most singular and the most inexplicable that we may encounter"
>
> Rainer Maria Rilke, 1975, p. 98

Introduction

For me, the Rilke quotation serves as a fundamental axiom both for life itself and, thus, for psychotherapy. How can life be lived at its deepest without the "courage for life"? And in psychotherapy also I do not see how either the therapist or patient can bear the emotional risks, turmoil, and profound uncertainty of the work without the virtue of *courage* (I use the term "patient" not in the medical sense, but with reference to suffering, patience, with what one has to undergo, experience, encounter). What Rilke says though is specific, he writes: "the courage for the most strange, the most singular and the most inexplicable". To allow for the "most strange, the most singular and the most inexplicable", the therapist has to abrogate omniscient "knowing", the patient too has to permit the therapist and him/herself not to know. Furthermore, psychological and psychotherapeutic theory has also to acknowledge its own limits, to refrain from the inflationary impulse to explain all things. Psychotherapy and psychology then need to give recognition to the Unknown, the Unknowable, and Unknowing. We can and do experience things without always being able to understand what they are. The rationalistic "explaining away" of some enigmas and anomalies leads to a falsification or denial of the very phenomena for which the explanation seeks to account.

One reason that Jung's psychology attracts me is that I find in Jung someone who, though deeply psychological, gave thought to what lay beyond the boundaries of psychology and to the problematic of the relationship between the psyche and nonpsychic reality [in Jung's threefold thinking: soul, body (nature), and spirit]. As he wrote in *Memories, Dreams, Reflections*:

> We know that something unknown, alien, does come our way ... What does happen to us in this manner can be said to emanate from mana, from a daimon, a god, or the unconscious ... I prefer the term "unconscious," knowing that I might equally well speak of "God" or "daimon" if I wished to express myself in mythic language ... I am aware that "mana," "daimon," and "God" are synonyms for the unconscious—that is to say, we know just as much or just as little about them as about the latter. [Jung, 1963a, pp. 336–337]

Jung's words allow for the possibility of a non-human agency at work in our lives, not everything being reducible to human subjectivity and acts. What I experience may be due to *unknown factors*. I can of course name such factors "the unconscious", thereby giving them a spurious explanation. When I psychologize in this way, I theorize the "unknown" in terms of human subjectivity and interiority; I internalize the "unknown". Thus I render life's unknowns "knowable" and "psychological", reinforcing and expanding psychology's explanatory domain.

The question underlying it all is whether what we speak of as the "parapsychological" can be derived solely from "unconscious" human behaviour, or whether we have to consider other forms of "agency", not immediately reducible to human subjectivity (though human subjectivity may participate in such paranormal events; Robertson, 1999; Turner *et al.*, 1992; Turner, 1996; Willis *et al.*, 1999)? In my work as a psychotherapist, I occasionally experience enigmatic, anomalous happenings, which, though possibly still accountable for psychologically, have a certain quality about them that feels more "borderline", that is, an "uncanniness" which seems to point beyond a strictly materialistic, rationalistic order of reality: some sense of a "beyond" that is operating in the highly intimate and emotional interchanges of the psychotherapeutic setting. At the very least, there is an indeterminacy about them, which engenders in me (and sometimes in the patient) an "imagination of the occult". They give rise to a quality of *imagin*-ability. Of course, this "proves" nothing, and its meaning may lie wholly in the subjective response. That I imagine something in a certain way, doesn't mean that is how things are. We always have to reckon with the potential duplicity of the psychic image. Yet even the "rationalistic" and "materialistic", insofar as they govern explanation and understanding, rest too upon the image, upon root metaphors that shape our experience, or put more strongly, *are* our experience. The whole discourse of psychotherapy and analysis no less operates through the images that we interpret and by which we interpret. In such instances, I prefer to hold to the uncertainty, to the unknown, by not trying to resolve or decide the domain of the enigmatic. So doing, I may well better serve the therapy and *logos* of the psyche. As Jung himself put it: "To assess psychic phenomena, we have to take account of all other phenomena that go with it, and accordingly we can no longer practice psychology that ignores the existence of the unconscious or of parapsychology" (Jung, 1964, para. 527). Admitting the parapsychological (or parapsychic), hence belongs to the very heart of psychological practice. The noun "psyche" can be suggestive of both the adjective "psychic" and "psychical" (so and so is definitely *psychic*; *The Society For Psychical Research*), and "psychic" in the meaning of "psychological".

To begin with, I want to describe a cluster of events, a certain complex of meanings which came about in my practice. Central to these, is a long-standing interest in the Grail legend and its significance in Jung's psychology. First, a dream from very early on in 1999:

> I'm in a room, which belongs to an unknown woman. There is a vague or confused sense about a film, TV programme, or actuality, in which reality is dualistic. On one side, is our ordinary world, the other is "Arthurian". A man is shifting between the two worlds. The woman shows us a long object, a stick with various small things attached to it. In the *other* reality, this is Arthur's sword, Excalibur.

With the occurrence of the dream, I returned to my interest in the Grail motif (shelved for several years). I also consulted the *I Ching* or *Book of Changes*, the Chinese oracle book (Jung wrote the "Foreword" to it, when originally published by the German scholar, Richard Wilhelm). This method of divination purports to show, utilizing sixty-four hexagrams, the particular configuration of meaning for any given moment of time. As one recent translation describes it, the *I Ching* "is a particular kind of imaginative space set off for a dialogue with the gods or spirits, the creative basis of experience now called the unconscious" (Ritsema & Karcher, 1994, p. 8). I asked my question concerning psychology and the Grail, the hexagram that came up was number sixty-one, "Centering Conforming" ("Inner Truth" in the English translation of the Wilhelm edition). The commentary goes thus:

> This hexagram describes your situation in terms of the relation between your inner core and the circumstances of your life. It emphasizes that bringing your central concerns and your life situation into a sincere and reliable accord is the adequate way to handle it. [*ibid.*, p. 638]

With the hexagram, there is the possibility of what are called "transforming lines". These give greater specificity to the reading, pointing to possible developments. I received "Nine at second", which states, "Calling crane located-in yin/One's sonhood harmonizing it/I possess a loved wine-cup/Myself associating, simply spilling it" (*ibid.*, p. 643). I want to mention two symbolic connections with this. In Celtic mythology, the crane is associated with magic cauldrons, which is one cultural source of the Grail as vessel. In Chinese mythology, the wine-cup signifies a vessel of libation, a sacred vessel like the Grail in Christian legend.

Nothing of this was ever expressed or discussed with any of the patients I saw at the time. Several experiences in my practice suggested, nevertheless, that these images and the associated "complexes", some of them having an intense, disturbing, and painful character, had been constellated. The following events happened over a period of around two weeks. One of the motifs I was interested in was that of a wounded masculinity connected with the Grail's guardian, the Fisher King. For weeks I had experienced an intermittent pain in both my hands, a feeling of soreness or burning, particularly in the palms of the hands. Then a patient had a dream in which my left hand had become red with soreness. It may well be that this woman, an experienced and intuitive therapist, was mirroring through her dream some aspect of my woundedness.

Shortly after, another woman, again a therapist, had the following dream:

> She is with me outside my house. There is a grassy bank leading to the door. On the left are two or three boys. Buried in the ground in front of my house is a sword. It is very shiny, splendid, bright silver with a seam down the centre. It has a silver, gold cross-handle with gems, a large ruby. From the handle hangs braiding, also silver and gold. The sword appears to the dreamer as important. It is connected with the earth, very solidly fixed in it.

The dreamer feels it won't easily extract and wants me to help, to understand its mystery. What does it mean? This individual said she had no especial interest in the Arthurian or Grail stories, and said she knew little about them. Her comment was "Something in my comical world about you being Merlin rather than Arthur."

And one further instance, another woman, who was also an intuitively-minded therapist, right at the start of a session, looked over from the couch at my catalogue of classical CDs. I was thinking about "woundedness" and the male psyche, whilst we were both being silent. The catalogue, she then said, had reminded her of her brother-in-law, for whom she had just ordered one. She recalled a dream from years ago, early on in the therapy. In the dream, he had pulled off a beard, to reveal a wound on his face. She associated the dream figure also with myself, having both a beard and a birthmark on my face. All of these happenings coming in this intense period, suggest to me that the intimacy of the relationships between us had served to channel a cluster of meanings, a network of complexes. Even if one speaks here of "projective" or "introjective" identification, this does not preclude their synchronistic nature, of both the psychological and the parapsychological. That more than one individual was involved, indicates a degree of "collectivity" or "sociality" in these constellations: the Grail and Arthur motifs were, as it were, "in the field".

If the reader can bear one last meaningful connection. I have an unusual surname, "Whan". It was only well into adulthood that I discovered it is Scottish: "MacWhan" or "MacQuhan", a variant of the name "MacQueen". The Gaelic root of these names derives from "Suibhne". This name is uncertain in meaning, but possibly denoting "ease and motion, or gentle flowing" (Black, 1965). Years after finding this out, I came across a reference to this name in connection with the Grail legend. For "Suibhne" or "Suibne" was a legendary Irish figure, considered one source for the Merlin figure, both connected with shamanism (I'll spare the reader such further intertwinings and links, though there are others). I hope the reader accepts, I am not claiming a lineage of descent from Merlin, though these "connections" have lead into some very personal areas connected with my family background, and of a very painful nature. But without taking this further, I feel they suggest something of what Jung called "transpsychic reality". I want now to go onto this, discussing it in the context of Jung's notion of the archetypes, the alchemical symbol of Mercurius, and the idea of synchronicity.

Psyche and spirit

For Jung then, psychology and parapsychology are inextricably entwined. But this mutual entwinement implies that psychology enfolds a subtle element not wholly of itself, its subject matter (psyche or soul), but rather of a transcendent character: something which is found in it, yet is not of it. In traditional (theological) language, if psychology signifies the *logos* of the psyche or soul, then parapsychology may indicate *the workings of the spirit or spirits* (at least a certain manifestation of them). In a somewhat hunter–

gatherer fashion, I want to follow a spoor, a trace of this elusive interplay between psychic and spiritual factors. A connection between psyche and spirit(s) runs throughout Jung's psychology. The expression *para*-psychology points to what lies "by the side of, beside", or "alongside of, by, past, beyond" the psychological. Parapsychology indicates a "beyond", a borderline, an "inbetween" or liminality. The sense of, or intimation, or image of, a "beyond" is one of the spatial metaphors that announces the realm of spirit or spirits. Parapsychology belongs both at the edge or periphery of psychology, but, as Jung states, also at its very heart or centre. Jung's claim, nevertheless, begs the question of what he meant by the "psychological"? The relationship between psyche and spirit generates an instability regarding the meaning of the psychological, correspondingly giving rise to a complex, shifting notion of what constitutes parapsychic phenomena in Jung's thinking.

Many of Jung's statements on the nature of psychology strongly suggest he understood it almost as a "cult of the dead", psychology as an expression of our obligations to the world of the dead and spirit(s). Psychology's is a haunted language, interrupted and disrupted often by S/spirit presence (with a capital or small "s"). It is a language resonant with ghostly voices, one open to parapsychic events and experiences. The notion of an "unconscious" draws us into hauntings and mediumistic communication. Consider, for instance, Jung's reflections on the "loss of soul". Jung connects this with the anima, the psyche's "feminine" self-personification. Loss of soul entails an absence of animation, as one may encounter in certain depressive states and other conditions. Jung explains this further in terms of the "dead":

> the soul, the anima, establishes the relationship to the unconscious. In a sense this is also a relationship to the collectivity of the dead ... the land of the ancestors. If, therefore, one has the fantasy of the soul vanishing, this means that it has withdrawn into the unconscious or into the land of the dead. [Jung, 1963a, p. 191]

Even so, what appears as a loss to consciousness, offers the dead a way of expression: "Like a medium, it gives the dead a chance to manifest themselves" (Jung, 1963a, p. 191). The needfulness of a dialogue with the dead then comprises a critical element in the constitution of depth psychology for Jung.

The experience of a loss of soul may signify the anima's connection with the "unconscious", which, "(i)n a sense", is a "relationship to the collectivity of the dead". But in what "sense", how are we to understand, to decide, what Jung is getting at when he says "like a medium"; is he speaking purely in metaphor and analogy? Psychology, Jung continues, is "fundamentally nothing but attempts ever renewed, to give an answer to the question of the interplay between the 'here' and the 'hereafter' ". Psychology represents a dialogical opening between life and death, time and eternity, spirit and soul. The returning dead have real claims upon us; we have a responsibility to them. Jung spoke of his feeling of their abiding presence, of the necessity that we listen to and address them: "I frequently have the feeling that they are standing directly behind us waiting to hear what answer we will give to them, and what to destiny (*ibid*., p. 299).

Jung's own "answer" was his "psychology of the unconscious":

> the dead have become ever more distinct for me as the voices of the Unanswered, Unresolved, and Unredeemed; for since the questions and demands which my destiny required me to answer did not come to me from the outside, they must have come from the inner world. These conversations with the dead formed a kind of prelude to what I had to communicate to the world about the unconscious. [*ibid*., pp. 191–192]

Psychology, for Jung, derives from a mediumistic exchange, the deep ancestral memory of a soul-speech, by which the living and the dead, spirit and soul, enter into and sustain their dialogues, the questions and answers.

Jung's references to such experiences and events, whether to actual spirits or to psychologically derived phenomena, remains equivocal, partly a reflection of his understanding of the psyche's "autonomy". By this, Jung meant psyche's own intentionality, distinct from that of the conscious ego-personality. The soul functions on its own accord. It is self-moving and may not align with conscious purpose and will, but may serve a different intent. Parapsychic phenomena may be one form in which the psyche manifests autonomously, which for Jung still allowed a psychological interpretation. Hence, in 1919, Jung wrote:

> parapsychic phenomena seem to be connected as a rule with the

> presence of a medium. They are, so far as my experience goes, the exteriorized effects of unconscious complexes ... exteriorizations ... I see no proof whatever of ... real spirits, and until such proof is forthcoming I must regard this whole territory as an appendix of psychology. [Jung, 1960, para. 600]

Jung held to this declaration—at least, as far as I know—in his public statements. Nevertheless, he did eventually modify it radically, as we shall shortly see.

Jung's theory of the psyche's autonomy derives partly, in the account given in *Memories, Dreams, Reflections*, from the experiences following on from his separation from Freud. After this break, Jung describes a period of great psychic upheaval. As a way of relating to these considerable tensions and upwellings, he developed a mode of dialoguing with the imaginal figures that came his way in dreams and fantasies. Out of these dialogues, Jung found his way to a deeper understanding of the nature of the psyche. The psyche became his teacher. Such imaginal figures were themselves involved in "the making of a psychology", as much as "Jung" himself. To one such "personality", Jung gave the name "Philemon", whom Jung described thus: "Philemon was a pagan and brought with him an Egypto–Hellenistic atmosphere with Gnostic coloration". Jung's first encounter with Philemon came through a dream:

> Suddenly there appeared from the right a winged being sailing across the sky ... it was an old man with the horns of a bull. He held a bunch of keys, one of which he clutched as if he were about to open a lock. He had the wings of the kingfisher ...

The encounter taught Jung about the psyche's autonomy, for:

> Philemon and the other figures of my fantasies brought home to me the crucial insight that there are things in the psyche which I do not produce, but which produce themselves and have their own life. Philemon represented a force which was not myself ... It was he who taught me psychic objectivity ... [Jung, 1963a, pp. 182–183]

The psyche is not reducible to human subjectivity; it has its own "objectivity", its own being in and for itself. When Jung speaks of the figures of this difficult time in his life, they are presented in terms of his developing notions of the psyche and psychology, as the stuff of fantasy, as personified unconscious contents, which he later conceived of as archetypal or transpersonal.

Philemon appeared to offer Jung help in handling the experiences and fantasies, as if the psyche were itself, as personified through this numinous figure, enabling Jung to relate to its own overwhelming stream of psychic contents. Jung regarded Philemon as representing "superior insight. He was a mysterious figure ... At times he seemed ... quite real, as if ... a living personality" (*ibid.*, p. 183). Philemon brought a healing element:

> In my darkness ... I could have wished for nothing better than a real, live guru, someone possessing superior knowledge and ability, who would have disentangled for me the involuntary creations of my imagination. This task was undertaken by the figure of Philemon, whom in this respect I had ... to recognize as my psychagogue. [*ibid.*, p. 184]

Jung's account of Philemon implies a certain equivocation about his "nature", about what kind of reality he is. On the one hand, he describes him in terms that suggest Philemon as a symbolic creation of the psyche, compensating and helping to contain the uprush of bewildering fantasies and affects. Yet, is there not a hint of a transcendent aspect, when Jung points to Philemon as "quite real ... as if he were a living personality?" Can Philemon be accounted for purely psychologically?

In the following paragraph, Jung takes this matter up. He recounts how, during a meeting with a friend of Gandhi, they discussed the guru relationship. Having asked his companion about his guru, the other replied: "Shankaracharya". Jung further inquired: "'You don't mean the commentator on the Vedas who died centuries ago?'" Jung's companion confirmed this. Again, Jung questioned him: "'Then you are referring to a spirit?'" At that point, Jung recalled Philemon. Jung's companion added: "'There are ghostly gurus too ... there are always some who have a spirit for a teacher.'" Jung found this answer "illuminating and reassuring", indicating perhaps that it gave further insight into who and what Philemon was. There are two further references to Philemon, which point in this direction. These references appear in two letters to the Catholic priest, Father Victor White. In the first (December 19th, 1947), Jung writes about a dream, of "a most venerable looking, very old man with white locks and a long flowing white beard". In the second letter (January 30th, 1948), he refers to the same dream figure: "While I stood before the bed of the Old Man, I thought and felt ... I know Him very well: He was my 'guru' more than 30 years ago, a real ghostly guru—but that is a long and—I am afraid—exceedingly strange story" (Jung, 1976, pp. 479–481, 490–493). If Jung were referring simply to a "straightforward" psychological, symbolical figure, why speak of it as an "exceedingly strange story"? Isn't Jung voicing his feeling of the mysteriousness of Philemon, maybe even of Philemon as a "spirit presence"—"a real ghostly guru"?

In the 1919 passage already quoted, from Jung's talk to the Society for Psychical Research—"The psychological foundations of belief in spirits"—he appeared to discount a spiritist explanation. Fifty years later, Jung published a revised statement, added as a footnote. The reasons given indicate not only the possibility of actual spirits, thereby rejecting a psychologistic reduction, but Jung here employs the term "transpsychic reality". He writes: "... I no longer feel as certain as I did in 1919, when I wrote this sentence ... I doubt whether an exclusively psychological approach can do justice to the phenomena ...". Making his retraction, Jung continues:

> Not only the findings of parapsychology, but my own theoretical reflections ... have led me to certain postulates which touch on the realm of nuclear physics and the conception of the space–time continuum ... open[ing] up the whole question of the transpsychic reality ... underlying the psyche [Jung, 1960, para. 600, note 15]

What I find interesting in Jung's thought is that his revised position results precisely *through* his psychological reflections, not in opposition to them. It was psychology itself, as it were, that lead Jung to its own boundaries, the liminal interplay between soul and spirit, that manifests in paranormal and parapsychological events. The paradox of Jung's psychology is that to be truly psychological, one must admit the limits of psychologism. Further, implicit in psychology is a *cosmology*, which Jung here is trying to make explicit. Such a cosmology (including spiritual as well as physical aspects) underlies all psychological statements. In bringing this cosmological ground to light, Jung took account of developments in contemporary theoretical physics. Jung's psychology thus transgressed its own boundaries, attempting to intuit a "beyond". To put this another way, Jung's thinking carries over from psychology into a pneumatology, the science of spiritual being(s), as well as to theoretical physics.

Mercurius, archetype, and synchronicity

Parapsychological phenomena had and have a special significance in the relationship between psychology and physics. According to Aniela Jaffe, Jung's colleague and personal secretary, he regarded parapsychology as "the bridge between the psychology of the unconscious and microphysics" (Jaffe, 1982, pp. vii–viii). Jung's interest in physics followed in part from his notion of the "objective" psyche, that the psyche has an autonomous reality, involving, but not reducible to, human subjectivity. Controversially, in parapsychology, Jung found phenomena suggestive of the psyche's "objective reality". In a late essay, "On the nature of the psyche", Jung quotes the Nobel physicist, Wolfgang Pauli, just on this point:

> It is undeniable that the development of "microphysics" has brought the way in which nature is described in this science very much closer to that of the newer psychology: but whereas the former, on account of the basic "complementarity" situation, is faced with the impossibility of eliminating the effects of the observer by determinable correctives, and has therefore to abandon in principle any objective understanding of physical phenomena, the latter can supplement the purely subjective psychology of consciousness by postulating the existence of an unconscious that possesses a large measure of objective reality. [Jung, 1960, note 130]

Physics offered Jung a theoretical basis for postulating an underlying connectivity between psyche and *physis*, nature. Such a deep level connection served psychology, not only in thinking further the mind–body relationship, but by suggesting hypothetical support for the possibility and understanding of parapsychic and paranormal experiences.

Physics, however, isn't the only fruitful area of Jung's psychology for researching into questions of parapsychology and the paranormal. For Jung found in his study of alchemy an historical antecedent of his own psychology of the unconscious, which thus granted him a wealth of insights into the psyche. His alchemical studies comprise the major portion of his late psychological reflections. The historical and symbolical parallels to his own thinking evidenced to Jung a kind of "proto-psychology", an implicit psychology which did not yet know itself as such. In their experiments, the alchemists, in their conceptions about the various substances, ideas about the transmutation of metals, and understanding of the developmental stages of the alchemical process, Jung saw as projecting their own psychic contents onto nature, or "unknown matter". Its relatively "unknown" character left it open to psychological projections. In other words, Jung regarded alchemy (the supposed transformation of "base metal" into gold) as a symbolic activity, in which the psyche was essentially depicting its own transformative processes. Jung interpreted this process of transformation specifically in terms of the psychology of individuation, the psychology of "becoming" most deeply and fully who and what one is; the actualization of the Self in relation to one's conscious personality.

A key element in alchemical theory was the relationship between spirit and nature. For the alchemist who understood his practices in spiritual terms, alchemy was a means to recover and release the divine spirit entrapped and hidden in materiality. As the alchemists put it: the "spirit in the stone". For orthodox Christianity, nature was "fallen". The alchemist then saw his task, his *opus*, as continuing the work of Creation. For him or her, the alchemical work was a work of redemption: Christianity was still in the making. Alchemy therefore complemented the Christian standpoint regarding nature, and through its workings sought to heal the rift between spirit and nature. The collapse of alchemy signalled, in Jung's mind, a critical event in the history of Western metaphysics and science: for with "the decline of alchemy the symbolical unity of spirit and matter fell apart, with the result that modern man finds himself uprooted and alienated in a desouled world" (Jung, 1959, para. 197). Behind this rupture, Jung perceived the cause of Christian metaphysics. Jung felt that Christianity had opened a "gulf ... between nature and spirit", enabling "the human mind to think not only beyond nature but in opposition to it" (Jung, 1958, para. 261). In alchemy, this thinking beyond or in opposition to nature was expressed as the *opus contra naturam*, "the work against nature". The "gulf" allowed the emergence of scientific experiment and thought: "man entered a new and independent relation to nature whereby the foundation was laid for natural science and technique" (Jung, 1991, para. 130). Alchemy, the "occult science", then, for Jung, addressed the very question of the riven or unified state of ultimate reality (the *unus mundus*), and, in my view, may well have contributed to his postulate of a "transpsychic reality".

At this point, I want to return briefly to the personal examples from my work, as a way into the subject of the alchemical Mercurius and parapsychology. I understand these synchronicities in terms of an *archetypal* configuration of the "transference" and "counter-transference". This entails an interrelating of feeling, behaviour, and intentionality, which though personally experienced remains essentially *transpersonal*. The particular images concerning the Grail and "wound" symbols constellated between myself and the patients belong, I feel, to this level. They carry a profound cultural history implicate in the momentary surfacing in the transference/counter-transference relationship. In his major essay, the "Psychology of the Transference" (Jung, 1953a), Jung drew upon a series of alchemical woodcuts, taken from the text, the *Rosarium philosophorum*. Jung employed these to illustrate the psychology of the various transferential phases in the individuation process, as these manifested in the analytic setting. Central to Jung's archetypal conception of the transference, is the alchemical notion of the "conjunction" between the therapist and patient (the alchemical *coniunctio*, or "union of opposites"). The transference itself was identified with the alchemical figure of Hermes–Mercurius:

> The elusive, deceptive, ever-changing content that possesses the patient like a demon now flits about from the patient to doctor and, as the third party in the alliance, continues its game, sometimes impish and teasing, sometimes really diabolical, the alchemists aptly personified it as the wily god of revelation, Hermes or Mercurius ... it would be an altogether unjustifiable suppression of the truth were I to confine myself to the negative description of Mercurius' impish drolleries, his inexhaustible invention, his insinuations, his intriguing ideas and schemes, his ambivalence ... I can well understand why the alchemists endowed their Mercurius with the highest spiritual qualities, although these stand in flagrant contrast to his exceedingly shady character. [Jung, 1953a, para. 384]

Understood symbolically, I regard this imaginal figure as also encompassing parapsychic phenomena in the transference relationship. As we shall see, the Mercurius symbol shows up as well in relationship to physics and synchronicity. First, however, I want to say a little more about Mercurius in connection with Jung's psychology, indicating not only why Mercurius symbolizes the transference, but why he constellates such paranormal phenomena as telepathic and synchronistic happenings.

In alchemy, Mercurius was a multifaceted symbolic figure, representing the arcanum of the work, its agent of transformation, the transformative process itself, and its goal. Mercurius was described as a divine spirit concealed in nature's depths, a kind of earth-spirit, the "stone that hath a spirit", in contradistinction to the rupture between nature and spirit in Christian metaphysics. For alchemy, he bore the title of *anima mundi* or "soul of the world" (Jung, 1963b, para. 643). Having also a triadic character—animal, vegetative, and mineral—Mercurius embodied an earthly complement to the heavenly Trinity. In an essay, "The Spirit Mercurius", Jung explored the complex facets of this symbolic figure. In the section on Mercurius as soul, Jung suggests that he is "to all appearances ... connected with the *inflatio* or *inspiratio* of the Holy Spirit" (Jung, 1967, para. 263).

In the next section, on the spiritual as distinct from the soulful aspect of Mercurius, Jung cites the alchemist Gerhard Dorn, who described the "abstract" quality of the symbol: "the qualities of an incorruptible spirit, which is like the soul, and because of its incorruptibility is called intellectual" (Anon., 1659, p. 419; Jung, 1967, para. 264, note 27). Jung notes other adjectives: "incorporeal", "ethereal", "rational", and "wise" (Anon., 1659, *III*, pp. xxxviii, 5; *ibid.*, *IV*, pp. xiii, 3; Jung, 1967, notes 33–35). As its transformative agent, Mercurius spiritualizes matter, and materializes spirit, thus symbolizing a kind of "subtle body" and "energy", a conjunction between "soul" and "spirit", "soul" and "body", and "spirit" and "matter", a "contamination—inconceivable to the modern mind—of separate realms, spirit and matter" (Jung, 1967, para. 261). The dual-natured, elusive, duplicitous, mischievous Mercurius also brings together the realms of life and death, thus we can locate him in mediumship, in the communications between the living and dead (Von Franz, 1975, p. 209). Finally, Jung notes that the symbolic image of Mercurius gives personified form to "soul" and "spirit". The Mercurial anatomy lets the imagination into what otherwise would have been consigned to "the abstraction of ... two-dimensional metaphor of dry-as-dust philosophical dialectic". Expressed imagistically, spirit and soul take on an "almost physical, plastic form, like tangible breath-bodies, and refuse to function as component parts of our rational consciousness" (Jung, 1967, para. 286). One facet then of the irrational, tricksterish behaviour of Mercurius, his refusal to be rationalized away, is his subtle-bodied liminality, his manifestation parapsychically in synchronistic phenomena, as in the psychotherapeutic setting.

Mercurius, synchronicity, and Wolfgang Pauli

A vividly disruptive and creative manifestation of Mercurius occurred in the life, work, thought, and dreams of the Nobel physicist, Wolfgang Pauli. In his *Psychology and Alchemy* (Jung, 1953b), Jung records and analyzes a number of Pauli's dreams (Pauli spent some time in analysis with Jung and later with Jung's colleague, Marie-Louise Von Franz). Subsequently, he and Jung collaborated on the question of psyche's relationship to matter, and thus on the relation between psychology and physics. The collaboration resulted in their jointly authored *The Interpretation of Nature and the Psyche* (Pauli & Jung, 1955). Both his analyses proved crucial for Pauli, who aspired to develop a theoretical physics that included psychic reality.

In a letter to another physicist, Markus Fierz, Pauli refers to certain dream images, which he associates with his aspiration:

> My search is for a process of conjunction (unification of opposites), but I have only partly succeeded in this. Nevertheless first an exotic woman (... Chinese) ... appeared in my dreams, and later a strange, light–dark man who seemed something about the unification of opposites ... [Lauirkainen, 1988; quoted in Van Erkelens, 1991, p. 35]

In one series of dreams, a figure appeared that Pauli named "The Persian". This dream figure sought entry where Pauli taught, so as to "cause a lot of tumult there". In one dream, Pauli conversed with him as follows:

I: "You are not allowed to study?"
He: "No, therefore I study in secret."
I: "What subject are you studying?"
He: "Yourself!"
I: "You speak to me in a very sharp voice!"
He: "I speak as someone to whom everything else is forbidden."
I: "Are you my shadow?"
He: "I am between you and the light, so you are my shadow, not the reverse."
I: "Do you study physics?"
He: "There your language is too difficult for me, but in my language you do not understand physics!" [Van Erkelens, 1991, p. 36]

This mysterious dream presence brought together physics and psychology. He appears to be a repressed, deeper awareness ("forbidden" to study, but doing so "in secret"). He not only "studies" the dreamer (his psychological side), characterizing the conscious ego-personality itself as "the shadow", thus reversing the usual perspective, but, in some unstated sense, transcends the dream figure of Pauli's understanding of physics. Indeed, he points to a failure of understanding. Van Erkelens, himself a theoretical physicist, suggests that to interpret this dream, it needs to be placed alongside another. In this other dream, a man, looking like Einstein, informed Pauli "that quantum mechanics only describes a one-dimensional intersection of a two-dimensional, more meaningful reality". In this second dream, the "second dimension" no longer comprises "an area of psychophysical connections", rather, now personified, it represents the "hidden dimension of nature", revealed "itself as a spirit" (*ibid.*, p. 38). Later, the "Persian" merged with the figure of "a light-skinned, blond man", whom Pauli called "the light–dark stranger" (*ibid.*, p. 39).

Attempting to construct a "unified field theory", inclusive of both physics and psychology, Pauli developed "a neutral language in which physical processes are described in such a way that the new formulation also applies to psychology and parapsychological processes". Van Erkelens suggests that one reason the project failed was its omission of the dimension of *feeling*, a factor he associates with the alchemical Mercurius. Only when Pauli had experienced an erotic transference to Von Franz, did the feeling function become conscious. The Mercurius figure is also evident in Pauli's notion of the "light–dark stranger", embodying the tension of opposites. Hence, in both Pauli's dreams and analytic life, the symbol of Mercurius arose, connecting the dissociated elements of Pauli's personality, his life, and work. The Mercurial transference functioned to bind him more erotically to his task: "Like Mercurius in medieval alchemy ... the stranger tries to commit Pauli to his inner destiny through the experience of love" (*ibid.*, p. 43). The Mercurial eros here serves a purpose which goes beyond the analytic dyad, beyond the erotic attraction of the couple for each other. Rather it uses the transference for a transpersonal aim, that of deepening the work and relation to the world, physics, and psychology. Mercurius' erotic subtle body brings together spirit, body, and soul, seeking a conjunction between these two disciplines, a restoration of what was lost with the decline of alchemy.

As well as through the erotic transference, Mercurius appeared in another way in Pauli's life, namely, in various parapsychic disturbances. Pauli, writing to Jung's wife, Emma, said of "the light–dark stranger": "If you take too little notice of him, he draws attention to himself by any means, for instance through synchronistic phenomena ... or depressive states or incomprehensible emotions" (quoted in Van Erkelens, p. 40). In this letter, Pauli refers to the peculiar effects that occasionally happened in his proximity. When Pauli went near experimental equipment, his presence exerted a destructive effect: "equipment sometimes spontaneously exploded into many pieces!" For this reason Pauli was forbidden to enter the laboratory of his friend, Otto Stern.

Pauli himself always felt, at such times: "an unpleasant inner tension before the actual *Pauli-effect* [as it became known] occurred; afterwards, he felt relieved and freed from tension" (*ibid.*, p. 41). As with Jung, Pauli saw in parapsychological occurrences an interconnectedness between the psychic and physical. As he observes in his letter, the failure to attend to a psychological factor could provoke it into taking a parapsychic form, so as to gain recognition and attention. It could instantiate itself either through a "psychopathological" form, such as with depressive states, or through a synchronistic event, as if what one didn't meet "within", would return from "without".

Just as Pauli, in his deep exploration of matter encountered, like the alchemists, a spiritual factor, so too Jung, in his psychological investigations, had to take account of the relation between psyche and spirit. The notion of synchronicity formed a crucial part of this recognition. It led Jung to conclude that the archetype extended beyond the psyche. Thus, latterly, for Jung, the archetype was not wholly psychological, and this had a bearing on the failure of psychology to fully account for the phenomenology of spirit and spirits. The archetype is fundamental to Jung's notion of synchronicity. He first publically used this expression in a 1919 paper entitled "Instinct and the unconscious". The archetype, he suggested, functioned analogously to instinct. The difference between them lay in "instinct" being "a purposive impulse to carry out some highly complicated action", an archetype is an "intuition" or "unconscious, purposive apprehension of a highly complicated situation" (Jung, 1960, para. 269). At the heart of archetypal activity was the "primordial image". Jung elaborates this as "the *instinct's perception of itself*, or the self-portrait of the instinct" (*ibid.*, para. 276). Hence, the archetype is intrinsically linked to instinctuality and so to nature, adding teleology and meaning.

In a latter essay, "On the nature of the psyche", Jung again discusses his theoretical understanding of the archetypal, but now points to its metapsychic nature. Jung's theorizing here represents a delimitation of psychology, thus crossing over the borderline into the realms of microphysics and synchronicity. Jung describes the archetype as embodying an autonomous spiritual factor: "the archetypes have, when they appear, a distinctly numinous character which can only be described as 'spiritual'". Furthermore, this spiritual character may take a decidedly parapsychic form: "It not infrequently happens that the archetype appears in the form of a spirit in dreams or fantasy-products, or even comports itself like a ghost" (Jung, 1960, para. 405). So, the archetype signifies a transcendent meaning *within* the psyche, which is not *of* it. It points beyond psychology, not only to parapsychology, pneumatology, and metaphysics, but to the very nature of reality itself.

Jung explains that his notion of synchronicity developed from his psychology of the unconscious, finding the principle of causality insufficient for certain experiences. For him, the psychology of the unconscious could not be understood solely from the causal principle. In his own words: "... there are psychic parallelisms which cannot be related to each other causally, but which must be connected through another principle, namely the contingency of events" (Jung, 1963b, p. 400). Jung used the notion of synchronicity to mean "a coincidence in time of two or more causally unrelated events which have the same or a similar meaning ..." (Jung, 1960, para. 849). Essentially, synchronicity is more about the correspondence of meaning, than coincidence of time, for certain meaningful connections may happen, but not necessarily at the same moment (Aziz, 1990). Jung's counter-proposal to causality was an "acausal principle", one not accountable in terms of chance or probability, rather an order of reality based upon the meaningful connectedness of the psyche, spirit, and the world:

> Meaningful coincidences are thinkable as pure chance. But the more they multiply and the greater and more exact the correspondence is, the more their probability sinks and their unthinkability increases, until ... no longer ... thought of as meaningful arrangements ... Their "inexplicability" is not due to the fact that the cause is unknown, but to the fact that a cause is not even thinkable in intellectual terms. [Jung, 1960, para. 967]

Underlying the synchronistic event, Jung formulated an archetypal factor. This factor "in its lower reaches ... loses itself in the organic-material substrate", whilst, in the upper reaches, it "resolves itself into a 'spiritual' form" (Jung, 1960, para. 380). He named this aspect of the archetype the "psychoid", which, unlike the archetypal image, was transcendent and irrepresentable In this sense, the archetype ceases to be psychic. Their locus transcends the psyche, depicted by Jung as "an infringement to which I would give the name 'transgressivity,' because the archetypes are not found exclusively in the psychic sphere, but can occur just as much in circumstances that are not psychic" (Jung, 1960, para. 964). Synchronicity is one such form of "transgressivity", suggesting that meaning is not only a "construct" of human subjectivity, but may actually subsist of its own accord in nature's realm.

I would like to end with a dramatic instance of synchronicity and transference, drawn this time from Jung's own work. Of transference and the parapsychic, Jung wrote, the "relationship between doctor and patient, especially when a transference on the part of the patient occurs, or a more or less unconscious identification of doctor and patient, can lead to parapsychological phenomena". Jung tells of a man whom he treated for "psychogenic depression". Later, the man married, and when Jung subsequently met his wife, he detected an animosity from her. He understood this as her jealousy of the man's relationship with Jung. Jung felt the marriage had placed a psychic burden which would lead again to depression. Foreseeing this, he arranged to make contact between himself and his patient, if the latter needed to. This failed to happen, partly, Jung felt, because of the wife's derision of his depressed mood.

Jung then heard no more. He goes on, however:

> At that time I had to deliver a lecture in B. I returned to my hotel around midnight. I sat with some friends for a while after the lecture, then went to bed, but lay awake for a long time. At about two o'clock—I must have just fallen asleep—I awoke with a start, and had the feeling that someone had come into the room; I even had the impression that the door had been hastily opened. I instantly turned on the light, but there was nothing. Someone might have mistaken the door, I thought, and looked into the corridor. But it was as still as death. "Odd," I thought, "someone did come into the room!" Then I tried to recall exactly what had happened, and it occurred to me that I had been awakened by a feeling of dull pain, as though something had struck my forehead and then the back of my skull. The following day I received a telegram saying that my patient had committed suicide. He had shot himself.
>
> Later, I learned that the bullet had come to rest in the back wall of the skull.
>
> This experience was a genuine synchronistic phenomenon ... in connection with an archetypal situation—in this case, death. By means of a relativization of time and space in the unconscious it could well be that I had perceived something which in reality was taking place elsewhere. The collective unconscious is common to all; it is the foundation of what the ancients called the "sympathy of all things." In this case the unconscious had knowledge of my patient's condition. All that evening, in fact, I had felt curiously restive and nervous, very much in contrast to my usual mood. [Jung, 1963a, pp. 137–138]

Jung's linkage of transference and synchronicity implies that the intimacy of emotion can open up a level of connection which transcends "ordinary reality", allowing a deeper parapsychic communication, a telepathic empathy. For myself, I conceive this metaphorically in terms of the "spirit Mercurius", who through the parapsychic and irrational, fractures our categories of "reason", breaking out of the vessel of psychology. As in alchemy, Mercurius demands recognition, which means attending to a transcendent level of meaning and happening not reducible to "psychologistic" interpretation—unless one distorts or denies the nature of the phenomenon. Mercurius represents a volatile, spiritual actuality, an "essentially antinomian dual nature" (Jung, 1967, para. 266), who, just as he disrupted the physicist's laboratory, exploding equipment, just as he beckoned the alchemist's attention to the "spirit in the stone", transgresses and escapes from whatever "containers" in which our theories and practices try rationally to bottle him.

References

Anon. (1659–1661). *Theatrum Chemicum Praecipous Selectorum Auctorum Tractatus ... Continens*. Strasbourg: Argentorati.

Aziz, R. (1990). *C. G. Jung's Psychology of Religion and Synchronicity*. Albany: State University of New York Press.

Black, (1965). *The Surnames of Scotland*. New York: New York Public Library.

Jaffe, A. (1982). *From the Life and Work of C. G. Jung*. Einsiedeln: Daimon Verlag.

Jung, C. G. (1953a). *The Practice of Psychotherapy. Collected Works Volume 16*. New York: Routledge.

Jung, C. G. (1953b). *Psychology and Alchemy. C.W., 12.*

Jung, C. G. (1958). *Psychology and Religion: West and East. C.W., 11.*

Jung, C. G. (1959). *The Archetype and the Collective Unconscious. C.W., 9i.*

Jung, C. G. (1960). *The Structure and Dynamics of the Psyche. C.W., 8.*

Jung, C. G. (1963a). *Memories, Dreams, Reflections*, Aniela Jaffe (Ed.). New York: Random House.

Jung, C. G. (1963b). *Mysterium Conjunctionis. C.W., 14.*

Jung, C. G. (1964). *Civilisation in Transition. C.W., 10.*

Jung, C. G. (1967). *Alchemical Studies. C.W., 13.*

Jung, C. G. (1973). *Letters, Volume 1: 1906–1950*, G. Adler & A. Jaffe (Eds.). London: Routledge and Kegan Paul.

Jung, C. G. (1991). *Psychology of the Unconscious*. London: Routledge.

Lauirkainen, K (1988). *Beyond the Atom: The Philosophical Thought of Wolfgang Pauli*. Berlin: Springer Verlag.

Main, R. (1997). *Jung on Synchronicity and the Paranormal*. London: Routledge.

Pauli, W., & Jung, C. G. (1955). *The Interpretation of Nature and the Psyche*. New York: Putnam.

Ritsema, R., & Karcher, S. (Trans.) (1994). *I Ching: The Classic Chinese Oracle of Change*. Shaftesbury: Elemental Books.

Robertson, F. (1999). *Beings, Powers and Agency: Theories of Hunter–Gatherer Cosmology*. Unpublished M.Sc. dissertation in Social Anthropology, London School of Economics.

Turner, E. (1996). *The Hands Feel It: Healing and Spirit Presence Among a North Alaskan People*. Dekalb: Northern Illinois University Press.

Turner, E., Bodgett, W., Kahona, S., & Benwa, F. (1992). *Experiencing Ritual: A new Interpretation of African Healing*. Philadelphia: University of Pennsylvania Press.

Wilhelm, R., & Jung, C. G. (1945). *The Secret of the Golden Flower*. London: Routledge and Kegan Paul.

Willis, R., Chisanga, K. B. S., Silazwe, H. M. K., Sikazwe, K. B., & Nanyangwe, S. (1999). *Some Spirits Heal, Others Only Dance: A Journey into Human Selfhood in an African Village*. Oxford: Berg.

Van Erkelens, H. (1991). Wolfgang Pauli's dialogue with the spirit of matter. *Psychological Perspectives, 24*: Spring–Summer,

Von Franz, M.-L. (1975). *C. G. Jung: His Myth in Our Time*. New York: G. P. Putnam.

CHAPTER FIVE

The "alien abduction" syndrome

Jean-Claude Maleval and Nathalie Charraud

> "From this ignorance of how to distinguish dreams, and other strong fancies, from vision and sense, did arise the greatest part of the religion of the Gentiles in time past, that worshipped satyrs, fauns, nymphs and the like; and now-a-days the opinion that rude people have of fairies, ghosts, and goblins, and of the power of witches"
>
> Thomas Hobbes, 1998, p. 14

October 3rd 1938: around two million Americans were convinced, by a radio broadcast devised by Orson Welles, that the Martians were invading Earth (Cantril *et al.*, 1940). The progress of astronomical knowledge has toppled the myth of the Martians. Nowadays we no longer hazard a guess as to the precise planetary origin of aliens. Nevertheless, since the 1980s numerous Americans claim to have been victims of abductions carried out by beings from other worlds. Firstly, there is the work of the New York sculptor Budd Hopkins, which serves to give the phenomenon objective form. In 1981, he published *Missing Time*, in which he studies, among other symptoms affecting certain subjects, periods of time that seemed to have disappeared from their memories. Hopkins assumes that such phenomena can be explained by kidnappings carried out by aliens. He returns to the theme in 1987 with *Intruders*, where he draws on various accounts to describe the sexual and reproductive behaviour linked to alien abductions. These things might have remained within the confines of one group of cranks among so many others, if they had not been given support by a major scientific authority. John E. Mack's book *Abduction* (1994) seems to be currently giving these phenomena an importance which recalls the effect of the "*Book of the Spirits*" by Allan Kardec (Kardec, 1857),[1] in the late-nineteenth-century, which gave birth to the doctrine of Spiritism and to many techniques for communicating with the spirits of the Beyond (which usually relied on revolving tables).

John Mack is not just anybody: not only is he the author of a reference book on the nightmare, in addition he gained a certain notoriety by receiving the Pulitzer Prize for a biography of Lawrence of Arabia; but above all he is a professor of psychiatry at Harvard University. To be sure, his work on the alien abduction syndrome still arouses considerable scepticism on the part of most of his colleagues, but it seems to be beginning to be echoed by some of them.[2] Besides, Mack had been preceded in studying alien kidnappings by a respectable professor of History at Temple University, Philadelphia, David M. Jacobs; in 1992, the latter published *Secret Life: First Hand Accounts of UFO Abductions*—with a preface by John Mack.

Subjects who, most frequently under hypnosis, report having been kidnapped by aliens, complain initially of a tendency to have terrible nightmares.[3] Sometimes, corresponding marks may appear on the body: bruises, grazes, various small lesions or even light haemorrhages. Such subjects sometimes observe the healing of some bodily trouble following the "abduction". They frequently experience, moreover, persistent feelings of solitude, of isolation or of becoming marginalized. Difficulties with relationships and sexuality are not unusual. The thirteen cases reported by Mack show themselves to be easily hypnotizable. Lastly, if one wished to see the episodes of "missing time" as merely ordinary memory difficulties, it would be possible to observe elements which point to a hysterical structure in these subjects. The considerably reduced field allotted to hysteria by North American psychiatry, the ignorance of it as a structure independent of manifest neurosis, makes it impossible for Mack to perceive it.

In the accounts reported by Mack, belief in extraterrestrial kidnappings does not present the characteristics of an insane idea: in the first instance, rather, the subjects tend to interpret them as nightmares, so that they doubt the reality of what they have experienced. Even when conviction sets in, many still consider that in these experiences they have had access to another reality,[4] in which the criteria for the objective apprehension of events do not apply. It is not impossible for insanity to take hold in this imaginary state, but in the great majority of cases these beliefs do not belong in the register of insane certainty.[5] They would have remained within the fantasy world of a few subjects if they had not taken shape in Mack's work, through which they became a social fact.

What evidence leads Mack to approve of the thesis of extraterrestrial kidnapping as a way of explaining the cases of the subjects who presented the symptoms we noted above? He admits that the material evidence appears too slender to be decisive, so that he does not hide the fact that the principle factors leading to his conviction are located in the lived experience and its narration under hypnosis (Mack, 1994, p. 410). The two major pieces of evidence are, firstly, the emotional intensity of the events "relived" under hypnosis and secondly, the correlation of independent witnesses with one another. The first of these is very weak: it is well known that forceful conviction and the impression of reality are characteristic of the nightmare. "The hallucinations which are produced are perhaps the most extraordinary feature of the nightmare", notes Macnish in 1836; "often, they make such a strong impression on the mind that we find it impossible not to think them real, even when we are awake ... In many cases, there are no arguments nor efforts of the understanding which can convince us that they were nothing but the chimeras of sleep" (Macnish, 1836, p. 143, quoted in Jones, 1931, p. 67). Waller writes:

> I do not know any means in man's power to convince oneself that the vision which appears during the paroxysm of a nightmare is not real, unless he is given evidence to the contrary by other people who were present and awake at that moment. [Waller, A treatise of the incubus, or nightmare, quoted Jones, *loc. cit.*]

Indeed, far from doubting the reality of the visions of extraterrestrials experienced under hypnosis, Mack gives them credence and lets them take shape consistently. And so the most plausible explanation for the persistence of sleep in the subjects during the abductions would be that they were "unplugged" by the extraterrestrials. He claims, nonetheless, to be careful not to influence the subjects. When the latter tell him of their doubts about the reality of these phenomena, he "could only tell them that the details of their stories had been found again and again in the accounts of other kidnapped people who had not been declared mad." Note that the use of the term "kidnapped" already entails a position taken; but he does not hesitate to give his opinion still more clearly:

> likewise, I note that the feelings and the emotions which they showed seem completely real to me, and for my part I asked them if they can offer any explanation for such intense feelings. In the end, I tell them that I do not have all the answers to these questions, and ask them to consider these "memories" as a reality. [Mack, 1994, p. 32]

Since it does not sweep away all the doubts of the subjects themselves, the intensity of the experience, Mack has to stress, can only be decisively established by an observer. From then on, the only evidence with a semblance of consistency lies in the correlation between different witnesses. Let us recall, firstly, that the irrefutable proof of the reality of witchcraft, between the fifteenth- and the seventeenth-centuries, rested on the same principle: "the almost unanimous correspondence of the sayings and the spells of sorcerers and witches throughout Christendom." Now, remarks Baissac:

> it follows from the accounts of the verbal interrogations and judgements we possess that most of the time those subject to the inquisition, if left to give their own accounts, would frequently contradict one another; and that the correspondences spoken of are only set up when the judge, directing the questioning along established lines, makes the accused answer yes or no. The conformity of the statements was thus nothing but a mirage of the uniformity of the questions, along with the beliefs of the period. [Baissac, 1982, pp. 164–165]

The relative conformity of evidence about witchcraft was produced by a pre-existing discourse, essentially that of the *Manuals of the Inquisition*.

Who speaks today through the mouth of extraterrestrials? What do John Mack's "kidnapped" people reveal? They have usually been picked up from their beds by alien creatures who took them through the air, out of the window, up to a space ship. There, they were subject to medical and surgical operations, similar to rape, with a view to generating a new breed of hybrid beings, half human and half alien. Lastly, still moving through the air, they were put back to bed, without anyone else being aware of their disappearance. The majority of accounts agree that the message of the extraterrestrials consists in warning us against the dangers which threaten the ecological balance of the planet. Moreover, they are astonished at the aggressiveness of humans, and urge them to open themselves to communication based on love. The conformity is certainly somewhat astonishing, but it is immediately clear that the alleged message is made up of nothing but very well-known information. When, by chance, it becomes original, it does not gain in credibility: according to certain aliens, dinosaurs, despite their minute brains, were in fact highly intelligent! The core of the message is no more creative than the mediocre television programmes it takes its material from; what gives it its consistency lies in the scene of seduction, which we will come back to.

On the other hand, if these narratives only consist of fantasy inventions, there should be a great variety of secondary themes to be observed. In fact, this is the case as soon as we examine more closely the major themes, such as the description of the inside of the space ships or the appearance of the alien beings. On this last, most spectacular point, the imagination is given free rein: sometimes the hair is blond, sometimes silvery, often absent; the head is sometimes triangular, sometimes in the shape of an inverted drop of water; the colour is grey, green, white, etc. Let us stop our list of the variations right there, it only proves one thing: the capacity of extraterrestrials to metamorphosize. They are even able, it seems, to transform themselves into animals.[6] Note the common characteristic of these aliens and the "bad angels and demons" studied by De Lancre in his investigation of magic in Labourd at the beginning of the seventeenth-century: "inconstancy". To explain the variety of the evidence about the appearance of the devil and the practices of witchcraft, where unanimity is lacking, a unanimous view of the inconstancy of the devil and his minions allows universality to be reintroduced (De Lancre, 1982). The comparison would doubtless not appear completely inappropriate to John Mack, as he takes it for granted that extraterrestrials open us to a dimension closer to the spiritual source of being, on the basis of which he sets up correspondences with Shamanism, Tibetan Buddhism, Karate, lucid dreams, former lives, parallel universes, synchronicity, etc. He even accepts that in certain cases "the extraterrestrials themselves can appear as a split-off part of the soul or ego of the kidnapped person" (Mack, 1994, p. 496). Henceforth, their "inconstancy" causes him no trouble: a long time ago, he developed the habit of warding off any rigorous approach to the phenomenon by invoking the need to transform the paradigm of rationality in order to apprehend it. Who speaks, then, by means of extraterrestrial messages and their commentator, to give us news bulletins about the ecological dangers facing the planet, and assert the need to open ourselves to communication based on love? No longer the Manuals of the inquisitors, but the ideology of the "New Age" movement, the contemporary religion of American yuppies, which urges us to seek God within ourselves, by means of altered states of consciousness and ecological concerns.[7]

The thirteen cases reported by Mack, concerning subjects under hypnotic treatment who exemplify the alien abduction syndrome, amounts to a clinical document not without interest. It constitutes a contribution to the study of hysterical delirium and to that of the mechanisms at work in psychotherapies.

The "inconstancy" of extraterrestrials knows one major exception; that is, most accounts agree on one point: the initial encounters are traumatic, and almost always centre on a scene of rape. The demonic image of aliens produced by the discourse of science easily stages a kind of surgical rape: it is carried out in some kind of operating theatre by a leader who is often called "doctor". Jerry describes under hypnosis how the creatures open her legs "like the gynaecologist does" (Mack, 1994, p. 163). Stirrups were not needed because she was paralysed; a long tube was inserted into her vagina and she felt a pinching—then she knew that an embryo had been implanted in her. In the same circumstances, Catherine feels incapable of offering the least resistance. A kind of cone with something on the end of it is inserted into her. It's freezing—it goes in as far as her intestines, but it doesn't hurt, it's just a bit uncomfortable (Mack, 1994, p. 191). When the subject in question is a man, it becomes a scene of anal rape. Dave feels that a flexible instrument, over a metre long, is inserted into his anus. "It slides into me," he reports. "It pushes up into my bowels well beyond the anus." There is, at any rate, a sympathetic female creature there to comfort him. Then a kind of suction machine is placed on the tip of his penis, which makes him ejaculate with a pleasure he has never experienced before (Mack, 1994, p. 339). Other experiences, in which the subject feels an object implanted in his or her skull or in other parts of the body, are far less pleasant.

For whoever has not completely forgotten Freud's discovery, such fantasmagoria are familiar: we are dealing with variants of the scene of seduction which the hysteric is so keen to locate at the origin of his or her trouble. Mack uses hypnosis to make this scene reappear in subjects who would have forgotten it. He certainly doesn't need to suggest it explicitly to obtain it from those who seek him out as a specialist in alien abductions. The people who go to see him mostly seem to have had from childhood a tendency to have nightmares fuelled by science fiction stories. Let us note once again the similarities between these accounts and those gathered on witchcraft: in the latter, the devil copulates with sorcerers and witches "carnally and sodomitically", with a twisted, scaly member which produces freezing semen (Baissac, 1982, p. 114). Diabolic and alien seductions are negative images of a scene of shameful pleasure.

If the majority of hysterical deliriums (Maleval, 1981), as was already noted by Henri Ey, borrow their form from suggestion or possession, the scene of passive seduction is their imaginary armour. Rather than subjecting her castration to the desire of the Other, in assuming willingly her lack-of-being, the hysteric puts her body forward in an attempt to make up for the lack of the Other. Henceforth, as Perrier puts it in a striking formula, she can only be raped, and only by Jupiter (Perrier, 1978, p. 66). The scene of seduction is the last fantasmatic screen to mask off the encounter with the real. This screen is obviously not opaque: it allows what it veils to more or less show through. It has a tendency to be broken through. At this point the nightmare appears—both at night and during the day. The latter occurrence points, for Freud, to a failure of censorship; for Jones, to a lecherous incestuous passion; while according to Lacan, the subject experiences the *jouissance* of the Other there (Lacan, 1962). It is in this domain, beyond the pleasure principle, again notes Freud, that we must locate the demonic—which is absent from the *Traumdeutung,* we recall (Freud, 1900). From this point on, everyone agrees in seeing in the nightmare a fluctuation of fantasy, so that it ceases to protect the subject from the *jouissance* of the Other. The most typical form of this phenomena is some imaginary vampire, a demonic figure who extracts the object of his *jouissance* from the body of the subject. Thus the fantasy is no longer situated in the subject's window onto reality: it is no longer framed by the imaginary and symbolic outlines which allow it to construct that window. No longer masked, the object a emerges through traumatic images that unravel reality.

The scene of seduction is a primal fantasy, which is no doubt the source of the affinity between hysteria and the emergent forms of psychosis; it can certainly be developed to give rise to pleasant and voluptuous scenes, but above all it tends to break down, allowing what it barely conceals to show through: the real object and the *jouissance* of the Other. One of the most frequently-occurring features in the descriptions of aliens lies in the appearance of the object-gaze at the heart of their image: most hypnotized subjects mention the strange, uncanny quality of their huge, black, lidless eyes.

The alien abduction syndrome is a modern form of hysterical delirium which allows us to grasp some of its specific features. Mack's clinical document illuminates in particular the difference between the acute and chronic forms of the syndrome.

Paradoxically, subjects who go to see Mack (often after the failure of other psychotherapies) feel relief from their nervous troubles, and sometimes even a resolution of their sexual problems, insofar as their conviction is consolidated—not only that they have been victims of alien abductions, but beyond this, that they are permanently at the mercy of these all-powerful beings. Catherine reports:

> I feel powerless. They can very easily catch me at any time they like, and make me do practically whatever they want, and I can do nothing about it. The very idea is terrifying. [Mack, 1994, p. 197]

Jerry writes:

> I ask myself whether anyone who has not been kidnapped can understand what it means to have no idea when the next abduction will happen . . . I'd like to see how the brain would function when a person is permanently subjected to traumas which she has no idea will ever stop. [Mack, 1994, p. 160]

Mack writes:

> The majority of individuals who have been dealt with in this book have suffered traumas with ramifications directly linked to their extraterrestrial misadventures—a feeling of solitude and being abandoned deriving from the terror felt during the frightening operations inflicted on their bodies, isolation in the very midst of families and social life, the inevitable choice at an intellectual level and profound convictions, and finally the horrible awareness that such dramas could happen at any time in the future, and also to their own children. [Mack, 1994, p. 484]

It is true that if all this were not fantasmagoric, the subjects should become increasingly terrified to the extent that they manage to convince themselves that what they took to be dreams are no such thing. Mack himself remarks that "it is surprising that the kidnapped people as a group are not more anxious" (Mack, 1994, p. 55). It is, at first glance, still more surprising that a psychotherapy which approves of the idea of possession could produce effects of the reduction of anxiety. What appears paradoxical to a rational approach to the phenomenon ceases to be so if we take into account the logic of the unconscious. It is because hypnotic psychotherapy is used here to give the fantasy consistent form that it allows the subject to develop a defence against the surging-up of the real. Of course, each individual produces his or her own construction with the aid of narcissistic elements. Some discover little by little that they are "double agents", half-human and half-alien, others content themselves with taking part in creating a new race of hybrid beings; most feel that they have expanded their consciousness, have become the bearers of a message of hope, gladly becoming teachers or therapists. Thus, groups of the "kidnapped" start to proliferate, in which one can find mutual comfort in one's beliefs. Polls seem to show that these have a glorious future, since several million

Americans feel that they have been victims of alien abductions or related experiences (Mack, 1994, p. 544).

Approving of the abduction fantasy is incontestably beneficial to the subject. He feels integrated in the community of the kidnapped, with whom he feels he shares the secret truth. The narcissistic image of each person is exalted by finding support in a common ideal. Nightmares and the fluctuation of fantasy ease off, while the hystericization of discourse takes hold. The subject's division is foregrounded: everyone denounces the limitations of the ego and declares that these experiences "destroy our illusion of control". Attacks on the Master and the denunciation of his knowledge are manifest: we must abandon the dominant paradigm of rationality, says Mack; while he considers that "these problems are a challenge thrown down to mental health professionals". The result of this discourse is supposed to be a new kind of knowledge. Such a knowledge, in the end, can only emerge through hearing what each person has experienced.[8]

The beneficial effect obtained by the practice of exorcism in cases of possession sometimes seems to have been of the same order: that of not stamping out the devil, but accepting it more easily. Those who caused Urbain Grandier to be condemned, at Loudun in 1634, continued in large numbers to have themselves exorcized after his death. "Indeed", reports Baissac, "when a priest who met them in the street asked them if they were still possessed, they used to reply with a sort of proud satisfaction: "Thank God, yes!"—"Ah!", the other would answer, "we're not so lucky; God does not love us that much!" (Baissac, 1982, p. 535). When integrated into the beliefs of a community, possession can lead to appreciable secondary benefits.

Chronic forms of the hysterical delirium sometimes seem, therefore, to allow the anxiety of the subject to be reduced. When we see this result obtained, as it were despite the consolidation of the notion of possession, how can we fail to invoke the "beautiful indifference" of hysterics? It was in connection with conversion symptoms that this description was employed, after observing their aptitude for binding anxiety; which once again confirms that the psychical troubles of hysteria share the same dynamic as somatic troubles. The balancing-act of the two disorders has moreover very often been noted.

Mack's clinical practice is exemplary concerning what differentiates psychotherapy from psychoanalysis. As we know, it is not on the terrain of therapeutic effectiveness that the divergences are most profound, but on the question of ethics. A treatment can only claim to be psychoanalytic when the one directing it holds the ethical position of object *a*, which leads him to want nothing for the analysand, and to do without the resources of the discourse of the Master. In contrast, Mack clearly calls for the inclusion of the therapist's subjectivity in the treatment. "In these alternative therapies", he writes, "the feelings and the state of mind of the one who helps, as well as his rationality and his skills of observation, represent the vital aspects of the therapeutic or investigative method." He reproaches Freud for having abandoned hypnosis, precisely because it brought a subjective element into play, which bore witness on his part to an infatuation with the subject/object duality belonging to Western science (Mack, 1994, p. 475). Apart from the solipsistic quality of such an argument, whose only support is an adherence to the naiveties of the "new paradigm" of the "New Age",[9] it is worth considering its consequences. The establishment of sects glued together by the fantasies of some therapist is one of them. In the specific instance of Mack's practice, he notes himself that he fosters in his patients the narcissistic sense of being different. Such experiences give rise to problems in the home and with relatives, "for", he remarks, "it is obvious that from now on the kidnapped person is most often concerned only with himself and what has happened to him" (Mack, 1994, p. 487). Sometimes these experiences go along with the fantasy of the family romance: "I have seen children", he reports, "who now consider the aliens to be their 'true' parents". Other hypnotherapists are convinced that the multiple personality syndrome, which has had an unprecedented expansion in the USA since the 1980s, is caused by another scene of seduction, this time enacted by the subject's parents. They often manage to persuade their patients of this, which gives rise to lawsuits, sometimes even to wrongful convictions. Mack's work shows in a striking way how the cost of alienation to be paid for by therapeutic benefits in psychotherapy is always exorbitant. In one sense, all forms of psychotherapy make aliens exist. It is only by introducing ethics to clinical practice that these fantasmagoria might fade away, and allow the truth of the subject to emerge.

Notes

1. We know that Allan Kardec was the pseudonym of Doctor Hyppolite Rivail, which he adopted following a communication with a spirit which revealed that this had been his name in a former existence at the time of the druids in Gaul. The anachronism is obvious: the distinction between the patronymic and the forename appears much later.
2. The authorities at Harvard, reports E. Behr, do not otherwise seem troubled by such convictions on the part of one of their most famous professors: "there are many great idea which start out by seeming crazy", the current director of Harvard's department of psychiatry, Malka Notman, confides to the *Wall Street Journal* (14th May, 1992). "Whatever one thinks of it, I believe it is useful to encourage creative work, so long as it does nobody any harm" (Behr, 1995, p. 162).
3. Mack's book on nightmares (Mack, 1970), is no doubt the most complete clinical study of the issue carried out in the field of psychoanalysis. It considers the nightmare to be the result of especially difficult problems in the subject's environment, or of traumatic memories. His work on the alien abduction syndrome is thus perfectly compatible with his previous research. It is notable, in this early work, that he shows a tendency to read Freud too swiftly and, following Rosen, assimilate dream and psychosis.
4. They perceive extraterrestrials and their own experiences as situated in another reality which will remain however extremely tangible for them, as much as—if not more than—the familiar physical world" (Mack, 1994, p. 493).
5. A completely different logic seems to govern the extraterrestrial message picked up by Claude Vorilhon in 1973. Named "Rael" by these beings (the "Elohims"), he assembled their Tables of the Law in a work entitled "Geniocracy and sensual meditation", the foundational text of a sect which he directs, the French Raelian Movement.
6. Jones notes, with regard to the nightmare:

   > The fact that metamorphosis has been so widely and closely associated with the worship of animals is of particular interest for our subject and leads us to deduce a relationship between these two ideas. There is little doubt that the idea of metamorphosis has important sources in the experiences of dreaming, since, there, the real transformation of a human being into an animal and the appearance of composite beings, part animal and part human, very often happens directly before the eyes of the dreamer. [Jones, 1931, p. 57]

7. "New Age" takes the transition in the astrological calendar from the zodiac age of Pisces to that of Aquarius as the pretext for announcing

the dawn of an era of love and enlightenment. Humanity is supposed to be in the process of entering a new age of spiritual and planetary, ecological and mystical awareness, marked by profound psychical changes. Social transformation is supposed to be subordinated to personal transformation. One of the central aims lies in exceeding the surface of material and visible things in order to attain the Essential which is Consciousness and Spirit. It is in fact a fairly vague current of thought, which entails the (no doubt ephemeral) coagulation of many free-floating religious motifs.

8. It can be seen that the discourse of the kidnapped can be precisely written in the matheme of the discourse of the hysteric (Maleval, 1981).
9. "New Age" is opposed to the dominant materialist and mechanist paradigm, wishing to substitute for it a spiritual and synthetic approach. It proposes a holistic vision of the world, based on the single origin of the energy which animates the totality of human and cosmic phenomena, and on the correspondences between the different orders of reality. This new paradigm seems not to be troubled by its *petitio principii.*

References

Baissac, J. (1982 [1890]). *Les Grands Jours de la Sorcellerie.* Marseille: Laffite Reprints.

Behr, E. (1995). *Une Amérique qui Fait Peur.* Paris: Plon.

Cantril, H., Gaudet, H., & Hertzog, H. (1940). *Invasion from Mars.* Princeton, NJ: Princeton University Press.

De Lancre, P. (1982 [1612]). *Tableau de l'Inconstance des Mauvais Anges et Démons.* Paris: Aubier Montaigne.

Freud, S. (1900). *The Interpretation of Dreams. S.E., 4&5.*

Hobbes, T. (1998 [1651]). *Leviathan.* Oxford: Oxford University Press.

Hopkins, B. (1981). *Missing Time: A Documented Study of UFO Abductions.* New York: Richard Marek.

Hopkins, B. (1987). *Intruders: The Incredible Visitations at Copley Woods.* New York: Random House.

Jacobs, D. M. (1992). *Secret Life: Firsthand Accounts of UFO Abductions.* New York: Simon & Schuster.

Jones, E. (1931). *On the Nightmare.* London: Hogarth Press.

Kardec, A. (1857). *Le Livre des Esprits (The Book of Spirits).* Paris.

Lacan, J. (1962). *L'Angoisse.* Unpublished seminar, 12 December 1962.

Mack, J. E. (1970). *Nightmares and Human Conflict.* London: Churchill.

Mack, J. E. (1994). *Abduction*. New York: Scribners.

Maleval, J-C. (1981). *Folies Hysteriques et Psychoses Dissociatives*. Paris: Payot.

Perrier, F. (1978). *La Chaussée d'Antin*. Paris: Union Générale d'Editions.

CHAPTER SIX

Developments in the concept of synchronicity in the analytic relationship and in theory

J. Marvin Spiegelman

Since Jung introduced his concept of synchronicity a half-century ago, the idea and the word have taken wing in the popular imagination and entered into general consciousness. Even popular songs make use of it. Despite general recognition and understanding, however, there has been little follow-up research into this idea in academic and analytical circles, other than to explain it or present examples. M.-L. Von Franz provides a major exception in her works *Number and Time* (1974) and *On Divination and Synchronicity* (1980) which elaborate the concept in both mathematics and fairy tales. Another exception is found in the work of the astrophysicist Professor Victor Mansfield of Cornell University, who has written an excellent book on the topic with many examples and significant criticism of the concept (Mansfield, 1995). My own work on synchronicity in the transference relationship, as a variant on the mind–body, matter–spirit issue addresses the topic in the analytic process itself (Spiegelman, 1996). The following remarks on the further development of Jung's concept of synchronicity will summarize the work of all three of the foregoing authors and are divided into two sections: (1) synchronicity in the analytical relationship and (2) theoretical questions.

Examples of synchronicity in the analytical relationship

Most Jungian analysts have experienced synchronicity in the context of their own analyses or their work with analysands. Indeed, Jung's description of this phenomenon is replete with examples: e.g., a patient, dreaming powerfully of an Egyptian scarab, was interrupted in her telling this dream by the beating at the window pane of just a similar beetle. Many synchronicity experiences are linked to post-mortal images and events (Von Franz, 1988). First-generation Jungian analyst Liliane Frey told me of a dream in which her deceased husband promised, just before his death, to make himself known to her postmortally, thus affirming the existence of life after death. Her telling of this dream to someone shortly after his death was interrupted by a bird appearing at the window, pecking at the glass. Only when Dr Frey recognized this bird as the message promised by her husband did it seem to nod and fly off. My wife and I had a similar experience with regard to the "other world". A few years after my mother-in-law's death, we sat on the cliffs overlooking the ocean at Pacific Palisades in Santa Monica, feeling our continuing love and appreciation of her and remembering how much she had enjoyed walks and picnics there. We were quiet for a few moments, then wondered aloud if she would visit us again as she had done in the weeks just after she died. Suddenly, a butterfly landed on my wife's foot, remaining for a long time. "Rose?" we both asked. The butterfly fluttered a little but remained poised there for several minutes, even though my wife now moved her foot a bit. After we felt the power of her mother's "presence", the butterfly flew off. Neither we nor Dr Frey believed that these winged creatures were manifestations of deceased loved ones, of course, but we powerfully felt a synchronistic meaningfulness of those events.

Such experiences convince participants, beyond any kind of rational or theoretical explanation, of the reality of a psyche–matter connection and the presence of meaning in the empirical universe. Indeed, the prevalence of animals in such synchronistic events—although far from being the only type of connection—may attest to this phenomenon having an instinctual basis, since our fellow creatures carry a symbolic meaning for us humans. This prevalence may also suggest that our capacity for symbolic intuition and sense of harmony with the universe lies far back in our evolutionary development, older than our rational cortex. Indeed, it may be consciousness itself which adds the "miraculous" flavour to the experience of such events, themselves natural in the non-human world. That is why Jung added the psychic connection—meaning—to these events which seem to involve both spirit and matter, both the individual and a larger cosmos.

Three instances of meaningful, sequential synchronistic events with insects/animals come to mind relevant to the individuation process in my own experience. Shortly after I began my analytic training in Zürich in the mid-1950s, I dreamed of seeing a huge ant colony, laid out geometrically and engaged in awesome activity. On my way to my analytic session, I stopped at a city bench at a quiet side of the Zähringerplatz to do a bit of active imagination with this dream. Within seconds, ants began crawling on my dream book. Some minutes later, in my analyst's office which overlooked a wood, I was relating this dream and my experience on the bench when a troop of ants came across the little table between us. This had never occurred before, said my analyst, C. A. Meier. We understood the dream to be a meaningful beginning of my training analysis which emphasized the orderedness and structure of the objective psyche itself and compensated for the "great work" of individuation which I was then undertaking—or rather, resuming—after spending two, pleasant but socially conventional, years as an Army psychologist, which themselves followed the completion of my initial three-year analysis. In retrospect, the dream also suggested the communal, impersonal, and non-individual nature of the psyche and that aspect of the objective Self which underlies it.

More than fifteen-years later, long after I had become an analyst and had temporarily resigned from my local analytical society, I was riding my bicycle through the hills near my home in Studio City, internally struggling with a problem of feeling a lack of recognition and being alone professionally. On this ride, surprisingly, I encountered an old high school chum who had become famous. He told me a sad tale of being cheated by his publishers and betrayed by his followers, evoking compassion from me, but also providing a compensation for my reciprocal complaints about lack of publication of my books and feeling of betrayal by my teachers. Struck by this apparent synchronicity and chastened by an awareness of the lack of fulfilment given by fame, I bicycled onward. A couple of miles later, on that same Mulholland Drive, I was amazed to see a large buck deer standing in the centre of the road. I stopped to stare at this great-antlered stag, who stared right back at me. Did I see a crown on his head? I bowed before his dignity and he seemed to nod back, slowly returning to the peace and safety of the hills. I often hiked the paths in those hills and bicycled the road; I had seen deer now and then, but never had I seen one on the road and certainly no stag ordinarily would so endanger himself. This image of lonely, kingly grandeur, keeping one's sovereign path in the midst of a hostile, dangerous urban environment, yet crossing its roads, was a fitting sequel and opposite, I think, to my dream of the collective ants of long ago. It helped me maintain my individual path at a difficult time. Such synchronistic experiences are not especially rare in many people's lives, we know, and they help us find our own meaning at times of significant change and difficult solitude.

The third example comes from my work with patients. I often experience synchronicities in analyses, but this one occurred relatively early in my practice. I was working with an Asian man, religious in orientation, but who had not thought to become an analyst. Some months into the work I dreamed that he had the mark of a fox on his face, and that this mark suggested that he should become a healer. The next day I received a copy of a journal which described an ancient cult in his country, called the Fox cult, which trained in shamanic healing. The following evening, during my drive home from the office, I caught sight of a fox in the headlights of my car. I stopped and watched it slowly go off into the hills. I had often seen coyotes on or near the road, but never a fox. When I informed my analysand of these experiences at our next meeting, he told me that he had indeed been thinking about becoming a healer, but had thought it presumptuous. These experiences were surprisingly supportive and convincing to us both. Subsequently, his own dreams suggested this path and ultimately he became a healer.

In the years since these particular synchronistic experiences, I have not infrequently shared others with analysands, not only in their reportage of incidents outside the consulting room, but in the office as well. Often these include either animals, or religious imagery and texts. Hence the importance, perhaps, of having at least a window onto nature when we work. In another incident, a man dreamed of a squirrel which revealed itself to represent a wise man. At that moment there appeared, on the neighbouring roof, a squirrel, making a considerable racket. It so happened that this neighbouring house was the residence and office of a person world-famous in the occult field, Israel Regardie, a fact unknown to my analysand. My telling him of this meaningful coincidence of wise man and animal had a powerful impact on him. The manifestation of a squirrel in that way had never happened before, nor has it since. Such examples can be multiplied, I am sure, in the experience of other analysts and analysands.

The psychoid nature of synchronicity and the analytic process

We generally surmise that animals appearing in dreams and fantasies signify our own instinctual processes. Often they are linked with the animals who accompany the gods in many traditions. Von Franz and others (Von Franz, 1973), amply develop such interpretations: bears, various cats, such as leopards and lions, snakes, horses and dogs, elephants and crocodiles, all inform us about unconscious strivings and existences in the Mother world, the Feminine, the autonomic nervous system, and the chakras of Kundalini, for example. They also portray qualities, such as independence, loyalty, courage, dedication, and the devouring, aggression and sexuality that we experience with them and project upon them. Less frequently noted is that when such images appear, there is likely to be some kind of body response as well. In his discussion of the archetypes, Jung notes that the consciousness–unconsciousness polarity is both dual and continuous. He draws on the image of the spectrum of light in physics, which is a continuum yet has an infrared and ultraviolet end. That is strikingly parallel to the invisible, instinctual basis of the archetype on the infrared side, while the ultraviolet reflects its spiritual aspect, as Jung describes in his essay, "On the nature of the psyche" (Jung, 1946). This image of the spectrum led Jung to conceive of the archetype *an sich* as an unknown, psychoid quality, showing itself in both mind and matter and revealing to us the background from which synchronistic events arise. Mythological images, such as the World Tree, with its roots going deeply into the earth and its branches reaching into heaven, are forerunners of this idea. Indra's Web is another. Jung's elaboration of the conception of the archetype, along with validation in the experiences of three or four generations of analysts, has made it something of general understanding in Jungian circles and the larger world. More recently, the concept of synchronicity is also receiving attention in the larger scholarly community (Mansfield, 1995), which I will address later on.

In the last dozen years, I have begun to recognize, at another level, the significance of such synchronistic animal/instinctual images and experiences for the analytic relationship. Such synchronicities occur not only in connection with outer incidents or figures, but also transpire within the analytic session and are experienced in the bodies of the two participants. Before describing this, however, I preface it by a discussing how my understanding of the transference has developed over the years.

After completing my training in Zürich in 1959, I found that my practice increasingly took on the character of being a "mutual process", one in which both parties were effected and transformed, just as Jung had described as far back as 1929 and had spelled out in his *Psychology of the Transference* (Jung, 1948). This was after I had experienced early analysands in much the same way that I had the clinical psychotherapy cases I had treated in the Veterans Administration and the Army years before. These latter relationships had a more clinically traditional asymmetrical character. As a new analyst, I discovered that the exhaustion I had felt after such sessions was more connected with my efforts to "be an analyst" rather than attributable to energy-draining from the work itself. I had tried to be objective, detached, and "analytical", yet still deeply connected with the work. I was modelling myself on both my ancient grandfather and my analyst C. A. Meier, I realized, and this identification was draining me. My father, however, my first analyst, Max Zeller and C. G. Jung himself were spontaneous, responsive and different from that austere image. The point is ultimately to be one's self in analytical work, despite the natural desire to model one's self on one teacher or another. When I gave up my identification with a persona image of the analyst—even though it was treasured and legitimate—and became more spontaneous myself, the exhaustion vanished and analytical processes became more symmetrical. This was in line with the addendum by C. A. Meier to what Jung wrote about this phenomenon (Meier, 1959), noting that the analyst's attempt to penetrate the psyche of his analysand resulted ultimately in losing the demarcation point of where the "cut" between the two consciousnesses lay. One no longer knew what belonged to whom. This state of affairs provides a fertile condition for the activation of the archetypes of the collective unconscious and results in the kind of situation that Jung wrote about in his *Psychology of the Transference* (1948). This also became my experience, not with every analysand, but with increasing frequency, depending upon the length of work and the particular individuals who came to me.

From my contribution to the 1965 *Festschrift für C. A. Meier* (Spiegelman, 1965), onward, I addressed myself to this interrelationship in a series of papers brought together in my book, *Psychotherapy as a Mutual Process* (Spiegelman, 1996). In the earlier years, I experienced this mutuality in imagery, fantasy, dreams, and even telepathic events, as well as the occasional synchronicity. Such experiences have been reported by others in the literature and are by no means rare. In the last dozen years or so, this simultaneity of experience on the part of both analyst and analysand has included a bodily and energy aspect which is more compelling in that there is an "incarnation" of the archetypal images in the participants and in the relationship itself (see last several papers in the aforementioned book). In my case, I think, this is partially the result of eight years of Reichian body work, as both patient and therapist. More recently, the additional experience of mutuality, as well as "body", has been subsumed under the idea of the analytic "field", a concept gradually being understood as encompassing both transference and counter-transference. Notably, Marie-Louise Von Franz (Von Franz, 1974, p. 124) was the first to understand the unconscious itself as a field generated in analytical work.

When initially I experienced bodily symptoms while listening to the analysand, I attributed them to my complexes being activated or to the presence of what Kleinian and Object Relations analysts refer to as projective identification—the unconscious of the patient "putting into" the analyst contents the analysand needs to have carried, or made conscious and healed. When I began to tell patients about such activations within me, say of stomach ache, heartache, anxiety trembling, headache, or other bodily responses, these were commonly associated with what was happening in the patient himself/herself at the moment or what had taken place during the previous days. The bringing to consciousness of such conditions, however, not only dissolved my symptoms but often also resulted in an experience of what can be called the "subtle body"—tingling, streaming and energy—which is neither mental nor physical alone but constitutes a "third" which is both, yet neither. This kind of energy has been experienced in Reichian therapy as "streamings", as well as in Kundalini Yoga, and in Tai Chi. Perhaps my Reichian work enabled me to be more open to such experiences, but I did not have a differentiated consciousness about them in my work with Jungian patients until years after I completed my Reichian analysis, even though "streamings" had frequently taken place earlier.

Uncertain as to whether others were having such experiences, I read that Nathan Schwartz-Salant encountered such things and wrote deeply about them (Schwartz-Salant, 1996). He not only connected these experiences with the archetype as a "third" between two participants in the analytical process, as had I, but he noted that this "third" could become an alchemical "fourth", via the image of an archetypal "couple" in the room, which could be visualized and readily experienced along with the energy by both parties. Schwartz-Salant linked this to Jung's *Rosarium Philosophorum* (Jung, 1948) pictures and his diagram of the analytical relationship. Other therapists were having such experiences, too, but failed to report them since they did not know what to do with them! Was this a kind of mysticism, a peculiar quality of analyst or patient, of no use analytically, they wondered? I also found that many analysands had experiences of the subtle-body, such as tingling in the palms or feet, not linked directly with general or external somatic conditions, but with autonomic nervous system events, such as excitement, love, passion, and meaningfulness. More importantly, there is an experience of transcendence with this activation. Clearly, the archetype is revealing itself as energy, in addition to the already experienced imagery that, along with Jung and others, I had known in the past.

Over the years, I knew analysands who engaged in work with these "subtle-body" energies in their lives, but this did not usually come up in the context of the analytic work. More recently (synchronistically?) two shamans came separately to work with me, one of whom is a lifelong healer who uses such energy, and I have an intuition that something more may happen between us. With other analysands, usually psychotherapists or artists or religious, the energy manifests as well. Most recently, a person who was trained in and practices energy work has appeared, and I am grateful for a continuing possibility of enlightenment in my own process, although this sort of energy awareness/interchange did not occur successfully with two previous energy healers with whom I worked. I do not know why.

Attention to such energy and images, in any case, is still in its preliminary stages in analytic work. But these experiences clearly demonstrate the mutuality of the process and our dependence upon the archetype for the development of consciousness in this activity. The astrophysicist, Victor Mansfield, and I have investigated the physics and psychology of such manifestations (see the last paper in *Psychotherapy as a Mutual Process* which also appears in Mansfield & Spiegelman, 1996) and we present the reasons we think that such events are another indication of synchronicity taking place in the analytic transference (while not confined to that kind of relationship). Clearly a synchronicity occurs, and includes mind and body, taking place within each participant and between them. Matter and spirit are united within the relationship itself. Meier, early on, hypothesized that mind–body events in analysis, and even psychosomatic connections, might be synchronistic (Meier, 1959).

The feminine aspect of the divine

I think that understanding of such events and the fact that this energy awareness occurred only later in my development as an analyst, rests on what Jung referred to as the historical coming-into-being of the feminine aspect of the divine. Jung wrote powerfully about this in *Answer to Job* (Jung, 1952a). Jung had the prescient intuition that the elevation of Mary into the Godhead in the collective western consciousness (as indicated by the Papal Bull so pronouncing it in 1950) meant that the body, matter and the feminine would also be so "divinized". His understanding of the elevation of the feminine principle into our image of the Godhead has been evidenced amply by the surging feminist movement and remarkable changes in western society. The popular spiritual/ psychological revolution of the 1960s made possible the collective entrance into western culture of the spiritual treasures of the East, such as Kundalini, Zen, Taoism, etc. A different relation to the feminine in these cultures and religions has also made possible significant changes which go beyond whether or not these faiths take root in the West as alternate ways to the divine.

In my opinion, one such manifestation is the continuing incarnation of the feminine—Goddess images, for example—in the analytic work in which Jungians engage. It is as if Aphrodite made her appearance in the offices of Freud and Breuer in the last decade of the nineteenth century, accompanying women who suffered from hysteria and fell in love with their doctor. Freud was courageous enough to try to understand this form of love made manifest in analytic work, to both learn from it and thereby heal, while Breuer fled in terror. The century following has seen all sorts of work on the unconscious. Particularly apparent has been an endless examination of the mother–child relationship in all analytic schools. Even Jungians have been attracted by Kleinian and Object Relations analysis, which pay special attention not only to infancy, but to the analytic relationship itself. This focus on *relationship*, beginning of course with mother and child, truly is the realm of the Goddess, where healing and development take place. Does this not compensate for continual working with the spirit, particularly from *within*, powerfully demonstrated by Freud and even more deeply, by Jung?

Understanding, consciousness-raising, the "word" and meaning surely belong to Logos, the world of the Father-principle or Masculine, in contrast to relatedness, love, experience and body-awareness of the Mother-principle or Feminine. The dual pair in Hindu Kundalini come to my mind: each chakra is a manifestation of Shiva (the God as form) and Shakti (the Goddess as energy), the latter being all-powerful in the lower, instinctual chakras, while the former, weak and new (child, youth), grows stronger later on. The two divinities united constitute a whole, both in the beginning chakra—Muladhara at the base of the spine—and the "end" or crown chakra of Sahasrara, as well as every centre in between. Form and energy, male and female, undergo changes and differences in power in the Ascension, but wholeness is present at each level.

In short, one might speculate that the continuing development of consciousness is demonstrating itself in the deeper aspects of the analytic process, which makes it a valuable container for such events when it is recognized as a spiritual endeavour as well. While the feminine aspect of the divine is gradually making itself known in western culture particularly, but also in the East, the focused-upon individuation process of analysis is an excellent place for such conditions to become apparent. Furthermore, thanks to Jung's discovery of the alchemical basis of such psychic work and the powerful image of the *coniunctio*, which manifests in such endeavours, we are twice-blessed with a continuing individual and cultural pressure toward the union of opposites and wholeness.

It is exciting to think that the gradual coalescence of spiritual traditions—part of the syncretism of the end of the Piscean age which also occurred at its beginning, two thousand years ago—shows itself in the psyche, even as one patiently unravels the memories and pains of childhood, where the archetypes originally were experienced in relation to the parents. Many people now also undergo analysis as a spiritual path of development of consciousness, beyond childhood repair exclusively. We have developed a kind of western Yoga, as Jung intuited. Thus we gradually get hints as to how the above coalescence comes about. [Several papers in *Psychotherapy as a Mutual Process* (Spiegelman, 1996) take up this theme.]

The combined work of C. G. Jung and his followers, particularly Marie-Louise Von Franz, Erich Neumann, and C. A. Meier, provides the groundwork for understanding the evolutionary unfolding of the development of consciousness quite beyond the needed repair of the damaged childhood psyche. It remains for us all to integrate this material and to add our own understanding, in order to enhance this awareness in the aeon just beginning. In this respect, synchronicity as both fact and theory is an excellent stimulant for reflection.

Theoretical questions

There has been recent questioning of the generalizability of Jung's concept of synchronicity to all parapsychological events. The astrophysicist Victor Mansfield has been particularly adamant about separating "meaningful coincidences"—which, as Jung demonstrated, are linked with the individuation process—from parapsychological events which carry no such significance, such as typical target-guessing events in experiments (Mansfield, 1995, 1998, 1999). No true meaning is to be found in these experiments, bravely inaugurated by J. B. Rhine (1934), except that which might be engendered in people being tested for unusual skills or perceptive capacity. Emotional heightening is occasioned by such testing, however, providing fertile ground for archetypal activation and parapsychological events, but no meaning can be linked to the individuation process. True, the frequency of "hits" decreases over time, correlative with a decrease in emotion; thus connection with the archetypal dimension diminishes, as well. Although synchronicity certainly includes archetypal activation, not all such activation is accompanied by synchronicity, nor are all such events automatically meaningful in the sense of individuation. Central to synchronicity is the experience of the union of psyche and matter, as Von Franz clearly describes:

> The most essential and certainly the most impressive thing about synchronicity occurrences ... is the fact that in them the duality of soul and matter seems to be eliminated. They are therefore an *empirical indication* of an ultimate unity of all existence, which Jung, using the terminology of medieval natural philosophy, called the *Unus Mundus*. [Von Franz, 1975, p. 247]

Von Franz took pains to show that central characteristics of synchronicity were personal meaning and acausality. She said:

> For Jung, individuation and realization of the meaning of life are identical—since individuation means to find *one's own* meaning, which is nothing other than *one's own* connection with the Universal Meaning. This is clearly something other than what is referred to today by terms such as *information, intelligence, cosmic or universal mind*—because feeling, emotion, the Whole of the person is included. This sudden and illuminating connection that strikes us in the encounter with a synchronistic event represents, as Jung well described, a momentary unification of two psychic states: the normal state of our consciousness, which moves in a flow of discursive thought and in a process of continuous perception that

> creates our idea of a world called "material" and "external"; and of a profound level where the "meaning" of the Whole resides in the sphere of "absolute knowledge". [Von Franz, 1992, p. 258]

Mansfield points out that such conditions do not ordinarily occur in most parapsychological events; such events may often not involve synchronicity, and equally synchronicity may often have no parapsychological aspect. My experience of my old school chum and the stag is an example. The synchronistic experience of an image of union of the material and spiritual worlds, at the deepest levels of our being, is what makes synchronicity such a revolutionary idea, and an experience of the *Unus Mundus* is both central and intimately connected with individuation. These conditions are usually absent, not only from card guessing, but even from most experimental work with telepathy, psychokinesis, clairvoyance, etc.

What is at issue here may be the problem of causality itself. Mansfield points out that Jung was reluctant to bring out his discoveries in synchronicity because he lacked a scientific handle for discussion. He latched onto Rhine's work as an entry point, despite the fact that this psychological scientist never really understood synchronicity at all and remained attached to some possible explanation which connected parapsychology with causality.

Jung was especially impressed that Rhine's correlations did not fall off with the distance between sender and receiver, nor did it matter whether the order of cards was guessed even before they were turned. This gave strong evidence of acausality, despite Rhine's resistance. But Jung's understanding of causality was not the same as Rhine's, nor that of most contemporary working scientists. Roger Newton (1970; as quoted in Mansfield) refers to Jung's use of causality as "historical causality", which means that one can establish a causal connection in a single *chain* of events. Scientific causality, however, establishes a connection in *repeatable* events: "jiggling" A produces B, for example. Rhine's experiments and others like them are scientific in that the results can be reliably repeated over time, whereas synchronistic events are unique and non-repeatable expressions of an experience of the *Unus Mundus*. The latter is thus both historically and scientifically acausal, whereas the former remains simply scientifically causal. They share scientific causality with numerous instances in quantum physics in which many phenomena have no well-defined causes for individual events, but exhibit regularity and lawfulness. These, too, are historically acausal, but scientifically causal. In short, synchronicity, connected with the archetype of meaning and individuation, and thus the Self, is relatively acausal, whereas parapsychological phenomena may exhibit scientific causality. The former are sporadic and creative, whereas the latter are constant and reproducible.

Where both types of phenomena may be reconciled perhaps resides in the idea of "acausal orderedness" in general. Jung says:

> I incline to the fact that synchronicity in the narrow sense is only a particular instance of general acausal orderedness—that namely, of the equivalence of psychic and physical processes where the observer is in the fortunate position of being able to recognize the *tertium comparationis*. But as soon as he perceives the archetypal background he is tempted to trace the mutual assimilation of independent psychic and physical processes back to a (causal) effect of the archetype, thus to overlook the fact that they are merely contingent. This danger is avoided if one regards synchronicity as a special instance of general acausal orderedness. [Jung, 1952b, p. 516]

Mansfield agrees with the overall concept here, but is clear in insisting that strict synchronicity is totally acausal, unlike other parapsychological events.

Is this differentiation merely trivial or of importance only to scholars and scientists in some minor way? I do not think so. The intrusion of both psyche and acausality into science is ultimately paradigm-shaking and, therefore, of enormous importance. We must continue to search for both clarity and precision in order to make advances. That quantum physics continues to break the older scientific demand for "objectivity", well beyond what the relativity of the psyche of the individual observer brings to observations, opens the door for Jung's larger perspective, but it is not decisive.

It is psychologically interesting that the causal problem should also be related to the issue of ego and Self. Is there a "willed", hence causal, aspect to some parapsychological activity, or is it fully acausal and under the rubric of the Self? The siddhis, which Asian masters discuss, are in the ancient tradition of the wilful direction of parapsychological activity, such as psychokinesis, willed telepathy, and clairvoyance, and the active use of occult powers. Magic, both black and white, is in this province. Jung and Von Franz are adversaries of the wilful direction of parapsychological or occult powers on scientific grounds and on the ground of immoral usurpation of ego where the Self belongs.

There is, as yet, no acceptable scientific explanation for the apparent causal transmission of energy or image in the occult and parapsychological fields, since neither measurement nor understanding of this process is available. Causality cannot be abandoned here, but the problem may be resolved by further developments in quantum physics. Unlike Newton and Kepler modern scientists transgress what Jung and Von Franz see as a psychological ethic—that such magical practice is an unwarranted and dangerous usurpation by the ego's aims, in place of submission to the Self. God is left out of the equation in modern materialism. Yet quantum physics, with its non-locality, choice by experimenter etc., brings that science closer to the psychological connection adumbrated by Jung and Pauli a half century ago. Progress in both satisfactorily demonstrating parapsychology and providing adequate theoretical comprehension, alas, remains slow.

A possible area for research and discussion may reside in divination, where the ego wills participation, yet leaves the result to the Self or other constellated archetypes. Von Franz says:

> Since synchronistic events seem to be irregular, they cannot be grasped statistically; nevertheless acausal orderedness can be investigated experimentally, because it is something general and regular. [Von Franz, 1992, p. 237]

Von Franz proposes an experiment in a more generally defined synchronicity (general acausal orderedness), as suggested by Jung toward the end of his life. Jung thought that once it was clear that an archetype had been constellated—e.g. in a person undergoing serious stress—then several divination methods whose functioning depends on synchronicity could be used. Divination clearly is an intermediate position in this area, since it necessitates a willed procedure, but cannot predict or determine the precise outcome or meaning of any event it examines. Jung thought that the multiple use of Tarot, *I Ching*, astrology, etc., each separately focused on the situation examined, might reveal symbolic commonality, despite their methodological and other differences.

Mansfield saw difficulties in such experiments, e.g. the typical critiques of non-believers which always undermine results, but he thought that if knowledgeable sceptics were employed throughout the experimental design, useful results could be obtained. Because of the continuing gap between academic and depth psychology, however, it still seems a long time before such work can be done, although here and there ever more refined experiments in parapsychology continue. Whether enough of these will shift the paradigm or whether the paradigm will shift on its own is still a mystery, even though half-a-century has elapsed since Jung's theory was formulated and it is sixty-five years since Rhine's work began. The term synchronicity is now in common use, but we are still far from having Jung's brilliant concept accepted as part of the structure of science.

I will end these reflections with a hint at what may be in store for the entire basis, in physics and in psychology, of the phenomena included in the concept of synchronicity. In the last ten to twenty years there has been a rapid development in physics of what is called "String Theory", or sometimes, "The Theory of Everything". I am unable to explain the particulars of this theory here, but I am struck with the realization that physicists have gone far beyond both Einstein's Relativity Theory and Quantum Physics, to find themselves with the notion of vibrating strings at the heart of matter, not particles or waves at all! These vibrating strings resonate or harmonize with each other in such a fashion as to produce, ultimately, our experience of three- or four-dimensional space and time, so that eleven such dimensions are now understood to exist. The notions of space and time, as these were known in Relativity and Quantum Mechanics, are practically eliminated. The ancient Greek idea of the Harmony of the Spheres comes to mind, and Indra's Web from India, to say nothing of Jewish, Christian, and Islamic mysticism which invoke a similar perspective. In the not-too distant future, these theoretical concerns about the unitary background of synchronistic events may well be in accord with the leading edge in science.

References

Jung, C. G. (1946). On the nature of the psyche. In: *Collected Works, Volume 8*. New York: Routledge.

Jung, C. G. (1948). *Psychology of the Transference. C.W., 16.*

Jung, C. G. (1952a). *Answer to Job. C.W., 11.*

Jung, C. G. (1952b). *Synchronicity: An Acausal Connecting Principle. C.W., 8.*

Mansfield, V. (1995). *Synchronicity, Science, and Soul-Making*. Chicago: Open Court.

Mansfield, V., & Spiegelman, J. M. (1996). On the physics and psychology of the transference as an interactive field. *Journal of Analytical Psychology, 41*: 179–202.

Mansfield, V., Rhine-Feather, S., & Hall, J. (1998). The Rhine–Jung letters; distinguishing parapsychological from synchronistic events. *Journal of Parapsychology, 62*: 3–25.

Mansfield, V. (1998). Distinguishing synchronicity from parapsychological phenomena: an essay in honor of Marie-Louise Von Franz, Part One. *Quadrant: Journal of the C. G. Jung Foundation of Analytical Psychology, XXVIII*(2): 17–37.

Mansfield, V. (1999). Distinguishing synchronicity from parapsychological phenomena: an essay in honor of Marie-Louise Von Franz, Part Two. *Quadrant: Journal of the C. G. Jung Foundation for Analytical Psychology, XXIX*(1): 37–45.

Meier, C. A. (1959). Projection, transference and the subject-object relation in psychology. *Journal of Analytical Psychology, 4*: 21–34.

Neumann, E. (1954). *The Origins and History of Human Consciousness*. New York: Bollingen–Pantheon Books.

Newton, R. (1970). Particles that travel faster than light? *Science, 167*: 1569–1574.

Rhine, J. B. (1934). *Extra-Sensory Perception*. Boston: Boston Society for Psychical Research.

Schwartz-Salant, N. (1996). On the interactive field as the analytic object. In: *The Interactive Field in Analysis* (pp. 1–36). Wilmette, Illinois: Chiron Publications.

Spiegelman, J. M. (1965). Some implications of the transference. In: T. Frey (Ed.), *Festschrift für C. A. Meier*. Zürich: Rascher Verlag.

Spiegelman, J. M. (1996). *Psychotherapy as a Mutual Process*. Nevada: New Falcon.

Von Franz, M. L. (1973). *An Introduction to the Interpretation of Fairy Tales*. Zürich: Spring Publications.

Von Franz, M. L. (1974). *Number and Time*. Northwestern University Press.

Von Franz, M. L. (1975). *C. G. Jung, His Myth in Our Time*. London: Hodder and Stoughton.

Von Franz, M. L. (1980). *On Divination and Synchronicity*. Toronto: Inner City Books.
Von Franz, M. L. (1988). *On Dreams and Death*. Boston: Shambala.
Von Franz, M. L. (1992). *Psyche and Matter*. Boston: Shambala.

CHAPTER SEVEN

The ghost in the mother: strange attractors and impossible mourning

Edward Emery

I: The scene of haunting

> The secret we don't know we're trying to find, the thing *un*-seen,
> the suction-point of which we now are trying to feed our lives ...
> —the secret—the place where the words, twist,
> ... we try the nipple ...
> —we look away—
> ...into the edifice of your whisper ... [Jori Graham, *The Errancy*, 1997]

The ghosting of the mother deranges the psychic economy of the child who has been nominated to carry the spectral prefigurations of the ghost. The one so haunted is spooked by two impossibilities: impossible mourning and impossible longing. While these two impossibilities are inseparable, I wish to begin with the second first as impossible longing shapes and deforms the first impossibility.

There are many ways to ghost the mother. The one that I shall focus on is the inscription of a dead child in the maternal psychic economy and its elegiac transmission as an atmospheric surround of a subsequently born child, the so-called replacement child. Abraham and Torok (1986), who are the first since Freud to take psychic haunting seriously as foundational to the problematic structurations of psychic life, distinguish between two modes of inscription: introjection and incorporation.

Introjection is like swallowing with digestion. Incorporation is like swallowing with indigestion. Incorporation is the negative of introjection. Central to introjection is the space of the buccal orifice, for it is this silent spot of the body that assimilates prior to the subsequent use made of this silent space as the material matrix for systems of representation (Derrida, 1986). One who is lost but not mourned and so subsequently deposited in its nominated replacement is not introjected but incorporated.

That which is lost but not mourned cannot be taken in to the psychical equivalent of the buccal space. A loss that is frozen in time and encased intrapsychically is not subject to the work of metaphorization. One lost and beyond mourning is subject to the work of incorporation to which Abraham and Torok ascribe a very specific meaning: the lost object is de-metaphorized; it is taken into the body as a "thing". This concretization of the unmourned one is subsequently located in mental space as a discretely preserved secret personification. This object is not assimilated into the web of identifications so much as it is, in the words of Jacques Derrida, "vomited into the inside, into the pocket of a cyst" (1986, p. xxxviii). What introjection allows for—the taking into the mouth in order to subsequently express—is in incorporation transformed into a forbidden speech, a certain non-speaking through which what is taken in is now done so on the level of fantasy in order to be preserved as an unnamable Thing.

The dead child, preserved in the intrapsychic enclave of the mother, transfigures the intersubjective field and atmospheric surround of the child designated as heir apparent and erasure of this trauma. The incorporated dead object, shrouded in both secrecy and a reverential aura, is persevered in something like a secret pocket in the psyche, an enclave or a crypt. The encrypted lost object registers in the atmospheric surround as a certain sense of haunting, as a disquieting, uncanny sense of elusive presence that thickens the intersubjective with an unlocatable but visceral beckoning. Something is wrong, but its nature and its locus can never quite be identified. It is neither "this" nor "that", neither "here" nor "there". This ghosting of the intersubjective transforms a sense of place into no-place, creating a background ill-at-easness that disturbs any sense of home with mute suffocation: something is at once too present and too absent.

The haunting effects of an unmourned presence registers as mute attention to something like an apparitional longing bereft of an object. If this state of haunting, which is the outcome of incorporation, takes on form it is through the evocations of images that are like the ghost of a ghost, disappearing as soon as they manifest, leaving a trace only through a series of erasures. That which is incorporated is encased in such a way in the unconscious vault of the ego and so sealed over that its presence is known only as a double secret: the secret of a secret.

Jason, whose older brother died at birth, describes this sense of ghostly double secret in mirror phase visual renderings. His brother, he said, was always hovering at the edge of awareness as something like the effect of someone's breath on a mirror—someone who is nameless and never present yet elemental, present like air, yet also like someone who is hidden as in a secret that itself must be kept secret. This breath-effect of the ghost distorts Jason's image of himself as he is shrouded under the force of an occult companionship that renders him not quite actual before his own self-presentation. Jason appears to others full of potential yet always elusive, darting in and out of the actual. Jason is more ghost than person. He finds respite from the pressure of being-ghost and intimations of being-person in periods of solitude, that are also double: they open him, in one instance, to profiles of the infinite, to the unbounded free-flow of spirit and, in other moments, they beckon him back into a privately idealized cryptic communion with the ghost-within.

The incorporation of the psychic body of the mother's extruded object of impossible mourning exerts a force on all relational and intrapsychic economies that is like a strange attractor. Strange attractors are one outcome of non-linear systems. Non-linear systems act in ways that appear as if compelled to repeat certain behaviours. The ghost-within haunts the subject and the intersubjective through the evocation of non-linear repetitions. Consider, first, these analogies. Water draining from a tube does so with characteristic spirals. A hand placed in the vortex disrupts it, only for the vortex to again resume its characteristic spiral. This motion that sustains this pattern is called a limit cycle attractor. Predator–prey systems can also be limit cycle attractors. Pike, for example, like to eat trout. Year after year, the number of pike and trout oscillate in exactly repeatable ways. Too many pike, the trout population falls and pike go hungry. As pike die out, the trout population flourishes. Pike and trout follow each other in endlessly repeating limit cycles.

Cryptic inscriptions of the object of impossible mourning establish exactly this dynamism within the being of the subject. The ascendance of the ghost-within depletes the ego of the subject and the ghost, seeking from its enclave incorporative affiliates, begins to hunger for connection. Inspired by an envy of existence the ghost-within goes, as it were, hungry and wanders the intersubjective, fuelling the affective in-scapes of desire with predator–prey turbulence. The hungry ghost in search of relational linkage feeds through projective and eviscerating identifications, sucking, in the extreme, the life out of the other or, alternatively, enshrouding the other in excitable idols of mourning (Emery, 1997). The other becomes an object of veneration before whom I worship and grow through adoration increasingly passive. Within this shaming passivity—more passive than the passivity that has activity as it's opposite—the other is configured as disturbingly malevolent, feared, and privately hated. In this turbulent evisceration of self one is rendered worthless, condemned to an abjection whose shame is pervasive and that further feeds these predator–prey hungry ghost dynamics.

One who is haunted by the mother's impossible mourning often has an uncanny ability to seek out as partners persons who are equivalently haunted or who have at least a kinship with feeling ghosted through the inscription of a parental secret. Jason, for example, was drawn to a woman who was talented, accomplished, and exquisitely grounded in the real. Only after they were together for some time did he discover that they shared a salient biographical symmetry: each were born in the shadow of a previous child's death. This they held together as a privileged curiosity as they established a rhythm to their life built around parallel work addiction and a shared overlap of what, at first, was mythologized as a kind of mute blank at-one-ment, as if they were living in the Grand Silence of the monastic cloister.

She managed the inscription of the maternal crypt through encapsulation in ego efficacies. He, for a while, achieved the same, but in Jason's case the crypt was more porous, more subject to leakage into the intersubjective and more desirous of perfect reparative adhesive union through affect intensifications that grew, under the force of other regressive pressures, into demands with ever heightened desperation. In regression to need as demand, his pursuit of relief from the somatized painful haunting from the ghost-within, drove her into deeper states of encapsulation (she experiencing this pursuit as her brother—who also never mourned their conjointly held dead sister—his breathing, as she once said, down her neck). The results of this mutually allergic dance were tragic and inevitable: implosive breakdown.

The ghost-within intruded into the cloister of intersubjective compensations. Each became flooded by what the system, in its predator–prey amplifications, could no longer contain. There was a contagion of the uncanny, a miasma of pollution as impossible loss became impossible longing. Muteness gave way to mad passion. The logic of asymmetry that supports the resilience of contact barriers was subsumed under the symmetry of an explosively implosive non-differentiation. The intersubjective became a prison in which the ghost-within is the warden. The work of haunting forecloses difference and instills, in its place, mutual but oscillating confusional states of contamination, possession, torment, and depletion. Life becomes a twisted dream. When the effraction of contact barriers serves the hungry ghost, there is a deformation and ultimate breakdown of potential space. The ensuing interpersonal violence commemorates further the loss of what cannot be remembered nor experienced except through the derangements of hyperbole.

When the ghost in the mother activates an intersubjective crypt, the relational system of compromises and quiet attention deforms into vortices of turbulence that turns difference into humiliating betrayal. Trajectories of privacy and autonomy become disconnected from the rhythms of relating and reduced to signifiers of abandonment, which in turn inspire the violence of the shame–rage cycle. What is sought as a curative phantasy to this intersubjective realization of the logic of symmetry is a better version of the same: something between the myths of twinship mirroring and merger, understood as a "holding" that is a hermetically sealed totalization, one without lack. The hungry ghost views lack as assault and responds to intolerable deficit through strategies that create relational pandemonium.

When the ghost-within inspires predator–prey totalizations the states of upheaval, of intensity, and of mad passion often, after the fact, seal over through a stoic amnesia that is in turn overlaid with the pseudo-innocence of disavowal. This tendency to forget—to not learn from experience—is due, in part, to the fact that, under the spell of the intersubjective crypt, what is lived is not experienced so much as it is endured in a state of suspended animation. There is, in this ghosting of the intersubjective, no history, only the non-experienced commemoration of turbulence. Mourning becomes a pre-emptive strike—assaulting in advance the anticipated loss of what was, in the first instance, frozen in the double secret of a preserved dead object that cannot be psychically killed off or elaborated. Subsequent "understanding" does not link up with the reflective space of psychic responsibility. It feeds, instead, the –K linkages of further violent projective accusation.

Yet, ghostly desire, for it to succeed, must not totally eviscerate or completely incorporate the other. Enough otherness must be preserved so that the other's life can recover sufficiently to be available for future commemoration of these endlessly repeating strange attractor limit cycles. What often keeps fuelling this system is that the shared amnesia of the intersubjectively actualized crypt—reflected in the differential isomorphisms of the respective biographies—allows for the emergence of what appears like reparation and repair, though in fact it is more like resuscitation for the next—always surprising and always disorienting—irruption of turbulent haunting.

The logic of non-linear regularity defines the work of the ghost. The eviscerative intention of the hungry ghost takes its prey to the edge where intimations of psychic death are possible. Yet, the dead must not be killed off. The work of the ghost does not want to completely destroy its prey. Having fed off the other through dissociative trajectories of turbulence, the ego again becomes more robust. The hungry ghost now has, as companion and source of nurture, a replenished ego on which internal feeding may resume inside the space of erasure until the plenitude of the ghost-within again permeates the intersubjective.

The haunting of the intersubjective creates a world of vortices and of vortices within vortices within vortices. The ghost-within has a privileged relationship to determinate but unpredictable compulsions toward repetition. The ghost is *le revenant*, "that which returns''. In speaking of the ghost, in speaking as if it is possible to speak of that which exists only as the secret of a secret and as the incorporated erasure of an introjection, we must say that the ghost exists only as the effect of a certain return. The ghost supplements the present with irruptions of the unexpected. These psychical ghosts—inscribed as inflammatory foreclosures of difference in the intersubjective—have, then, a curious kind of ''body''. It is one that is, as Jacques Derrida (1994) suggests, ''an *a-physical* body''. The ''body'' of the ghost is present as the force of a determinant, but always unpredictable, return.

Certain isomorphisms shape the contact barrier between the intrapsychic and the intersubjective (Emery, 1992). It is this contact barrier and this space of translation that the a-physical body of the ghost renders turbulent. One outcome is the formation of something like an ''I'' without a self. This haunted ''I'' links to the negative outline of a self. This process is analogous to what Maurice Blanchot (1992) describes as ''a non-personal punctuality oscillating between no one and someone, a semblance that only the exigency of the exorbitant relation invests silently and momentarily with this role.'' When the ghost-within circumambulates the fields of affective sensibility and relational intentionality, the relation to loss is curiously ironic. Under the ghost-effect one is always *in potentia* amenable to losing what in fact one never had and which was, in the first instance, never one's ownmost, what was never from the beginning properly mine nor what might legitimately fall under the nomination of one's proper name. This institution of a loss that is impossibly mourned forms a fissure or fault line between the ''I'' and the self in which each is the other's loss for which there is an impossible mourning, expressed as uncanny longing. The ghost-within returns neither as presence nor as it's opposite—absence—but as the loss of loss, as the hollowed out space of the negative between no one and someone.

Ethan, whose older brother died four years prior to his birth, sits in his usual pose of a stilling rigor mortis and describes—after twelve years of therapy—how for the first time he has caught a glimpse of himself, has seen some appresentation that he thinks of as himself as he walks down a hall and, for the first time, notices something other than tormenting nothingness and accusatory nothingness that shames to near-death. Ethan notices an emptiness beneath this companionable nothingness of dread-filled mood and he finds, for the first time, the revelation of something he conceives of as the fullness of self-presence, in which there is not only at-one-ment but also the abiding loneliness of difference, a loneliness which expresses that he might, in this moment and for the first time in an act of spectral recognition, be himself.

His "I" that is the crypt of the Other opens to a nascent self otherwise embedded in the implicate dimension and further covered over through mournful repetitions of deferral and of oppositional undoings, this second-order covering serving as foreclosure against a fruitful internal copulation between "I" and Self. And in this moment Ethan catches a glimpse of a gaze that witnesses this internal primal scene without the persecuting intrusion of the uncanny and accusatory atmosphere that is the formless form of the circumambulating spectre-brother. And he notices, too, and also for the first time, that this pleasurable repose in self-presencing emptiness can turn in an instant that is, he says, faster than light, into an accuser, a mocker, a depersonalizing commentator and then he is again outside himself. He then becomes the Outside experienced as the alien-within and as a body that also is curiously outside of itself, eccentric and taken over through libidinal evacuations.

There is, then, for the "I" that has contracted under the spell of the revenant an impacted density of nothingness akin to the sucking obliterations of a dense object (Emery, 1992), this forming against a ground without sustainable horizon or boundary. Ethan now recognizes this shift from I–self mating into I–spectre autistic copulation more easily. On a trip with his partner there is for him an expansiveness of relating and an appreciation of her otherness and her interest in him. When he returns home, however, it is as if he has been resigned to the crypt in a night where, as is typical, he and his partner sleep apart, for this is the only arrangement he can bear without the also faster than light shock of flooding and subsequent psychic haemorrhage. Despite this protective skin of apparent separation, Ethan is again visited by waveforms of the uncanny that shimmer over and through him, saturating him with dread and pressure.

Ethan feels, in these moments, the disturbing presence of the former owner of his home, beseeching, cold, longing. Thought of by him as a possible projection of an a-physical body from some remote time into the now, Ethan senses the appresentation of this hungry ghost as the feared dispersal of his own body, at once evacuated and tremulously overstimulated. The degree zero of the ghost-within inscribes as a trace on the ego the affective markings and the libidinal etchings of desire as haunting. Under the sign of *le revenant* the subject loses the ability to lose, so that what returns does not come back as that which one can have or recover but under the attainment of what Blanchot thinks of as some "non-power in some form that inscribes itself against any form" (1992, p. 86).

II: The virtual space of the ghost and the incestuous chora

> And the ribbony avenue of the possible dream frays, thins—what gate, where is the gate? [Jori Graham, *The Errancy*, 1997]

The trace of the ghost—the always returning erasure of an incorporated loss that was never properly mine—is present as a virtual reality that is of the order of impossibility, of impossible mourning in double reversal with impossible longing. Gilles Deleuze (1994) suggests that it is heuristically prudent to distinguish between the virtual and the possible. The possible expresses a form of identity in the concept while the virtual approximates to a pure multiplicity. The possible undergoes "realization". The virtual, in contrast, is not opposed to the real, but possesses a full reality in itself. The virtual, which is not realized, is, instead, actualized.

The ghost-within poses questions (think here of Hamlet's ghost, for example) from an order other than that of the possible and the real, for these dimensions require that existence is thought of as an eruption or the act of a leap occurring behind our backs and subject to a logic of all or nothing (Deleuze, 1994). There is, then, on the level of the possible, no difference between the existent and the non-existent as the latter is already possible. Within the order of the possible, difference is nothing but the negative of the concept (either as an opposition to the real or a limitation imposed upon the possible). Actualization of the virtual, in contrast, always takes place through a process of multiplication that is differentiated from identity. The actual never resembles the singularities they incarnate.

The virtual actualizes the non-existent as an immanent haunting of the real by the reality of the impossible. The ghost-within figures another difference and differs otherwise, as it is the non-substantial actualization of the impossible. The ghost-within is of the order of the virtual.

The always-returning non-present actualization of the virtual ghost-within gives distinctive shaping to psychic space and to its deformations. We are, in psychoanalysis, comforted by and familiar with what, following Winnicott, is thought of as potential space with its simulacra of generative illusions and imaginative pre-figurations. This is the space out of which is shaped "holding environments", surrounds of attention, useable silence, and affect metabolization. Potential space and holding environments take shape in overlapping mental space that is of three dimensions. It is my view that this shaping of potential spaces in three dimensions is contingent on evolution out of another more elusive spatiality that is difficult to talk about but, I believe, foundational to all dimensions of psychic life.

This pre-originary space that is the background matrix of potential space is more like Blanchot's form that has no form. It is more like a background pre-personal generative emptiness whose explication actualizes in the domesticated form of potential space. Without this background emptiness, which is not nothingness, and which is also antecedent to the enframing structure of the face (Green, 1987; Emery, 2000) potential space is not possible. It is, I believe, this pre-originary foundational emptiness that Plato spoke of when he described a space that is the matrix out of which all other spatialities take form.

Plato called this space the *chora* (Hamilton & Cairns, 1961). The *chora*, he said, is neither sensible nor intelligible, neither inside nor outside. It is, he added, speaking through analogies with which we are all familiar, the matrix, nurse, and mother of all space. For potential space to form on the plane of the intersubjective there must be, in the first instance, a healthy *chora*. The force of different affect states can feedback through non-linear dynamics and damage the generative integrity of the *chora* which in turn can constrict the resiliency of derivative potential spaces. Kristeva (1989), for example, building on the work of Andre Green, links collapse of the *chora* to blank mourning. The ghost-within exerts, I believe, other equally distinctive effects on this pre-originary spatial matrix. There is, in my view, a strange attractor affiliation between the space of the *chora* and the virtualization of the ghost. Prior to encapsulation into what Abraham and Torok (1986) think of as a crypt, an imagined little grave of the impossibly mourned other housed in the unconscious sector of the ego, the haunting effect of the ghost-within permeates the generative manifold of the *chora*.

Intrapsychic crypts manifest in the intersubjective as a certain flattening and deadening of potential space. When the *chora* is subject to deformation under the force of impossible mourning, potential space collapses into its background emptiness—realized, in this collapse, as the negative of nothingness—and an intersubjective crypt forms in its place. Intersubjective crypts are the internally projected loci of the ghost in three dimensions.

Through linkage to the space of the *chora*, the ghost-with erupts into three-dimensional psychic space as the signifier of infinity. This overflow of the infinite amplifies through the ghost-within and shapes the intersubjective into a version of the negative sublime. As a consequence of this linkage between intimations of the infinite and the intergenerationally transmitted spectre, the ghost-within haunts through intimations of the uncanny. Linkage between precocious intimations of the infinite and the ghost-effect fuels the internal dissociation between the "I" who acts and the self who is in the mode of "is-not".

Telescoping the multi-dimensional pre-originary space of the *chora* into the relational three-dimensionality of potential spaces intensifies the haunting of the intersubjective into a passion for form as compensation for the collapsing effect of haunting on potential space. The ghost-within twists and fractures potential space into component formal signifiers, behind which are intimations of the formless void infinite. Irruption of the pre-originating spatiality of the *chora* into the bounded world of three-dimensionality results in the formation of a position that is intermediate between an autistic one and the positional dynamism's of object relating. This third space is the space of haunting. One so haunted longs for an impossible perfect love—perfectly spacious and perfectly solicitous—that is found less on the plane of existential embodiment than on the spectral plane of image. Because the ghost-within is conduit for intimations of the infinite, activation of the libidinal body in the subject who is so haunted transmutes the swoon of pleasure into a potentially uncontainable *jouissance* of flooding mad-passion and subsequent aggressive reactivity to this momentous at-one-ment.

One who is under this force field is subject to a certain non-domestication of the instincts. The capacity to renounce incestuous desire is often severely curtailed for one who is in mythologized communion with the ghost-within. Communion with the ghost-within also floods with precocious intimations of the infinite, the latter force intensifying the haunted attachment to the eroticized body of the mother. The sensitive loving child, who has been nominated as the deposition for the parental complex of impossible mourning, has a mad passion for the haunting incestuous object that includes not only divinization of the body of the mother, but also of her preserved secret—the dead object of her passion and the parts of her that have been damaged by this possession. There is a wild determination, often at the expense of all manner of suffering, to keep the mournful mother alive, preserved from the circulating complex of a guilty aggressivity that is potentially differentiating, but feared as murderous This insistent desperate need to repair the mother and to secretly idolize the ghost-within shapes excitable permutations of the primal scene phantasy and the Oedipus complex.

Incorporation of the ghost-within fuels the furnace of incestuous desire in a manner that manifests not only on the level of phantasy—which is the primary emphasis of Andre Green (1987)—but also on the level of what Didier Anzieu (1990) identifies as formal signifiers. Unlike phantasy, formal signifiers lack a narrative structure and scenic elements. They have more to do with destabilization of the spatial background to the scenic. Formal signifiers are made up of images that express, for example, the postural senses (proprioceptive and tactile, for instance) rather than the visual and auditory senses of distance. Formal signifiers involve spatial transformations that distort or destroy container–contained relations in a manner that can be felt as irreversible: a surface puckers, a vertical axis is reversed, or a support collapses.

Formal signifiers involve such transformations as my double that leaves me, my shadow that accompanies me, or an external being is preserved inside. Incestuous investment in the ghost-within effects a double haunting because of the symmetrical alignment between the narratives of impossible longing and the formal signifiers of impossible mourning. Linkage between the ghost-within and the higher dimensional spatialities out of which is shaped mental space, destabilizes the container–contained/formal signifier–phantasy relationships. The pressure of the mad passion for the haunted body of the mother only seals this fate, making adhesion a primary strategy for the restoration of the damage haunting does to the resiliency of formal signifiers. Under the force of impossible mourning, container–contained relationships often consolidate into rigid and at times irreversible transformations whose higher level organization structures the frozen interplay between signifiers and scenarios. The mad passion for the ghost-within punctuates the "I" with the haunting of an absent "self". There is no agent of expressivity, only a discourse that forms an image-repertoire in the interstices between formal signification and phantasy. The result is a haunted narration spoken as through another's voice.

Jane speaks in long metaphoric ellipses and in exquisitely constructed formulations of poetic qualifications, always going for further nuance and marking each observation with a counterpoint or its exception. This flow that seems too beautifully narrated, but that never tells a story, has about it a strange space of repose and of stillness, a silence that is not so much a place of pause as it is a negative inhabitation in the words themselves. Her speech is Orphic and I listen to her like the lost Euridyce, waiting to be found. Her haunted narration is like a long deconstructionist exegesis on deferral and I feel in relation to it a poised provisionalism, an uncanny being otherwise. I listen not as myself or from myself, but as from some dark recess that has no inside and no bottom, that is more like a vortex within a vortex, an echo chamber of elegiac longing for what never was and that has no past tense. I listen as from a vast future tense to a return from some place that is close to what Freud thought of as prehistory.

Listening to her is lovely, entrancing, and as I listen I float along. At first this floating has about it the quality of following. There are, in relation to her modes of expressively representing herself, something like associations yet they never quite form, never quite take shape and the listening never quite centres in the heart or solar plexus or their in-between connections, which is where I find that, for me, the best spacious listening takes place. And so there is a gradual disturbance that inserts itself in my listening awareness.

There is no real calm in me as I listen, but like Euridyce I long, with some irritability, for a form to grasp on to, for a meaning that stops sliding and slipping along polysemic trails. I long for something substantial, for some object to master or to understand.

I long for landmarks, for a sign that there is a horizon or that figure-ground logic is not absurd. I long for a world that is not saturated with an unspeakable mad passion that shrouds meaning in the will to signify and I begin to dread Jane. The sight of her repulses me with a repulsion that is about more than her bird-like anorexia and yet somehow this same repulsion also beckons me on. She has about her the aura of an adhering stickiness, as she appears to want to feed me with words that cannot conceive or give birth to an alive object of meaning.

I am in a spell. I begin to intimate in relation to this entrancing erasure of self that is the other, a correlative presentation of myself, as if I am listening in the way an analyst might, but in fact I am becoming a simulacrum of my image of an analyst. I am becoming, I gradually realize, ghosted. And Jane? Her Orpheus is the poise of pure sound, of words that do not mean, that do not say so much as they sound like they mean and sound like they say. Jane speaks not to narrate nor to inform nor to inquire into herself. She speaks to build a scaffolding of formal signifiers to support her mute mad passion.

I know nothing, really, about her. She speaks as if she has no history and never references, in her self-performative, anything like memory or recollection. Neither is there any evidence of expressed wants or of wants that might be wanted or that she wants to express. It is as if she arrived from some elsewhere without trajectory. Jane, it seems, is a trace that erases itself in its apparent appresentation in the familiar mode often thought of as a subject, as one who can speak on behalf of other times and other voices. Jane, I gradually realize, does not speak but is the simulacrum of another voice. A few years later—though in such a therapy time is not marked nor does it pass so much as it punctuates the always returning spectre—Jane arrives with a present, not for me but one given to her for a birthday whose date I do not know, for such a biographical fact goes singularly unmarked. It is a ventriloquist's puppet, a dummy that today she places on the couch as she chooses the chair.

This puppet for which Jane speaks is a gift, she says, from her father. Father? She has a Father? I am relieved to know that she may have had one, that she might have been conceived, that she is the outcome of some possible desire, that she might be somewhere in some dimension of self something other than the actualization of the virtual or the empty space of non-meaning. But he—this Father, this one that she speaks of but does not name—is a mere aside and quickly forgotten, in a discourse of impossible mourning.

The ghosted personality speaks not as oneself but as the Other, on the other's behalf, being the virtual echo chamber of the other who cannot be represented so much as encrypted in self-performatives. The subject speaks for the dummy that deanimates the self and who preoccupies as if the subject is mother to the self as the embalmed lost object of impossible mourning. And yet this is not quite accurate, either. It is, I believe, that the dummy also speaks on behalf of the ventriloquist function of the crypt. For the ghosted personality, haunted by an impossible mourning, longs not for the Other but to be one who can only be themselves by serving the ventriloquist function for the impossibly mourned object. Jane can only be herself by being otherwise, speaking always through strategies of postponement as if her vocatives commemorate the death of one who has not died but has been embalmed in language. Her discourse is an idol to the mute mad passion for the beloved and despised spectre—the rival who cannot, it seems, be killed nor assimilated, but who, in a manner proper to the a-physical body of the ghost, always returns.

There is, for Jane, no development of meaning, no sense of deepening engagement. The density of her discourse is a symptom of the thinness of its meaning. There is, in relation to Jane, a vast chasm. It is compelling to think of this enacted appresentation of the dummy as an epiphany of representation on the way toward "thinking about" but this is a ruse of hope, for Jane just as soon "forgets" this event ever happened and treats it, from that time on, as an unremembered non-event that we, then, hold as *our* unspoken secret. The crypt is sealed.

Every lover, observed Plato, is mad, but some are madder than others and mad in distinctively ironic modes. For most, this madness is, as Roland Barthes suggests in his lexicon of love, merely metaphorical: one is driven "nearly mad". Jane, however, is mad differently, for her passion that she cannot speak, but only circumambulate through clouds of words, is that she is the Other, that she is the space of its virtual inhabitation, that she lives not as herself but as and for the Other she is not, but who possesses her. There is, as a result, little room for anything like object relating. The normalized madness of the lover is that they become more themselves as they seek and beseech the Other. The haunted madness, of one that has been nominated to become the space of incorporation for an impossibly mourned antecedent beloved rival, is that to be themselves is to betray this prior nomination.

The greatest threat to this devotional integrity is that the haunted, in fact, might become themselves and discover their own desire exempt from the inflammatory mad passion of an endlessly exciting haunted mother, a passion that is sparked again and again through enlivening acts intended to resurrect an internal dead object or to fill a blank space of inconsolable loss. The "madness" of one who is a subject is the realization that they are, in a sense, condemned to be themselves and not another. Self, in this instance, takes on a quality of dense resilience, as it becomes the conduit of I-am-ness. The "madness" of one who is in secret communion with the ghost-within is that their intrapsychic relational space is already inhabited and subject to the claustrophobic saturation of internal overstimulation. The "madness" of one who is yoked to the circumambulating ghost-within is the madness that they are condemned to be the Other. Their wish, then, is the wish to kill the dead yet this achievement in fantasy and, *in extremis*, in derivative enactment is no liberating exoneration, for the ghost is "that which returns". The ghost-within, in other words, is not finite but comprises an unconscious infinite set of circumambulating affective figurations whose "presence" is never definitively regulated to the hygienic category of the "absent".

In the first "madness" there is the solitude of relational singularity. In the second haunted madness, one who lives a secret tandem relation to the ghost-within is never, in a sense, solitary, for they are never alone. For one who lives in relation to the spectre, the achievement of solitude, as distinct from a certain withdrawn preoccupation, relies on episodic internal space clearing tactics whose more regressive forms include the passive modes of numbing and blanking-out and the more active modes of opposition and projective evacuation. These more regressive expressions are often desperate manoeuvres to gain intrapsychic distance from intersubjective insistence. Impossible mourning seeks cure through a longing for a certain relational emptiness that often appears interpersonally as avoidant rejection, but that is in fact an effort to rehabilitate the Other to whom they relate to its proper position across the caesura of alterity.

The ghost-within collapses contact barriers intrapsychically between topographies and intersubjectively between the Other and the image-repertoires of the spectre. The need for a space apart, for a kind of non-schizoid hermitage, that is also not another version of a crypt on the part of the replacement child, often can be generative in that it allows for the emergence of a spacious silence that is not another face of blank mourning. Out of this redemptive silence other contact barriers take shape. Alterity is born.

Sylvie is at a party. There is around her a swirl of activity, of exuberant play, of boisterous engagements, of chatter, of mergings and meldings and blendings that are both high-spirited and high pitched. The other children are romping and jumping and throwing things and eating each other's food. Sylvie, born after the death of a sibling, retires to an unoccupied bedroom where she quietly and with gracious delicacy eats her dinner while following intently and with laser-like attention, for at least the twelfth time, Pocahontas II. Sylvie is discovered by another girl who enters as from a whirlwind, commenting, asking questions, poking, and otherwise insisting on "contact". Sylvie is disturbed, frowns, and makes it clear that she is to be left alone. The ball of energy wanders off. When free from impingement, there is around Sylvie something like an aura of light, a clearing in which her being shines forth and she appears, to those who can see, like an angel, radiant and deeply wise for a four-year-old. She sits still with the delicate poise and the gracefully resigned attentive knowing of a monk.

The ghost-within fetishizes the potential spaces of relating and of creation, while it stretches this generative psychic spatiality across simultaneous implicate dimensions. Telescoping this multidimensional pre-originary space of the *chora* into the relational three-dimensionality of potential spaces intensifies the haunting of the intersubjective field into a passionate aesthetic of image. The position of haunting locates the subject at the level of image as it forecloses generative contact with the imaginal, the former being linked to repetitive fragments of instinct while the latter is more akin to the creative visions of culture. This form of the spectre that is no-form is neither fantastic nor imaginary, but is of the order of an image: it compels yet is without dimension or of depth.

III: The image-repertoire of the ghost: the silent cure

> So in the cave of the winds he prisoned the north wind … and the north wind and the west wind and such other as … cause the clouds of the sky to flee, and he turned loose … turned the southerly loose and the southerly came … came out streaming, with drenched wings … [Jori Graham, *The Errancy*, 1997]

Image is the privileged semiotic of haunting. Image, suggests Roland Barthes, is pre-emptory: it always has the last word.

> The image is presented, pure and distinct as a letter … Precise, complete, definitive, it leaves no room for me, down to the last finicky detail: I am excluded from it as from the primal scene … Here then, at last, is the definition of the image, of any image: that from which I am excluded. [1978, p. 132]

To be haunted is to be caught in a web of exclusionary images, and of images of images, an endless iteration of images. Barthes' definition of image takes on further specificity in the genealogy of image Gilles Deleuze (1989) developed in his work on film. Deleuze distinguishes, for example, between the perception-image, the affection-image, the impulse-image, the action-image, and the reflection-image. The projected actualization of the ghost-within is of the order of an impulse-image and is intermediate between affection and action. It is, according to Deleuze, an image akin to a fetish. The ghost-within made spectral through the activation of the impulse-image repertoire constitutes a world that is often subject to a claustrophobic sensibility and sensuality that captivates and pressures as it effects an intolerance for the pragmatics of extraverted relating.

The ghost-within haunts desire and compels compulsive realizations as in a spell or under the influence of a magical incantation that is not unlike an epiphany. One day Ethan observes in a film the image of a woman who is, to him, not particularly beautiful but who had, he said, a certain diaphanous presence and a certain wispy aura of spirit that absolutely riveted him, that held him in this spectral gaze of ghostly density. He had found his Beatrice and in relation to this contra-sexual figuration of the ghost-within, all else paled. His life and his living relationships became what they always were to him but now only more so: necessary demand, occasionally invigorating, but more frequently filled with the double loss of intrusion and lack. His relationships both competed with and commemorated his relationship to the ghost-within (at times idealized as Saviour, at others suffered as Tormentor, at still others transformed into the Crucified One). Ethan's relation to the ghost shifted its centre of gravity with his Beatrice epiphany. The ghost-within found its consummate realization in this most poignant image whose haunting presence Ethan found both transcendent, excitingly preoccupying and, strangely, deeply soothing.

For Ethan, his Beatrice-spectre does not compete with orders of the real. She is superordinate. He is "held" by his Beatrice. Her apparitional embrace completes him. This epiphinal virtualization of a spectre impulse-image gave coherence to otherwise destabilizing formal signifiers of I-ness. Ethan, for the first time, was happily haunted. He does not phantasize about this spectre-Beatrice, so much as her discovery is installed as a cohering abiding presence—an assimilated good ghost. Having found his Beatrice, Ethan is now less prone to an envy of existence. The hungry ghost has become a holy one. In relation to this good spectre, that completes him and that adds prosthetic stability to the formal significations of his psyche, Ethan is now more like Sylvie, the wise child open to the elemental subtle energies of the infinite.

Yet, we must not equate the mutation of a moment with a transformation. If phantasy is subject to a certain monotony of form in its repetitions, the spectre-image is subject to iterations of the same that give rise, not to the monotony of the singular, but to the flow of the multiple. The ghost-within finds its realization in an image that is multiple. Haunting begets haunting as this system of incorporative secrets intensifies the pull into vortices upon vortices of turbulence. I believe, then, that we cannot speak of the ghost-within in the singular, nor in terms of anything remotely like another internal identity, nor even as a series of encrypted identifications. I differ, in this regard, from Abraham and Torok and their profoundly important work on psychic haunting. The ghost-within, precisely because it is a strange attractor, has nothing about it that we can equate with the singular or think of only in terms of a historically determined internal signifier despite the obvious contribution history makes to the prefigurations of psychic haunting.

Encryptions of the un-mourned Other in the subject constrict the expansiveness of difference into a corrosive object of abandonment. The work of the negative subsumes the growth of meaning, through an identification with and allegiance to the ghost-within, that places Eros in bondage. It is the erotic that is, in the haunted subject, under the force of the repetitious impulse-image repertoire. The compulsion to repeat operates under the force of the negative. The tyranny of the Same privileges fusion and possessive allegiance over the radical alterity of the Other, the non-dialectical difference fundamental to the formation of a generative contact barrier. The negativity in the tyranny of the Same, that is at work in the haunted image-repertoire, collapses the dynamism of relational difference into a negation that cancels out oppositional negativities, reducing the subject to eclipse under incipient implosion–explosion patternings of nothingness. The ghost-within leaves its crucifying trace on the biographic assertions of the "I".

As image is inherently spectral, it is the privileged vehicle for apparitional significations. In the haunted primal scene, the subject feels incapable of awakening the part of the mother, who is lost in a mournful swoon with her beloved absent, and who, in turn, soothes herself in narcissistic identification and in internal mirror transferences. The ghost in the mother exerts, in the intersubjective systematics established with the nominated replacement child, deterministic but unpredictable jumps to levels of infinite complexity. In the replacement child, the strange attractor of infinite complexity is the preservative object of impossible mourning. This in turn inspires a certain hauntology of the visual and a consequent eccentric position: the haunted live in a position that is always outside of themselves.

Alexander, who was born three years after the death of his brother, is riveted by two scenes: the chance observation of a woman admiring her breasts in a mirror and the memory of cutting the tail off a cut out Halloween black cat, only to run to his mother in panic for magical repair. He has, in the beginning of analysis, this dream.

> He is in a temple, a place that has the aura of holiness about it, and he witnesses on a table, as on a sacrificial altar or a mortuary slab, the body of a woman who is laid out stone-still and rigid, as his gaze is drawn to her breasts in relation to which he becomes all eyes, attempting something like scopophilic enlivenment through the substitution of the eye for the mouth.

The scene with the mother in the crypt has for Alexander the aura of something holy, as if he is witness to the body of a goddess, a view that only belies the depth of his passion for her—dead.

Alexander's blankly excited gaze is less a position of desire than it is one of fascination in relation to which he feels pulled up and out of himself, ungrounded and without balance. This, he notes, also is manifested in his body, in a certain lack of coordination. It is as if his centre is always "over-there" where he is his not. The other holds Alexander in a spell from which he expects some variant of cure: to be enlivened, redeemed, and released only to in fact feel imprisoned in the aura of the object.

In the space of the spectre, Alexander is not singular, nor alone. He is, in the dream, surrounded by a community of witnesses, the multiplication effect of a condemning voyeuristic hauntology. The community of witnesses establishes the scene of haunting as it turns the libidinized vigil over the body of the dead mother into a case for the prosecution. "The violence of the mute forces that would thus be setting up the crypt does not end with the trauma of a single unbearable and condemned seduction scene—condemned to remain mute but also condemned as a building is condemned by official order of the court," writes Jacques Derrida (1986, p. xv). He continues:

> A forum is always defined, from the start—and this will be concretely verified in this case—as a politico–juridical instance, something more than a duelling ground, but like a duelling ground requiring a *third*, witness; a tribunal preparing a case, summoning before it for indictments, statements of counsel, and sentencing, a

> multiplicity of persons called up by subpoena … The seduction scene alone is not sufficient … What is needed, still mute, is the contradiction springing from incorporation itself. It ceaselessly opposes two stiff, incompatible forces, erect against each other: "deadly pleasure" … "two contradictory demands: that the Father's Penis should neither *come* … nor go." Without this contradiction within Desire, nothing would be comprehensible: neither the relative solidity of the crypt … nor the hermeticism and the indefatigable effort to maintain it, nor the failure of that effort, the permeation from within or from without, seeping through the crypt's partitions … engraving itself upon several surfaces along the angular lines that … always follow the division of a "fantasmatic double(ness)", each fantasy being "double and opposed". [*ibid.*, p. xv]

The body of the mother, poised in the rigor mortis of haunting, asserts the negative demand of desire—that the Father cannot penetrate her, that there is no inside, that there is only an inviolate outside, only this alterity of death that the witnesses are there to prepare the case for … and against. Life lived according to this logic of the ghost is an event of paralytic postponements, of endless witnessing, of always being the exiled "third" and in this position radically passive, yet not exempt from passionate communion with the mournful desire held in the morturial space of the body of the haunted mother.

This figuration of the maternal body, lush yet rigidly still, is for him an event of uncanny beauty, a beauty that he cannot shake. The aura that surrounds the body of the haunted mother inspires in Alexander the compulsions of the impulse-image system that populate the potential space in which he might otherwise develop what Kierkegaard calls a self: that relationship that relates itself to itself. The mother in the crypt is also for Alexander uncanny, creepy, disturbing, agitating, dread-filled, beyond contact or affective engagement. The autoeroticism in this troubled dream of a mother beyond contact is also hate-filled. He thinks of sacrifice, of the Lamb of God, of Isaac, of sacrifice that is not aborted, but that brings all life to a silence that is cold and flat, eviscerated. He thinks of a silence that persecutes. This sacrifice is also the sacrifice of meaning that turns language into a web of negative signifiers. The space of thought is decathected through inhabitations by the unthought phantasy from the crypt. In conjunction with this insistent primal scene, the image-repertoire organizes Alexander's psychic life into a web of spectral significations.

How does one mourn an impossible mourning? Of course, this has to do with an achievement: the murder of the image of the venerated dead. And of course this also has something to do with the analyst's aliveness, expressed in his communicative linkages and progressive relatedness (Green, 1987). For these two conditions to take hold, however, the space that is haunted must first develop out of its radical passivity toward an active–passive dialectic in which activity, action, and activation are not foreign states of self. This radical passivity that is beyond any activation of self is informed, as Derrida suggests, by the encrypted phallus within the body of the impossibly mournful mother: the one that neither comes nor goes.

Contrary to the current emphasis on the analyst as a person, on their realness, their generative counter-transferences, their love for their patient, their ability to engage and make contact, I believe that the "aliveness" that is transformational for the haunted patient is initially not the aliveness of the analyst's productivity (whether phallic or maternal) nor of their "experience" so much as it is the "aliveness" in the analyst's silence. Each patient that I have seen, for whom the ghost in the mother has been a central problematic, evaluates their being understood on ontological and not epistemological criteria. Does the analyst know in their person something about contact with the formless void infinite? Are they able to speak to "nothingness" from "emptiness?" Does their speaking respect a silence that makes room for endless traces of muteness while equally leaving room for vulnerable gestures and rhythms of something like contemplative relating. Is the analyst's "realness" unsaturated with respect to the drive toward an extraverted and ultimately hysterical relating? Is their "love" the love that waits patiently as it bathes the nascent baby-self in the attention of silent respect? Is the analyst's speech spoken from this silent love that also loves the patient's silence? Is the analyst's silence a tension point of contact without leaning toward the acquisitive or the productive or collapsing back into an ascetical absence?

Is, in other words and in other terms, the analyst in some self-accessibility to the space of the *chora*? It is this embodied silent contact with a beneficent background emptiness that, in my experience, determines whether the potential space between analyst and patient becomes recurrently ghosted or provisionally open to salutations of difference, the gradual tolerance of which ventilates the mythopoetic mergers with the incestuous object of impossible mourning. The silence that the analyst must find in themselves and occupy is not the silence of the crypt but the silence of the hermitage—the place not of hiding or withdrawal but of solitude-in-communion in dynamic development with the opposite position: with communion-in-solitude. This spaciously loving silence is the atopos where one does not seek in repetitious insistence infinity in a "breast" (this is the petrified silence of one who is passively haunted), but rather finds a "breast" in infinity (this is an open silence that sees in the signifying demarcations of being the "face" of the Other.

These two qualities of silence are linked, in my view, to two modes of mourning: to what I think of as mourning through the idol and mourning through the icon (Emery, 1997, 2000). In mourning through the idol, the Other is shrouded in a fascinating veneration. In mourning through the idol, one's mourning clings to its object. It is a mourning that is impossible, addicted, and adhesive. Before the idol, the gaze is frozen, concretized, and fixated as exemplified in Alexander's worship in the temple of the breast. The idol functions as an "invisible mirror", as one that blocks contact with the invisible (Marion, 1991). In mourning through the idol, I am locked in a tandem object relation with the dead. I am then heir to passivization, a reflection of the dead object's stoic immobility. I am frozen in a petrified silence. Mourning through the idol short-circuits and violates the glory of the infinite as it reduces the other to a precarious fetish of self-duplication, a prosthetic function in which the other is appropriated from exteriority into the cryptic enclaves of incorporation (Emery, 2000).

The Icon, in contrast, opens to the beyond, to the formless void as generative matrix, to the clearing in which the luminescence of being shines forth. In mourning through the icon, the visible that is open to the invisible has as its phonetic corollary the word that is open to a pre-originary silence. Silence before an idol is tremulous, saturated with envy, with the petrifying passivity of the uncanny. It is agitated, distracted, looking for what is absent, consumed in mimetic desire. Silence before an icon is filled with repose, with open attention, with intimations of "O", with the glory of the face of the Other. It is this silence that is also expressively contained in the silent spot in the body—in the space of introjection—and that foreshadows, once it is contacted, a series of transformations whose outcome is introjection of the crypt. Dread, then, gives way to wonder. The snares of encryption give way to the errant uncertain destination of becoming singular.

References

Abraham, N., & Torok, M. (1986). *The Wolf Man's Magic Word.* Minneapolis, MN: University of Minnesota Press.

Anzieu, D. (1990). *Psychic Envelopes.* London: Karnac Books.

Barthes, R. (1978). *A Lover's Discourse.* New York: Hill and Wang.

Blanchot, M. (1992). *The Step Not Beyond.* Albany, NY: State University of New York Press.

Deleuze, G. (1989). *Cinema 2: The Time Image.* Minneapolis, MN: The Athlone Press.

Deleuze, G. (1994). *Difference and Repetition.* New York: Columbia University Press.

Derrida, J. (1986). Foreword. In: Abraham & Torok, 1986.

Derrida, J. (1994). *Specters of Marx.* London: Routledge.

Emery, E. (1992). On dreaming of one's patient: dense objects and intrapsychic isomorphism. *Psychoanalytic Review, 79*: 509–535.

Emery, E. (1997). Mnemosyne: death, memory, and mourning. *J. Melanie Klein and Object Relations, 15*: 397–416.

Emery, E. (2000). Facing "O": Wilfred Bion, Emmanuel Levinas, and the face of the Other. *Psychoanalytic Review, 87*: 799–840.

Graham, J. (1997). *The Errancy.* New Jersey: Echo Press.

Green, A. (1987). *On Private Madness.* New York: International Universities Press.

Hamilton, E., & Cairns, H. (1961). *Plato: The Collected Dialogues. "The Timaeus"* (pp. 1151–1211). Princeton: New Jersey.

Kristeva, J. (1989). *Black Sun.* New York: Columbian University Press.

Marion, J. L. (1991). *God Without Being.* Chicago: University of Chicago Press.

CHAPTER EIGHT

"Each single ego": telepathy and psychoanalysis

Nick Totton

"Have I given you the impression that I am secretly inclined to support the reality of telepathy in the occult sense? If so, I should very much regret that it is so difficult to avoid giving such an impression. In reality, however, I was anxious to be strictly impartial. I have every reason to be so, for I have no opinion; I know nothing about it"

Freud, 1922, p. 220

"Telepathy would be the name of an ongoing and groping research that—at the moment of its emergence and in the area of its relevance—had not yet grasped either the true scope of its own inquiry or the conceptual rigour necessary for its elaboration"

Maria Torok, 1986, p. 86[1]

Wenceslas

Following in its founder's often heavy footsteps, Reichian therapy—in which I had my original training—has tended to be sceptical of the paranormal. This scepticism often surprises non-Reichians, who (if inclined to be generous) usually understand Reich himself to be a shaman, alchemist or mystic who, at some point between the 1930s and the 1950s, came untethered from consensual reality and floated off into the stratosphere in a cloud of UFOs and orgone energy. The picture is not wholly unfair: Reich's later work does have fascinating and important parallels (of which he himself was largely unaware) with magical and alchemical traditions.[2] But it discounts Reich's own fierce insistence on his scientific materialism, and his lifelong hostility to what he defined as "mysticism".

Reich's misfortune was that the achievement which he himself saw as most solidly grounded in objectivity—the orgone accumulator and associated theories—was treated by the scientific community as mystical and illusory. Like Freud himself, Reich tried to appeal to Einstein as an iconic guarantor of scientific status; however Einstein found Reich less useful than Freud as a reciprocal guarantor.[3] Despite an initial interest in the orgone accumulator, Einstein decided, after perfunctory research, that because it couldn't work, it didn't work; and stopped answering Reich's letters—this (occult) correspondence, in other words, must cease.[4]

In his earlier work, Reich treats mysticism as "essentially the negation of sexual strivings ... essentially sexual defence" (Reich, 1975, p. 200). He emphasizes its reactionary social role as the opium of the masses which Marx describes, a means of palliative control. Later on, as Reich develops his bodymind energetics (Totton, 1998, pp. 142–143), he portrays "mysticism" as a confused apprehension of bodily energy—"primary biophysical sensations, plasmatic streamings ... experiences which are almost completely blocked off in the so-called normal human being" (Reich, 1972, pp. 399–400). Thus Reich interprets mysticism as a misunderstanding of perceptions which in themselves are more accurate than the average—what Jung might describe as a projection outwards of internal reality. For Reich, though, unlike Jung, the internal reality involved is not *psychic* but *psychosomatic*, organismic. The mystic, like the schizophrenic, in Reich's view suffers from a mind–body split:

> For the mystic, a soul "lives" in the body. There is no connection between body and soul except for the fact that the soul influences the body and vice versa. To the mystic ... body and soul are rigidly separated ... [Reich, 1983, p. 91]

Reich argues that the rigid separation of mind and body leads, in turn, to a confusion between inner and outer realities. In effect, any remainder which we cannot conveniently divide between these two artificially distinguished categories of psyche and soma gets projected outwards: powerful bodily sensations which disturb the mind-identified ego's precarious illusion of control, for instance, can be interpreted as the effect of influencing machines or other paranoid constructs. "The beginning of the loss of reality testing in schizophrenia lies in the patient's misinterpretation of sensations arising from his [*sic*] own body" (Reich, 1983, pp. 24–25; cf. Reich, 1972, Chap. 15). Reich argues, in fact, that:

> *the organ sensation ... is a true sixth sense.* Besides the abilities to see, hear, smell, taste, touch, there exist[s] unmistakeably in healthy individuals *a sense of organ functions* ... The schizophrenic has displaced this sense and has transformed it into certain patterns of his delusional system, such as "forces" ... [Reich, 1972, p. 454; original italics]

Hence, when I did my own training in Reichian therapy, my trainer initially insisted that all apparently "paranormal" experiences were distorted projections of bodily events onto the world. He encouraged us to re-own such events as aspects of our somatic energy. Unfortunately for this approach, his course had attracted a motley caravan of psychics, mystics, and fringe adventurers; we worked on him, and by the end he was at least as deeply involved in paranormal explorations as the rest of us. (In some ways rather more so—he took to dowsing with an invisible pendulum.)

My own experience, along with many other people, is that Reichian therapy tends to open one up to experiences of the sort generally defined as "paranormal": telepathy, clairvoyance, synchronicity, auras, strange energies, past lives, apparently discarnate beings. This happens at one end of a spectrum of new experiences set off by the focus on subliminal body sensation which is central to Reichian bodywork. In many ways—and here Reich is partially right—it feels much less important than the new sensitivities to emotion, bodily energy, sexuality and relationship which are part of the same spectrum. However, it can be quite impressive. To pick a relatively unsensational example, I became aware during my own training that I could feel water flowing underneath me, for instance when I was standing on a low bridge or above a culvert—a sort of "fizzing" sensation in my feet and legs.[5] This faculty very plainly developed as a consequence of work I did on my fear of falling, tracing it back to tension in my pelvis, related to castration- and orgasm-anxiety. As the muscular tension of my pelvis and legs began to relax, I became aware of all sorts of new sensations there, of which this "paranormal" sensitivity was only one.

In what follows, I will be trying to show both that it is important to insist on the *paranormal* status of such experiences, without reducing them to misperceptions or misinterpretations; and, at the same time, that there is an essentially unpunctuated continuum on the level of *causality* between "normal" and "paranormal" experience. In other words, the task is not to pick apart the subliminal sensory from the occult extrasensory—whether or not anything is left in the second category. Paranormality, like the closely related *unheimlichkeit*, is a matter, not of cause, but of effect (and affect). I shall be arguing that, despite Reich's own stated view, the increased openness to the paranormal which I have described is consonant with the goals and theory of Reichian therapy—rather than, as he himself would have argued, a side-effect of poorly conducted Reichian therapy (Reich, 1972, p. 403). I shall try to link this phenomenon up with Freud's own writings and ideas on the paranormal, in order to outline a general, Reichian-inflected theory of the metapsychology of the paranormal.

The real thing

> The reader of thoughts merely reads his own thoughts into other people. [Fliess to Freud, quoted by Freud in Masson, 1985, p. 447]

> We all have to be aware that patients are frightened of us. They are afraid because they think we are ignorant, and they are possibly even more afraid that we are not ignorant. [Bion, 2000, p. 152]

In what follows, I will sometimes let telepathy act as representative for the whole spectrum of paranormality. It is a paranormal phenomenon particularly relevant to psychoanalysis, since the latter is in a very real sense founded on the claim that "I know what you're thinking". This idea may seem immediately odd to analysts and psychotherapists who are all too aware of how often, and crucially, they *don't* know what the client is thinking. "I wish you could know without me telling you," clients say; or, occasionally, they believe that we do know everything they have been doing or thinking. We don't; sometimes, counter-transferentially, we wish we could.

However our very awareness of this ignorance, the perception of it as a *lack* in us or in the situation, indirectly demonstrates my point. In analysis or psychotherapy, the question, "Do I/you know what you are/I am thinking?" is constantly under review. From the analysand's side, this sets up two, usually oscillating, claims: "You know what I'm thinking" and "You don't know what I'm thinking". Either of these, or both at once, can become desperately important to maintain. Equally, there are points at which the analyst or therapist will very much hope that the client either does or does not know what she is thinking.

However much one elaborates the issue, it seems impossible for analysis to evade being implicated in a situation where privileged understanding of someone's conscious or unconscious thoughts is being claimed—or denied. This is particularly clear as regards the "English school", and gets conceptualized there in ways which are particularly close to telepathy: communicative counter-transference, metabolizing the patient's difficult feelings, projective identification, and other such ideas are all essentially "paranormal" concepts (and none the worse for it). And while Lacanians are dismissive of this sort of thinking—what we may call a "telepathy of the imaginary"[6]—they are surely themselves committed to a parallel telepathy of the symbolic, focused less on *who is thinking* than on *what is being thought*.

> That the unconscious of the subject is the discourse of the other appears even more clearly than anywhere else in the studies that Freud devoted to what he called telepathy. ... It is a case of resonance in the communicating networks of discourse. [Lacan, 1953, pp. 55–56]

Telepathy, it seems, is often what is being sought in therapy or analysis—sought and fled from in more or less equal degrees. So transference becomes a matter of *thought* transference, desired and resisted, decked out in fancy historic dress: one of the things my parents did was to know and not know what I was thinking, at all the right and wrong times. And, equally, I had to struggle with knowing and not knowing, understanding and not understanding, *their* thoughts and emotions. All this is replicated in the therapeutic relationship.

It will be clear from the above that I am not claiming for telepathy any intrinsically non-material mode of operation. As Freud says, telepathy concerns the idea:

> that mental processes in one person—ideas, emotional states, connotive impulses—can be transferred to another person through empty space *without employing the familiar methods of communication* by means of words and signs. [Freud, 1933b, pp. 69/39;[7] my italics]

What is essentially telepathic transmission can take place through the medium of language, as Lacan suggests—though not by language's "familiar means of communication"; or through the sorts of subliminal cues that certain theorists talk about in relation to projective identification; or through those quietly mysterious phenomena which we call "empathy" and "intuition"; or through intonation, body language, vitality affect, pheromones, subtle energy, or any other known or unknown channel. "What lies between these two mental acts [of telepathic 'transmission' and 'reception'] may easily be a physical process" (Freud, 1933b, pp. 85/55). What, then, identifies "essentially" telepathic communication? What I am calling "telepathy" is not the *modus operandi*, but its *result*: the "unfamiliar" experience of transparency between subjects. A telepathy of the real.

Lost in translation

> *Übersetzung* [translation] enjoys a comprehensive scope in the Freudian corpus ... Neuroses and symptoms for Freud are translations of unconscious material. ... The analyst's interpretations manifest his "arts of translation"—*Übersetzungskunste* ... Clearly, Freud's literal use of *Übersetzung* as translation and transposition ... demonstrates that he understood as a concomitant unifying activity the translation of ideas and affects into words and the translation or transposition of psychic materials from the unconscious to the conscious levels. [Mahony, 1992, p. 31]

The past participle of "transference" is "translation"—both terms come from the Latin *trans-ferre*, past participle *trans-latum*, to carry across. Freud's German term *Übertragung* can also be translated as "translation"—or, indeed, as "metaphor" (the same thing in Greek), or as a great number of other terms—"carrying over, communication, spreading; transmission, relaying; endorsement; conferring (of an office); transcription" (*Cassells New German Dictionary*, 1968; cf. Laplanche, 1976, p. 138). What a suggestive list! One could write a whole paper on each. The knot of English and German terms—transfer, translate,[8] interpret, *deuten*, *übersetzen*, *übertragen*—draws our attention to some key features of the analytic encounter: that something is being conferred and endorsed; that a role is being performed according to someone's conception; and, above all, that *translation* is going on—something is being carried over or across.

And while telepathy is often sought outside language, as an escape from language, "thought transference" is also an aspiration *of* language.[9] Just as the intelligible/unintelligible repressed always drives its way back into language, so that "truly the idea gets torpedoed in the heart of the sentence enunciating it" (Breton, 1978, p. 133)—so language is itself a telepathy-machine, a "communicating vessel" (*ibid.*, p. 127). A telepathy-machine, or an influencing-machine? And in which direction, in the analytic encounter, does or should the influence run? Which way is something being carried? And carried across where? Across a boundary, or boundaries. This is all a question of frontier control, of the customs inspectors who featured so strongly in Freud's dream life. Laplanche and others make the point clearly in relation to textual translation:

> A translation that stands up to "the test of alienness" [*l'epreuve d'etranger*] is one that makes no attempt to domesticate or acclimatise the text in order to provide some sort of analogy readily acceptable to our own expectations. [Laplanche *et al.*, 1992, p. 140]

Hence, in contradiction to Freud (who says that the two can "without much violence" be identified—Freud, 1933b, pp. 69/39), we can draw a distinction which amounts to an opposition between telepathy and "thought reading".[10] The latter, unlike the former, involves a process of *translation* which makes the material involved representable, or presentable—"readily acceptable to our own expectations"—a "familiar ... communication". At this point it loses its "paranormal" quality, and becomes a part of normality.

Freud is at times clear that every translation from the unconscious involves a *mis*translation.

> There is no doubt, then, that it is our normal thinking that is the psychical agency which approaches the content of dreams with a demand that it must be intelligible, which subjects it to a first interpretation and which consequently produces a complete misunderstanding of it. [Freud, 1900, pp. 642/500]

There is a difficult and at times tragic sense in which analysis and therapy are themselves caught in this trap: the more they attempt to offer *understanding* to the client's material, the more they *translate* it, and "consequently produce a complete misunderstanding". Freud goes on to compare this work of misunderstanding with a newspaper game which rearranges a passage of German to make it look like a Latin inscription.

> If we are to avoid being taken in ... we must ... look firmly at the letters, pay no attention to their ostensible arrangement, and so combine them into words belonging to our own mother tongue. [*ibid.*, pp. 643/501]

But isn't this equally a description of the work of misunderstanding itself, "firmly" recombining the client's communication into words from the analyst's own "mother tongue"?[11] Every analysand, then, perhaps on some level feels ultimately cheated—that their experience has been stolen, and replaced with a changeling, a perfect simulacrum neatly decked out in analytic clichés. The reader of thoughts has read their own thoughts once again into another person.

It can be argued, to the contrary, that this process of translation is not only the best option available, but also inherently of value. Laplanche and others say, again in the context of translating Freud into French:

> Any genuine translation is not only put to the "test" of that "alien" which is the work but also, in turn, puts the work to the test of that alien which is the experience of translation itself. What is latent in the work only an alien can discover and only the translation into an alien, foreign language can carry through the development and destiny of the work. [Laplanche *et al.*, 1992, p. 190]

In many ways this can be applied to the process of psychoanalysis, as a bracing retort to all the talk of "holding" and "understanding". The experience of psychotherapy will always combine feeling understood as *oneself,* and feeling understood as *other*—being assimilated into a foreign world-view, reflected in a strange mirror. This experience is shocking, difficult to bear, not always helpful; but it certainly can be transformative in ways which are at the heart of the Freudian project.

However, there is something *else* which can happen in analysis and in psychotherapy; something which many theorists refer to, each in their own way; and this is what I am stalking under the rubric of "telepathy"—an *untranslated* passage of information between subjects. The shock and excitement, at times trauma, of this passage is responded to like all "foreign bodies": with hysteria.

My private affair

> The subject [telepathy] must have fascinated, as well as repelled him. [Anna Freud to Ernest Jones, quoted Gay, 1995, p. 443]

"Dreams and telepathy" (1922) is one of Freud's most clearly hysterical works, in two senses: it communicates an excitement indistinguishable from anxiety, and it systematically subverts its own authority and the authority of others (cf. Fink, 1995, pp. 133–134, 149). "You will learn nothing from this paper of mine," Freud begins, "about the enigma of telepathy; indeed, you will not even gather whether I believe in the existence of 'telepathy' or not" (Freud, 1922, p. 197; the quotation marks here are masterly). I have already quoted the ending of the paper as the epigraph to this one—"I have no opinion; I know nothing about it" (*ibid.*, p. 220). Peter Gay is led to "wonder" primly "why Freud published the paper at all" (Gay, 1995, p. 444). An earlier paper on "Psychoanalysis and telepathy" (Freud, 1941), which Freud read to a meeting of the Central Committee of the IPA in 1921, was in fact not published during his lifetime. In it, Freud confesses, coquettishly, that he has forgotten to bring the notes of one case he had planned to present: "nothing can be done against such a clear resistance" (*op. cit.*, p. 190). Looking for the document, "in its place I found another sheet of indifferent memoranda on quite another topic" (*ibid.*);

naturally, one would love to know what this topic was. Now you see it, now you don't.

Of course Freud's game of concealment is also a game of revelation: we learn beyond all doubt that Freud is fascinated by telepathy (a state in no way inconsistent with having no opinion and knowing nothing about it). Only a few years later, Freud was writing to Jones that his thought transference experiments with Ferenczi and Anna "have gained such a persuasive power for me, that diplomatic considerations had to take a back seat"; while still arguing unconvincingly that "my adherence to telepathy is my private affair, like my Jewishness, my passion for smoking, and other things, and the theme of telepathy—inessential for psychoanalysis". This, at any rate, is how Gay translates the passage (Gay, 1995, p. 445); according to Jones (1957, pp. 423–424), and much more interestingly, Freud says that telepathy is "in essence alien [*Fremd*] to psychoanalysis":[12] a *Fremdkörper*, a foreign body. Jones also quotes Freud as saying that the subject of telepathy "always perplexed him to the point of distraction [*bringen mich immer aus der Fassung*]" (Jones, 1957, p. 419). The German phrase means to be brought out of control, out of the setting or frame, out of the script.

We can get a pretty good idea from "Dreams and telepathy" of why Freud is fascinated, and why out of control. Even beyond the intrinsic relationship between telepathy and psychoanalysis which I have already pointed out, and which Freud tries weakly to avoid in the passage quoted above, his account here and elsewhere is constructed so as to demonstrate that "the instances of telepathic messages or productions ... are clearly connected with emotions belonging to the sphere of the Oedipus complex" (Freud, 1922, p. 219). Freud slips this point in with studied casualness, insisting loudly that "I do not intend to give this out as a great discovery" (*ibid.*)—and reverts immediately to a constant theme of his writings on the topic:

> Telepathy has no relation to the essential nature of dreams; it cannot deepen in any way what we already understand of them through analysis. On the other hand, psycho-analysis may do something to advance the study of telepathy. [*ibid.*]

What are the implications of the connection made between telepathy and the Oedipus complex? Freud's focus is on the way in which telepathic "communications" function as primary process material, subject to exactly the same transformations and displacements as other charged thoughts and feelings; this is why he insists that it is "inessential"—it makes no difference to the construction of a dream, for instance, whether the dream matter is telepathically or otherwise derived. The dreamwork will be the same. "If the phenomenon of telepathy is only [*sic*!] an activity of the unconscious mind, then no fresh problem lies before us. the laws of unconscious mental life may then be taken for granted as applying to telepathy" (*ibid.*, p. 220).[13] Analysts, though, Freud implies, are well-placed to test the validity of supposed telepathic phenomena by subjecting them to the methods of psychoanalysis.

Why, though, *is* telepathy "connected with emotions belonging to the sphere of the Oedipus complex"—and in particular, as Freud points out, with "death or the possibility of death" (*ibid.*, p. 218)? Can we make any sense of this? I would suggest that we can, if we grant that the oedipal period is the time at which children seek to achieve *non-transparency*, to make themselves opaque to the adult gaze—to move away from the state of mind Derrida describes:

> The truth, what I always have difficulty getting used to: that non-telepathy is possible. Always difficult to imagine that one can think something to oneself, deep down inside, without being surprised by the other, without the other being immediately informed. [Derrida, 1988, p. 13]

This portrays very accurately, I think, the experience of small children. Freud himself explicitly connects it with telepathy: "Here we are reminded of the frequent anxiety felt by children over the idea that their parents know all of their thoughts without having to be told them" (1933b, pp. 86/55–56). This anxiety also contains, perhaps, a fear of the thought-reading which *creates* an already-known thought within its object. English psychoanalysis focuses on the earlier stages of childhood, at which the idea of "the other being immediately informed" has at least an element of comfort to it. At the oedipal threshold, though, it becomes intolerable, because what we are thinking and wishing feels so unacceptable and indeed dangerous: we are plotting mutiny and destruction. Through a combination of fear and guilt, we achieve that sealing of the borders which is regarded as a normal condition of adulthood. We attain the state which Freud refers to elsewhere as "the feeling of repulsion in us which is undoubtedly connected with the barriers that rise between each single ego and the others" (Freud, 1908, p. 153).

This phrase of Freud's has always fascinated me, with its implication of a process which is charged not just emotionally but almost physically, like the repulsion between the identical poles of two magnets. A felicitous similarity of phrasing by Anna Freud also brings home the connection with telepathy, and with Freud's strange treatment of it in his own work: "the subject," she tells Jones, "must have fascinated, as well as repelled him" (quoted by Gay, 1995, p. 443). Here the magnetism becomes Mesmeric, hysterical—the "fascination" of the transferential trance which generates its own "repulsion". How often, we realize, telepathy features in accounts of hysteria!

Royal roads

And realizing this, I also remember the thoroughly hysterical joke with which Freud ends "Psychoanalysis and telepathy". He claims to be telling it to illustrate why "thought transference" is worth investigating in its own right, despite being only a minor example of "the great world of occult miracles".

> St. Denis is said, after his head was cut off, to have picked it up and to have walked quite a distance with it in his arms. But the custodian used to remark: "*Dans des cas pareils, ce n'est que le premier pas qui coûte.*" The rest is easy. [Freud, 1941, p. 193]

This passage stuck in my mind for its apparent irrelevance and quirkiness. Looking at it again, though, it becomes apparent that it concerns a primary theme of hysteria[14]—*what one can do without one's head*: what the body can do on its own.[15]

Telepathy, and paranormal phenomena in general, are widely regarded as "disembodied"—events, real or imagined, on the "mental" side of the supposed mind–body divide. I said earlier that telepathy is both an escape *from* and an aspiration *of* language; in exactly the same way, it is both an escape from and an aspiration of the body. Telepathy is frequently defined, in fact, as the communication of information by *non-physical* means. The whole implication of the Reichian approach is that, to the contrary, the road to the paranormal is through the body.[16]

I write "to the contrary"; but, like Reich, I am trying to get beyond the *contrariety* of "mind and body", to work towards a non-dualistic conceptualization which can hold these two facets of experience together (Totton, 1998, Chap. 7). Part of the work of doing this, however, is to recognize that our *experience* is indeed of mind and body as in many ways contrary to each other; and that both this experience, and the reasons for it, must be incorporated (so to speak) into a theory of mind–body unity. The case of the paranormal is a helpful one for such a task, because in very complex ways it both demonstrates a continuity between "normal" and "paranormal", and "mental" and "material", phenomena; and also exemplifies the intense anxiety which can occur when "mind" is confronted directly by "body".

To begin with the continuity: the example of dowsing which I have already used is highly revealing. Water dowsing of the traditional kind is very plainly an *embodied* paranormal activity. It is the dowser's body which responds to the presence of underground water, without the intervention of consciousness, through muscle contractions that cause the forked twig to turn in the dowser's hands (Bird, 1980, pp. 5–7). The dowser experiences this as caused by an external force; but objective measurement clearly demonstrates that it is the dowser's own body which has reacted. It is not too hard to generate a fairly plausible theory as to the physical mechanism—some sort of electromagnetic sensitivity—by which the body becomes "aware" of hidden water. So here we have what is apparently a paranormal phenomenon right at the "material" end of the spectrum; until the very same dowser mentions that she can also find water on maps, rather than in the (literal) field; that in fact she can find not only water, but any substance or object she is asked to, present or absent, simply by adjusting her intention, but using the same involuntary muscular contraction as before (Bird, 1980, pp. 3–4, 225–228).

This notion of the "involuntary muscular contraction" is actually crucial in what follows. The ultimate example of such an event, of course, is the orgasm; and Reich pointed out in great detail the difficulty which the ego generally has in permitting such involuntary events to take place (e.g. Reich, 1983, pp. 306–309). One might push it to extremes and say that the ego finds it hard to permit the body to *live*—since involuntary activity of the heart, the diaphragm and lungs, the guts, is vital to physical existence. The body's fight for life in the face of the ego's paralytic panic is the matter of hysteria. The ego, we might say, misunderstands the mobility of life, and in particular of sexuality, as the threat of slipping apart into death: a threat to which it responds with a frozen, monolithic rigor (Totton, 1998, Chap. 6). This comes out very clearly in certain sorts of phobia, where the underlying fear is of *spontaneous movement*—most interestingly perhaps, in the case of ghosts: I am alone in my bed at night and *something moves* ... Or, in Freud's joke, a headless body moves of its own accord.[17] The phrase at the end of the St Denis passage, translated as "the rest is easy", is actually "*Das Weitere findet sich*": the rest takes care of itself, just as the body takes care of its own life without reference to the ego. If the "head" can allow itself to be carried by the "body" for one single step, then the rest will take care of itself.

I am suggesting, in fact, that this way of thinking about ghosts offers a model for the "paranormal" as a whole. The paranormal, the *unheimlich*, the unrepresentable, the real—all relate to and derive from the body; all of them describe our confused apprehension of Reich's "primary biophysical sensations, plasmatic streamings ... experiences which are almost completely blocked off in the so-called normal human being" (Reich, 1972, pp. 399–400). In speaking of our confused apprehension, though, I am not meaning to imply that these experiences are in any sense illusory or mistaken. Our bodies are not isolated one from another, or from the material and energetic world which gives birth to them. Information, in every sense, is the substance of our being; and information flows constantly through the world's networks, like the water which dowsers find beneath the ground. But much of this information, as psychoanalysis knows very well, is intolerable to us. "Intolerable information" is a possible definition of the unconscious; and the "paranormal" is one form of (almost) intolerable information—intolerable because it informs us of the intimate presence of the other, which signifies death to a self founded on separateness.

The foreign body

We are coming back now to the paradoxical connection Reich makes between a mind–body split, and a confusion between inner and outer reality. It is important to note that this confusion operates in both directions: not only may "inner perceptions ... be experienced as coming from the outer world", but also "stimuli from the outer world may ... be perceived as inner experiences" (Reich, 1972, p. 400). When we are embodied—which involves gracefully allowing our body the freedom from control on which it will in any case insist—we can distinguish between "in here" and "out there" in a secure but not over-rigid way: we can allow a "translation" between the two which does not overwhelm the borders.

Clearly, an objective of psychoanalysis in general is to enable us to accept without too much anxiety the existence of the unconscious—not just as a theoretical entity, but as co-inhabitor, co-possessor, of our bodies, our minds, our decisions, and self-presentations. Reichian therapy has the same objective, but carries it a step beyond: if successful, it creates sufficient strength and flexibility to endure our connectedness *through* the unconscious[18] with the rest of existence, including other people; to endure the actual uncontrollability of our experience, the actual impossibility of exclusive possession of our "selves". We can allow ourselves to be an *emergent* ego, a mutable and provisional summation of mind–body experience, rather than an *emergency* ego identified with the muscular tension that resists experience in the interests of survival.

Insofar as telepathy is a part of the real, it is problematic to the subject: resistant to symbolization. A struggle ensues, which is paralleled and reproduced in the political struggle between analyst and analysand over who controls the translating-machine. Usually, in analysis and in everyday life, telepathy is not *allowed* to be "real" (in either sense), but is forcibly aligned with the symbolic or the imaginary: in other words, it becomes either a *transmission of meaning* or a *mirroring of selfhood*. The most fundamental distinction, perhaps, between telepathy and thought-reading is that the latter has an arrow of direction attached to it: one reads the thought of the other. In true telepathy, there is no such direction, no such possession: both subjects are transparent to each other, under an open sky. It is through working with this distinction that psychoanalysis may hope to escape its fate as yet another form of border control.

Barriers that rise

If we cannot perform an arbitrary cut along the continuum of perception, severing the sensory from the "extrasensory", the normal from the "paranormal", then we need to conceptualize a more complex relationship between the two. In such a picture, the paranormal will, as Breton says of "surreality",

> reside in reality itself and will be neither superior nor exterior to it. And conversely, because the container will also be the contained. One might almost say that it will be a *communicating* vessel placed between the container and the contained. [Breton, 1978, p. 126; my italics]

This image of the "*vase communicante*" was supremely important to Breton. In his work of that title, he speaks of

> *a capillary tissue* in ignorance of which one works in vain to understand mental circulation. The role of this tissue is visibly to assure the constant interchange which must take place in thought between exterior and inner worlds. [Breton, 1978, p. 71; original italics]

I am assigning a very similar role to the paranormal: that it throws back into "circulation" whatever the ego attempts to bind to itself—or conversely, exercises a magnetic counter-force to the "repulsion" that Freud describes between "each single ego and the others". What the ego says is mine, the paranormal shows to be other; and what the ego says is other, the paranormal shows to be profoundly mine.

To understand the paranormal and our relation with it, then, we are brought back to the whole question of alienation, *Verfremdung*: the separation of our self from our self, the making foreign of the body, which originates, according to Freud, in *Urverdrängung*, primal or primary repression.

> It is highly probable that the immediate precipitating causes of primal repressions are quantitative factors such as an excessive

> force of excitation and the breaking through of the protective shield against stimuli [*Reizschutz*]. [Freud, 1926, pp. 94/245–246]

Freud also stresses, however, that "the protective shield exists *only* in regard to *external* stimuli" (*ibid.*/246; my italics): it is against being overwhelmed by excitation *from outside* that primal repression protects us. Paradoxically enough, primal repression, in Freud's model, is necessarily repression of the traces of the other (Laplanche & Pontalis, 1973, pp. 333–334).

This is clearly not what Freud consciously intends to suggest—but wouldn't telepathic sensitivity to adult psychic processes be a clear candidate for primal repression? Imagine: a baby born into a welter of incomprehensible data, including not only startling and painful physical sensations, but also conscious and unconscious thoughts and feelings of great intensity for which it has no referents. Enigmatic signifiers, indeed, from which no shield will protect you; the only way out is via a fundamental dissociation or repression, separating in a single act not only our self from our self, but also self from other self, and "head" from "body". This cutting of connection, synchronous with the cutting of the umbilical cord, also performs a primal cut upon our experience of self.

> Melanie Klein said—and I think it is borne out—at the very experience of birth itself, the full-term foetus feels castrated, mutilated, as if the mother's genitalia cut something off. Severed the umbilical cord? Severed the long-distance sense of smell? One would have to be this patient's analyst to guess, conjecture what the telephonic system is that has been cut off; what the messages are that she can't get. [Bion, 2000, p. 180]

Rank (1993 [1929], pp. 187–189) identifies primal repression/primal anxiety with birth trauma, and treats birth as the prototype for castration anxiety (*ibid.*, pp. 20–22; cf. Peerbolte, 1975, pp. 3–4). As Derrida says, "Difficult to imagine a theory of what they still call the unconscious without a theory of telepathy. They can neither be confused nor dissociated" (Derrida, 1988, p. 14). Might it be the repression of the one which brings the other into being?

Reichian work attests that cutting the head from the body is not a very good solution: *joining the two up* works better. Those who desire the paranormal more than they fear it generally reject the head—the hysteric strategy. Those for whom fear outweighs desire choose the obsessive strategy and reject the body. "I wish I could cut my head off," says an obsessive–compulsive client—cut off the obsessional thought patterns that drown out and protect against the real; but what she does in practice is to cut off the body instead, through ceremonies of decontamination and control.[19] Rejoining the two—recognizing the head as *constituted* by the body, the body as *constituted* by the head—opens us to Breton's "capillary tissue": to the barely bearable paranormality of the world.

Freud makes his joke in French partly because of the association with Charcot and hysteria; but also because it doesn't work properly in translation. In German, the idiom is *"Der erste Schritt ist der Wichtigste"*, the first step is the most important, or *"Es kommt auf den ersten Schritt an"*, it depends on the first step; in English, "It's the first step that counts"; but in French, "It's the first step that *costs*", that comes hard. But *"pas"* in French also means "not": it's the first negation, the primal repression, that costs us. The first cut is the deepest; as is the first step of reparation. The rest takes care of itself.

Notes

1. I have drawn heavily in what follows on linked work by Derrida (1988), Torok (1986) and Royle (1991, 1995). Despite their brilliance, however, these explorations stay wholly on the plane of language.
2. See Conger, 1988, Chap. 11; Mann and Hoffman, 1990, Chaps. 6 and 7.
3. Even so, although he was willing to conduct a public correspondence with Freud on the origins of war (Freud, 1933a), Einstein did not see him as "scientific" enough to merit his support for a Nobel Prize (Gay, 1995, p. 456 note).
4. See Sharaf, 1984, pp. 283–288.
5. Water-dowsing is one of the best documented "paranormal" faculties—see Bird, 1980, and references therein.
6. In this paper I will be using several Lacanian terms, since they are extremely useful for my purpose; but I will not be using them very accurately. They function more as loan-words than as translations—see below.
7. Wherever possible, I give references to texts by Freud with the Penguin Freud Library pagination followed by the Standard Edition pagination, as here.
8. "Translate" can refer to a transfer from one state to another—a bishop

to a new see, or a yokel to an ass ("Bless thee. Bottom! Bless thee! Thou art translated!"—Midsummer Night's Dream, III.i, p. 124).

9. This is applied specifically to literature by Royle (1991); see also my discussion below of Freud (1908).
10. Freud is using "telepathy" in something like its more literal meaning of "sensing from afar".
11. Literally the *mother* tongue in the case of many British analysts.
12. The Freud–Jones letters have "not related to psychoanalysis"—Paskauskas, 1993, p. 597.
13. This approach has been pushed to perhaps the ultimate extreme by Devereux (1953).
14. Freud is apparently describing a visit to the Abbey of St-Denis, made while he was studying hysteria with Charcot at La Salpetriere: the joke brings in the whole highly charged, "occult" atmosphere of Charcot's and Janet's hysterical investigations.
15. Of course, in the St Denis story the body does not abandon the head but takes it along for the ride: see below.
16. After writing this paper, I discovered Jan Ehrenwald's very interesting discussion of the role of "enkinesis":

> Enkinesis can be defined as the imaginative projection of our consciousness into another person's motor or psychomotor behaviour resulting in the actual sharing of some of his [*sic*] motor, vasomotor or glandular processes. One could say empathy is projection guided by perception; enkinesis is introjected action guided by empathy. ... Yet ... we must not forget that empathy and enkinesis are, nevertheless, nothing but the sensory and motor aspects of the identical process of social interaction ... We have to realize, furthermore, that there is no sharp demarcation line between the two marginal functions of the ego discussed here and *psi* processes in the stricter sense. [Ehrenwald, 1954, p. 144]

This is very close to the argument of this chapter.

17. In a footnote to the St Denis joke (Freud, 1941, p. 193), Strachey attributes it to Marie, Marquise du Deffand, speaking to Cardinal de Polignac in the late-eighteenth century. Oddly enough, searching for Deffand on the Internet led me to an editorial by Wendy Kesser from a magazine called *Hysteria*: "'Women', Madame du Deffand, friend of Voltaire, once said, 'are never stronger than when they arm themselves with their weakness.' In this spirit we take as our title what was once the gag of our silence" (Kesser, n.d.). Ironically, Deffand's St Denis quotation—"The distance doesn't matter; only the first step costs/counts/is difficult" (all three translations are used)—seems to be frequently included in lists of generally uplifting sentiments, as a

parallel to Mao's "The journey of a thousand miles begins with a single step", without anyone realizing that she was talking about a dead saint. And in an *unheimlich* synchronicity, a third *bon mot* of Deffand's is: "Do I believe in ghosts? No, but I'm afraid of them." (We may safely conclude from these three remarks that her structure is hysterical.) This set of occult correspondences is typical enough of how the paranormal inserts itself into the "communicating networks of discourse", of which the Internet is such a marvellous example.

There is at least one further twist: in 1996 Freud's punchline, "Ce n'est que le premier pas qui coute", appeared by apparently paranormal means on a piece of photographic film, as part of an elaborate set of communications from what claimed to be disembodied entities, intent on proving that human beings survive physical death (Solomon & Solomon, 1999, note 149). The sentence was significant because it appears in *Human Personality and Its Survival of Bodily Death* by F. W. H. Myers (Myers, 1903, p. 250)—a book which Freud would certainly have read. Both before and, it seems, after his death, Myers was a key contributor to paranormal research (see e.g. Saltmarsh, 1938).

18. Our preconscious (in the psychologist's sense) evaluation of perceptual data is strongly influenced by unconscious material (in the analyst's sense): Totton, 1998, pp. 21–22.
19. Williams (1997, pp. 103–107) describes a young female patient who developed a terror of having fleas penetrate her bodily orifices. She had been diagnosed as mentally defective because she was unable to let herself think.

References

Bion, W. R. (2000). *Clinical Seminars and Other Works*. London: Karnac.

Bird, C. (1980). *Divining*. London: Macdonald and Jane's.

Breton, A. (1978). *What Is Surrealism?* F. Rosemont (Ed.). London: Pluto Press.

Cassell's New German Dictionary (12th edn.) (1968). London: Cassell.

Conger, J. P. (1988). *Jung and Reich: The Body as Shadow*. Berkeley, California: North Atlantic Books.

Derrida, J. (1988). Telepathy. *Oxford Literary Review, 10*: 3–41.

Devereux, G. (1953). Extrasensory perception and psychoanalytic epistemology. In: G. Devereux (Ed.) *Psychoanalysis and the Occult*. London: Souvenir Press, 1974.

Ehrenwald, J. (1954). *New Dimensions of Depth Analysis: A Study of Telepathy in Interpersonal Relationships*. London: George Allen and Unwin.

Fink, B. (1995). *The Lacanian Subject: Between Language and Jouissance.* Princeton, NJ: Princeton University Press.

Freud, S. (1900). *The Interpretation of Dreams. Penguin Freud Library, Volume 4; Standard Edition, Volume 4* and *5*.

Freud, S. (1908). Creative writers and day-dreaming. *S.E., 9*.

Freud, S. (1922). Dreams and telepathy. *S.E., 18*.

Freud, S. (1926). *Inhibitions, Symptoms and Anxiety. PFL 10, S.E., 20*.

Freud, S. (1933a). Why war? *S.E.*, 22.

Freud, S. (1933b). *New Introductory Lectures on Psychoanalysis PFL 2, S.E.,* 22.

Freud, S. (1941 [1921]). Psychoanalysis and telepathy. *S.E., 18*.

Gay, P. (1995 [1989]). *Freud: A Life for Our Time*. London: Papermac.

Jones, E. (1957). *The Life and Work of Sigmund Freud, Volume 3*. London: Hogarth Press.

Kesser, W. (n.d.). Hysteria's got attitude. Quoted on the *Hysteria Books* website, http://www.hysteriabooks.com/name.html.

Lacan, J. (1953). The function and field of speech and language in psychoanalysis. In: A. Sheridan (Trans.), *Ecrits: A Selection*. London: Routledge, 1977.

Laplanche. (1976). *Life and Death in Psychoanalysis*. Baltimore: Johns Hopkins Press.

Laplanche, J., & Pontalis, J. B. (1973). *The Language of Psychoanalysis*. London: Hogarth.

Laplanche, J., Cotet, P., & Bourguignon, A. (1992). Translating Freud. In: D. Ornston (Ed.). pp. 135–190.

Mahony, P. (1992). A psychoanalytic translation of Freud. In: D. Ornston (Ed.), *Translating Freud* (pp. 24–47). London: Yale University Press.

Mann, W. E., & Hoffman, E. (1990). *Wilhelm Reich: The Man Who Dreamt of Tomorrow*. Wellingborough: Crucible.

Masson, J. (Ed.) (1985). *The Complete Letters of Sigmund Freud to Wilhelm Fliess*. London: Belknap Press.

Myers, F. W. H. (1903). *Human Personality and Its Survival of Bodily Death, Volume 1*. London: Longmans Green.

Ornston, D. (Ed.) (1992). *Translating Freud*. London: Yale University Press.

Paskauskas, R. A. (Ed.) (1993). *Complete Correspondence of Sigmund Freud and Ernest Jones, 1908–1939*. Cambridge, Mass: Belknap.

Peerbolte, M. L. (1975). *Psychic Energy in Prenatal Dynamics; Parapsychology; Peak Experiences: A Paraphysical Approach to Psychoanalysis and Transpersonal Psycho-dynamics*. Wassenaar: Servire.

Rank, O. (1993 [1929]). *The Trauma of Birth*. New York: Dover.

Reich, W. (1972 [1945]). *Character Analysis*. New York: Farrar, Strauss and Giroux.

Reich, W. (1975 [1933]). *The Mass Psychology of Fascism*. Harmondsworth: Penguin.

Reich, W. (1983 [1942]). *The Function of The Orgasm*. London: Condor.

Royle, N. (1991). *Telepathy and Literature: Essays on the Reading Mind*. Oxford: Blackwell.

Royle, N. (1995). The remains of psychoanalysis (i): Telepathy. In: N. Royle (Ed.), *After Derrida*. Manchester: Manchester University Press.

Saltmarsh, H. F. (1938). *Evidence of Personal Survival from Cross Correspondences*. London: G. Bell and Sons.

Sharaf, M. (1984). *Fury on Earth: A Biography of Wilhelm Reich*. London: Hutchinson.

Solomon, G., & Solomon, J. (1999). *The Scole Experiment: Scientific Evidence for Life After Death*. London: Piatkus.

Torok, M. (1986). Afterword: What is occult in occultism?. In: N. Abraham & M. Torok (Eds.), *The Wolf Man's Magic Word: A Cryptonomy*. Minneapolis: University of Minnesota Press.

Totton, N. (1998). *The Water in the Glass: Body and Mind in Psychoanalysis*. London: Rebus Press.

Williams, G. (1997). *Internal Landscapes and Foreign Bodies: Eating Disorders and Other Pathologies*. London: Duckworth.

INDEX